I0576939

Joanna Baillie

A series of plays

In which it is attempted to delineate the stronger passions of the mind

Joanna Baillie

A series of plays
In which it is attempted to delineate the stronger passions of the mind

ISBN/EAN: 9783744785662

Printed in Europe, USA, Canada, Australia, Japan

Cover: Foto ©Thomas Meinert / pixelio.de

More available books at **www.hansebooks.com**

A

SERIES OF PLAYS:

IN WHICH

IT IS ATTEMPTED TO DELINEATE

THE STRONGER PASSIONS OF THE MIND.

EACH PASSION BEING THE SUBJECT

OF

A TRAGEDY AND A COMEDY

———

LONDON:

PRINTED FOR T. CADELL, JUN. AND W. DAVIES, IN THE STRAND

1798.

INTRODUCTORY DISCOURSE.

I T is natural for a writer, who is about to
submit his works to the Publick, to feel a strong inclination, by some Preliminary Address, to conciliate
the favour of his reader, and dispose him, if possible,
to peruse them with a favourable eye. I am well
aware, however, that his endeavours are generally
fruitless : in his situation our hearts revolt from
all appearance of confidence, and we consider his
diffidence as hypocrisy. Our own word is frequently taken for what we say of ourselves, but
very rarely for what we say of our works. Were
these three plays, which this small volume contains,
detached pieces only, and unconnected with others
that do not yet appear, I should have suppressed
this inclination altogether; and have allowed my
reader to begin what is before him, and to form
what opinion of it his taste or his humour might
direct, without any previous trespass upon his time
or his patience. But they are part of an extensive
design : of one which, as far as my information
goes, has nothing exactly similar to it in any
language : of one which a whole life time will be

limited enough to accomplish; and which has,
therefore, a considerable chance of being cut short
by that hand which nothing can resist.

Before I explain the plan of this work, I must
make a demand upon the patience of my reader,
whilst I endeavour to communicate to him those
ideas regarding human nature, as they in some
degree affect almost every species of moral writings,
but particularly the Dramatic, that induced me to
attempt it; and, as far as my judgment enabled
me to apply them, has directed me in the execution of it.

From that strong sympathy which most creatures, but the human above all, feel for others of
their kind, nothing has become so much an object
of man's curiosity as man himself. We are all
conscious of this within ourselves, and so constantly do we meet with it in others, that like
every circumstance of continually repeated occur-
rence, it thereby escapes observation. Every
person, who is not deficient in intellect, is more
or less occupied in tracing, amongst the individuals
he converses with, the varieties of understanding
and temper which constitute the characters of
men; and receives great pleasure from every
stroke of nature that points out to him those
varieties. This is, much more than we are aware of,
the occupation of children, and of grown people
also, whose penetration is but lightly esteemed;

and that conversation which degenerates with them into trivial and mischievous tattling, takes its rise not unfrequently from the same source that supplies the rich vein of the satirist and the wit. That eagerness so universally shewn for the conversation of the latter, plainly enough indicates how many people have been occupied in the same way with themselves. Let any one, in a large company, do or say what is strongly expressive of his peculiar character, or of some passion or humour of the moment, and it will be detected by almost every person present. How often may we see a very stupid countenance animated with a smile, when the learned and the wise have betrayed some native feature of their own minds! and how often will this be the case when they have supposed it to be concealed under a very sufficient disguise! From this constant employment of their minds, most people, I believe, without being conscious of it, have stored up in idea the greater part of those strong marked varieties of human character, which may be said to divide it into classes; and in one of those classes they involuntarily place every new person they become acquainted with.

I will readily allow that the dress and the manners of men, rather than their characters and disposition are the subjects of our common conversation, and seem chiefly to occupy the multitude. But let it be remembered that it is much easier to express our observations upon these. It is easier to communicate to another how a man wears his wig and cane, what kind of house he inhabits, and what kind of table he keeps, than from what slight traits in his words and actions we have been led to conceive certain impressions of his character: traits that will often escape the memory, when the opinions that were founded upon them remain. Besides, in communicating our ideas of the characters of others, we are often called upon to support them with more expence of reasoning than we can well afford, but our observations on the dress and appearance of men, seldom involve us in such difficulties. For these, and other reasons too tedious to mention, the generality of people appear to us more trifling than they are: and I may venture to say that, but for this sympathetick curiosity towards others of our kind, which is so strongly implanted within us, the attention we pay to the dress and the manners of men would dwindle into an employment as insipid, as examining the varieties of plants and minerals, is to one who understands not natural history.

In our ordinary intercourse with society, this sympathetick propensity of our minds is exercised upon men, under the common occurrences of life, in which we have often observed them. Here vanity and weakness put themselves forward to view, more conspicuously than the virtues : here men encounter those smaller trials, from which they are not apt to come off victorious ; and here, consequently, that which is marked with the whimsical and ludicrous will strike us most forcibly, and make the strongest impression on our memory. To this sympathetick propensity of our minds, so exercised, the genuine and pure comick of every composition, whether drama, fable, story, or satire is addressed.

If man is an object of so much attention to man, engaged in the ordinary occurrences of life, how much more does he excite his curiosity and interest when placed in extraordinary situations of difficulty and distress ? It cannot be any pleasure we receive from the sufferings of a fellow-creature which attracts such multitudes of people to a publick execution, though it is the horrour we conceive for such a spectacle that keeps so many more away. To see a human being bearing himself up under such circumstances, or struggling with the terrible apprehensions which such a situation impresses, must be the powerful incentive, which makes us press forward to behold what we shrink from, and wait with trembling expectation for what we dread.* For though few

---

* In confirmation of this opinion I may venture to say, that

at such a spectacle can get near enough to distinguish the expression of face, or the minuter parts of a criminal's behaviour, yet from a considerable distance will they eagerly mark whether he steps firmly; whether the motions of his body denote agitation or calmness; and if the wind does but ruffle his garment, they will, even from that change upon the outline of his distant figure, read some expression connected with his dreadful situation. Though there is a greater proportion of people in whom this strong curiosity will be overcome by other dispositions and motives; though there are many more who will stay away from such a sight than will go to it; yet there are very few who will not be eager to converse with a person who has beheld it; and to learn, very minutely, every circumstance connected with it, except the very act itself of inflicting death. To lift up the roof of his dungeon, like the *Diable boiteux*, and look upon a criminal the night before he suffers, in his still

of the great numbers who go to see a publick execution, there are but very few who would not run away from, and avoid it, if they happened to meet with it unexpectedly. We find people stopping to look at a procession, or any other uncommon sight, they may have fallen in with accidentally, but almost never an execution. No one goes there who has not made up his mind for the occasion; which would not be the case, if any natural love of cruelty were the cause of such assemblies.

hours of privacy, when all that disguise, which respect for the opinion of others, the strong motive by which even the lowest and wickedest of men still continue to be moved, would present an object to the mind of every person, not withheld from it by, great timidity of character, more powerfully attractive than almost any other.

Revenge, no doubt, first began amongst the savages of America that dreadful custom of sacrificing their prisoners of war. But the perpetration of such hideous cruelty could never have become a permanent national custom, but for this universal desire in the human mind to behold man in every situation, putting forth his strength against the current of adversity, scorning all bodily anguish, or struggling with those feelings of nature, which, like a beating stream, will oft'times burst through the artificial barriers of pride. Before they begin those terrible rites they treat their prisoner kindly; and it cannot be supposed that men, alternately enemies and friends to so many neighbouring tribes, in manners. and appearance like themselves, should so strongly be actuated by a spirit of publick revenge. This custom, therefore, must be considered as a grand and terrible game, which every tribe plays against another; where they try not the strength of the arm, the swiftness of the feet, nor the acuteness of the eye, but the fortitude of the soul. Con-

sidered in this light, the excess of cruelty exercised
upon their miserable victim, in which every hand
is described as ready to inflict its portion of pain,
and every head ingenious in the contrivance of it,
is no longer to be wondered at. To put into his
measure of misery one agony less, would be, in
some degree, betraying the honour of their nation:
would be doing a species of injustice to every
hero of their own tribe who had already sustained
it, and to those who might be called upon to do
so ; amongst whom each of these savage tormentors
has his chance of being one, and has prepared
himself for it from his childhood. Nay, it would
be a species of injustice to the haughty victim
himself, who would scorn to purchase his place
amongst the heroes of his nation, at an easier
price than his undaunted predecessors.

Amongst the many trials to which the human
mind is subjected, that of holding intercourse,
real or imaginary, with the world of spirits: of
finding itself alone with a being terrifick and awful,
whose nature and power are unknown, has been
justly considered as one of the most severe. The
workings of nature in this situation, we all know,
have ever been the object of our most eager
enquiry. No man wishes to see the Ghost himself, which would certainly procure him the best
information on the subject, but every man wishes
to see one who believes that he sees it, in all the

agitation and wildness of that species of terrour. To gratify this curiosity how many people have dressed up hideous apparitions to frighten the timid and superstitious! and have done it at the risk of destroying their happiness or understanding for ever. For the instances of intellect being destroyed by this kind of trial are more numerous, perhaps, in proportion to the few who have undergone it than by any other.

How sensible are we of this strong propensity within us, when we behold any person under the pressure of great and uncommon calamity! Delicacy and respect for the afflicted will, indeed, make us turn ourselves aside from observing him, and cast down our eyes in his presence ; but the first glance we direct to him will involuntarily be one of the keenest observation, how hastily soever it may be checked; and often will a returning look of enquiry mix itself by stealth with our sympathy and reserve.

But it is not in situations of difficulty and distress alone, that man becomes the object of this sympathetick curiosity ; he is no less so when the evil he contends with arises in his own breast, and no outward circumstance connected with him either awakens our attention or our pity. What human creature is there, who can behold a being like himself under the violent agitation of those passions which all have, in some degree,

experienced, without feeling himself most powerfully excited by the sight ?   I say, all have experienced ; for the bravest man on earth knows
what fear is as well as the coward ; and will not
refuse to be interested for one under the dominion
of this passion, provided there be nothing in the
circumstances attending it to create contempt.
Anger is a passion that attracts less sympathy than
any other, yet the unpleasing and distorted features
of an angry man will be more eagerly gazed upon,
by those who are no wise concerned with his
fury or the objects of it, than the most amiable
placid countenance in the world.   Every eye is
directed to him ; every voice hushed to silence in
his presence ; even children will leave off their
gambols as he passes, and gaze after him more
eagerly than the gaudiest equipage.   The wild
tossings of despair ; the gnashing of hatred and
revenge ; the yearnings of affection, and the
softened mien of love ; all that language of the
agitated soul, which every age and nation understands, is never addressed to the dull nor
inattentive.

   It is not merely under the violent agitations of
passion, that man so rouses and interests us;
even the smallest indications of an unquiet mind,
the restless eye, the muttering lip, the half-checked
exclamation, and the hasty start, will set our
attention as anxiously upon the watch, as the

first distant flashes of a gathering storm. When some great explosion of passion bursts forth, and some consequent catastrophe happens, if we are at all acquainted with the unhappy perpetrator, how minutely will we endeavour to remember every circumstance of his past behaviour! and with what avidity will we seize upon every recollected word or gesture, that is in the smallest degree indicative of the supposed state of his mind, at the time when they took place. If we are not acquainted with him, how eagerly will we listen to similar recollections from another! Let us understand, from observation or report, that any person harbours in his breast, concealed from the world's eye, some powerful rankling passion of what kind soever it may be, we will observe every word, every motion, every look, even the distant gait of such a man, with a constancy and attention bestowed upon no other. Nay, should we meet him unexpectedly on our way, a feeling will pass across our minds as though we found ourselves in the neighbourhood of some secret and fearful thing. If invisible, would we not follow him into his lonely haunts, into his closet, into the midnight silence of his chamber? There is, perhaps, no employment which the human mind will with so much avidity pursue, as the discovery of concealed passion, as the tracing the varieties and progress of a perturbed soul.

It is to this sympathetick curiosity of our nature, exercised upon mankind in great and trying occasions, and under the influence of the stronger passions, when the grand, the generous, the terrible attract our attention far more than the base and depraved, that the high and powerfully tragick, of every composition, is addressed.

This propensity is universal. Children begin to shew it very early; it enters into many of their amusements, and that part of them too, for which they shew the keenest relish. It tempts them many times, as well as the mature in years, to be guilty of tricks, vexations, and cruelty; yet God Almighty has implanted it within us, as well as all our other propensities and passions, for wise and good purposes. It is our best and most powerful instructor. From it we are taught the proprieties and decencies of ordinary life, and are prepared for distressing and difficult situations. In examining others we know ourselves. With limbs untorn, with head unsmitten, with senses unimpaired by despair, we know what we ourselves might have been on the rack, on the scaffold, and in the most afflicting circumstances of distress. Unless when accompanied with passions of the dark and malevolent kind, we cannot well exercise this disposition without becoming more just, more merciful, more compassionate; and as the dark and malevolent passions are not the predominant inmates of the human breast, it hath produced more deeds—O many more ! of kindness than of cruelty. It holds up for our example a standard of excellence, which, without its assistance, our inward consciousness of what is right and becoming might never have dictated. It teaches us, also, to respect ourselves, and our kind ; for it is a poor mind, indeed, that from this employment of its faculties, learns not to dwell upon the noble view of human nature rather than the mean.

Universal, however, as this disposition undoubtedly is, with the generality of mankind it occupies itself in a passing and superficial way. Though a native trait of character or of passion is obvious to them as well as to the sage, yet to their minds it is but the visitor of a moment ; they look upon it singly and unconnected : and though this disposition, even so exercised, brings instruction as well as amusement, it is chiefly by storing up in their minds those ideas to which the instructions of others refer, that it can be eminently useful. Those who reflect and reason upon what human nature holds out to their observation, are comparatively but few. No stroke of nature which engages their attention stands insulated and alone. Each presents itself to them with many varied connections ; and they comprehend not merely the immediate feeling which

gave rise to it, but the relation of that feeling
to others which are concealed. We wonder at
the changes and caprices of men ; they see in
them nothing but what is natural and accountable.
We stare upon some dark catastrophe of passion,
as the Indians did upon an eclipse of the moon ;
they, conceiving the track of ideas through which
the impassioned mind has passed, regard it like
the philosopher who foretold the phenomenon.
Knowing what situation of life he is about to be
thrown into, they perceive in the man, who,
like Hazael, says, " is thy servant a dog that he
should do this thing ?" the foul and ferocious
murderer. A man of this contemplative character
partakes, in some degree, of the entertainment of
the Gods, who were supposed to look down upon
this world and the inhabitants of it, as we do upon
a theatrical exhibition; and if he is of a benevo-
lent disposition, a good man struggling with,
and triumphing over adversity, will be to him, also,
the most delightful spectacle. But though this
eagerness to observe their fellow-creatures in every
situation, leads not the generality of mankind to
reason and reflect; and those strokes of nature
which they are so ready to remark, stand single
and unconnected in their minds, yet they may be
easily induced to do both : and there is no mode
of instruction which they will so eagerly pursue,
as that which lays open before them, in a more

enlarged and connected view, than their individual observations are capable of supplying, the varieties of the human mind.   Above all, to be well exercised in this study will fit a man more particularly for the most important situations of life.   He will prove for it the better Judge, the better Magistrate, the better Advocate ; and as a ruler or conductor of other men, under every occurring circumstance, he will find himself the better enabled to fulfil his duty, and accomplish his designs.   He will perceive the natural effect of every order that he issues upon the minds of his soldiers, his subjects, or his followers ; and he will deal to others judgment tempered with mercy; that is to say truly just; for justice appears to us severe only when it is imperfect.

In proportion as moral writers of every class have exercised within themselves this sympathetick propensity of our nature, and have attended to it in others, their works have been interesting and instructive.   They have struck the imagination more forcibly, convinced the understanding more clearly, and more lastingly impressed the memory.   If unseasoned with any reference to this, the fairy bowers of the poet, with all his gay images of delight, will be admired and forgotten; the important relations of the historian, and even the reasonings of the philosopher will make a less permanent impression.

The historian points back to the men of other ages, and from the gradually clearing mist in which they are first discovered, like the mountains of a far distant land, the generations of the world are displayed to our mind's eye in grand and regular procession. But the transactions of men become interesting to us only as we are made acquainted with men themselves. Great and bloody battles are to us battles fought in the moon, if it is not impressed upon our minds, by some circumstances attending them, that men subject to like weaknesses and passions with ourselves, were the combatants.* The establishments of

---

* Let two great battles be described to us with all the force and clearness of the most able pen. In the first let the most admirable exertions of military skill in the General, and the most unshaken courage in the soldiers, gain over an equal or superiour number of brave opponents a compleat and glorious victory. In the second let the General be less scientifick, and the soldiers less dauntless. Let them go into the field for a cause that is dear to them, and fight with the ardour which such motives inspire; till discouraged with the many deaths around them, and the renovated pressure of the foe, some unlooked-for circumstance, trifling in itself, strikes their imagination at once; they are visited with the terrours of nature; their national pride, the honour of soldiership is forgotten; they fly like a fearful flock. Let some beloved chief then step forth, and call upon them by the love of their country, by the memory of their valiant fathers, by every thing that kindles in the bosom of man the high and generous passions: they stop; they gather round him; and goaded by shame and indignation, returning again to the charge, with the fury of wild beasts rather than the courage of soldiers, bear down every thing before them. Which of these two battles will interest us the most? and which of them shall we remember the longest? The one will stand forth in the imagination of the reader like a rock of the desert, which points out to the far-removed traveller the country through which he has passed, when its lesser objects are obscured in the distance; whilst the other leaves no traces behind it, but in the minds of the scientifick in war.

policy make little impression upon us, if we are left ignorant of the beings whom they affected. Even a very masterly drawn character will but slightly imprint upon our memory the great man it belongs to, if, in the account we receive of his life, those lesser circumstances are entirely neglected, which do best of all point out to us the dispositions and tempers of men. Some slight circumstance characteristick of the particular turn of a man's mind, which at first sight seems but little connected with the great events of his life, will often explain some of those events more clearly to our understanding, than the minute details of ostensible policy. A judicious selection of those circumstances which characterize the spirit of an associated mob, paltry and ludicrous as some of them may appear, will oftentimes convey to our minds a clearer idea why certain laws and privileges were demanded and agreed to, than a methodical explanation of their causes. A historian who has examined human nature himself, and likewise attends to the pleasure which developing and tracing it, does ever convey to others, will employ our understanding as well as our memory with his pages; and if this is not done, he will impose upon the latter a very difficult task, in retaining what she is concerned with alone.

In argumentative and philosophical writings, the effect which the author's reasoning produces on our minds depends not entirely on the justness of it. The images and examples that he calls to his aid, to explain and illustrate his meaning, will very much affect the attention we are able to bestow upon it, and consequently the quickness with which we shall apprehend, and the force with which it will impress us. These are selected from animated and unanimated nature, from the habits, manners, and characters of men ; and though that image or example, whatever it may be in itself, which brings out his meaning most clearly, ought to be preferred before every other, yet of two equal in this respect, that which is drawn from the most interesting source will please us the most at the time, and most lastingly take hold of our minds. An argument supported with vivid and interesting illustration, will long be remembered when many equally important and clear are forgotten ; and a work where many such occur will be held in higher estimation by the generality of men, than one its superior, perhaps, in acuteness, perspicuity, and good sense.

Our desire to know what men are in the closet as well as the field, by the blazing hearth, and at the social board, as well as in the council and the throne, is very imperfectly gratified by real history ; romance writers, therefore, stepped boldly forth to supply the deficiency ; and tale writers, and novel writers, of many descriptions, followed after. If they have not been very skilful in their delincations of nature; if they have represented men and women speaking and acting as men and women never did speak or act; if they have caricatured both our virtues and our vices; if they have given us such pure and unmixed, or such heterogeneous combinations of character as real life never presented, and yet have pleased and interested us, let it not be imputed to the dulness of man in discerning what is genuinely natural in himself. There are many inclinations belonging to us, besides this great master-propensity of which I am treating. Our love of the grand, the beautiful, the novel, and above all of the marvellous, is very strong; and if we are richly fed with what we have a good relish for, we may be weaned to forget our native and favourite aliment. Yet we can never so far forget it, but that we will cling to, and acknowledge it again, whenever it is presented before us. In a work abounding with the marvellous and unnatural, if the author has any how stumbled upon an unsophisticated genuine stroke of nature, we will immediately perceive and be delighted with it, though we are foolish enough to admire at the same time, all the nonsense with which it is surrounded. After all the wonderful incidents, dark mysteries, and secrets revealed, which eventful novel so liberally presents to us; after the beautiful fairy ground, and even

the grand and sublime scenes of nature with
which descriptive novel so often enchants us;
those works which most strongly characterize
human nature in the middling and lower classes
of society, where it is to be discovered by stronger
and more unequivocal marks, will ever be the
most popular.   For though great pains have been
taken in our higher sentimental novels to interest
us in the delicacies, embarrassments, and artificial
distresses of the more refined part of society, they
have never been able to cope in the publick opinion
with these.   The one is a dressed and beautiful
pleasure-ground, in which we are enchanted for
a while, amongst the delicate and unknown plants
of artful cultivation ; the other is a rough forest
of our native land ; the oak, the elm, the hazle,
and the bramble are there; and amidst the endless
varieties of its paths we can wander for ever.
Into whatever scenes the novelist may conduct
us, what objects soever he may present to our
view, still is our attention most sensibly awake
to every touch faithful to nature ; still are we
upon the watch for every thing that speaks to us
of ourselves.

The fair field of what is properly called poetry,
is enriched with so many beauties, that in it we
are often tempted to forget what we really are,
and what kind of beings we belong to.   Who in
the enchanted regions of simile, metaphor,

allegory and description, can remember the plain order of things in this every-day world ? From heroes whose majestick forms rise like a lofty tower, whose eyes are lightening, whose arms are irresistible, whose course is like the storms of heaven, bold and exalted sentiments we will readily receive ; and will not examine them very accurately by that rule of nature which our own breast prescribes to us. A shepherd whose sheep, with fleeces of the purest snow, browze the flowery herbage of the most beautiful vallies ; whose flute is ever melodious, and whose shepherdess is ever crowned with roses ; whose every care is love, will not be called very strictly to account for the loftiness and refinement of his thoughts. The fair Nymph, who sighs out her sorrows to the conscious and compassionate wilds ; whose eyes gleam like the bright drops of heaven ; whose loose tresses stream to the breeze, may say what she pleases with impunity. I will venture, however, to say, that amidst all this decoration and ornament, all this loftiness and refinement, let one simple trait of the human heart, one expression of passion genuine and true to nature, be introduced, and it will stand forth alone in the boldness of reality, whilst the false and unnatural around it, fades away upon every side, like the rising exhalations of the morning. With admiration, and often with enthusiasm we proceed on

our way through the grand and the beautiful
images, raised to our imagination by the lofty
Epic muse; but what even here are those things
that strike upon the heart; that we feel and
remember? Neither the descriptions of war, the
sound of the trumpet, the clanging of arms, the
combat of heroes, nor the death of the mighty,
will interest our minds like the fall of the feeble
stranger, who simply expresses the anguish of his
soul, at the thoughts of that far-distant home
which he must never return to again, and closes
his eyes amongst the ignoble and forgotten; like
the timid stripling goaded by the shame of
reproach, who urges his trembling steps to the
fight, and falls like a tender flower before the
first blast of winter. How often will some simple
picture of this kind be all that remains upon our
minds of the terrifick and magnificent battle,
whose description we have read with admiration!
How comes it that we relish so much the episodes
of an heroick poem? It cannot merely be that
we are pleased with a resting-place, where we
enjoy the variety of contrast; for were the poem
of the simple and familiar kind, and an episode
after the heroick style introduced into it, ninety
readers out of an hundred would pass over it
altogether. Is it not that we meet such a story,
so situated, with a kind of sympathetick good
will, as in passing through a country of castles

and of palaces, we should pop unawares upon some humble cottage, resembling the dwellings of our own native land, and gaze upon it with affection. The highest pleasures we receive from poetry, as well as from the real objects which surround us in the world, are derived from the sympathetick interest we all take in beings like ourselves ; and I will even venture to say, that were the grandest scenes which can enter into the imagination of man, presented to our view, and all reference to man completely shut out from our thoughts, the objects that composed it would convey to our minds little better than dry ideas of magnitude, colour, and form ; and the remembrance of them would rest upon our minds like the measurement and distances of the planets.

If the study of human nature then, is so useful to the poet, the novelist, the historian, and the philosopher, of how much greater importance must it be to the dramatick writer ? To them it is a powerful auxiliary, to him it is the centre and strength of the battle. If characteristick views of human nature enliven not their pages, there are many excellencies with which they can, in some degree, make up for the deficiency, it is what we receive from them with pleasure rather than demand. But in his works no richness of invention, harmony of language, nor grandeur of

sentiment will supply the place of faithfully delineated nature.　The poet and the novelist may
represent to you their great characters from
the cradle to the tomb.　They may represent
them in any mood or temper, and under the
influence of any passion which they see proper,
without being obliged to put words into their
mouths, those great betrayers of the feigned and
adopted.　They may relate every circumstance
however trifling and minute, that serves to
develope their tempers and dispositions.　They
tell us what kind of people they intend their
men and women to be, and as such we receive
them.　If they are to move us with any scene of
distress, every circumstance regarding the parties
concerned in it, how they looked, how they
moved, how they sighed, how the tears gushed
from their eyes, how the very light and shadow
fell upon them, is carefully described, and the
few things that are given them to say along with
all this assistance, must be very unnatural indeed
if we refuse to sympathize with them.　But the
characters of the drama must speak directly for
themselves.　Under the influence of every passion,
humour, and impression ; in the artificial veilings
of hypocrisy and ceremony, in the openness of
freedom and confidence, and in the lonely hour
of meditation they speak.　He who made us hath
placed within our breast a judge that judges

instantaneously of every thing they say. We expect to find them creatures like ourselves ; and if they are untrue to nature, we feel that we are imposed upon ; as though the poet had introduced to us for brethren, creatures of a different race, beings of another world.

As in other works deficiency in characteristick truth may be compensated by excellencies of a different kind, in the drama characteristick truth will compensate every other defect. Nay, it will do what appears a contradiction; one strong genuine stroke of nature will cover a multitude of sins even against nature herself. When we meet in some scene of a good play a very fine stroke of this kind, we are apt to become so intoxicated with it, and so perfectly convinced of the author's great knowledge of the human heart, that we are unwilling to suppose that the whole of it has not been suggested by the same penetrating spirit. Many well-meaning enthusiastick criticks have given themselves a great deal of trouble in this way ; and have shut their eyes most ingeniously against the fair light of nature for the very love of it. They have converted, in their great zeal, sentiments palpably false, both in regard to the character and situation of the persons who utter them, sentiments which a child or a clown would detect, into the most skilful depictments of the heart. I can think of no stronger instance to shew how powerfully this love of nature dwells within us.*

Formed as we are with these sympathetick propensities in regard to our own species, it is not at all wonderful that theatrical exhibition has become the grand and favourite amusement of every nation into which it has been introduced. Savages will, in the wild contortions of a dance, shape out some rude story expressive of character or passion, and such a dance will give more delight to his companions than the most artful exertions of agility. Children in their gambols will make out a mimick representation of the manners, characters, and passions of grown men and women, and such a pastime will animate and delight them much more than a treat of the daintiest sweetmeats, or the handling of the gaudiest toys. Eagerly as it is enjoyed by the rude and the young, to the polished and the ripe in years it is still the most interesting amusement.

---

* It appears to me a very strong testimony of the excellence of our great national Dramatist, that so many people have been employed in finding out obscure and refined beauties, in what appear to ordinary observation his very defects. Men, it may be said, do so merely to shew their own superior penetration and ingenuity. But granting this; what could make other men listen to them, and listen so greedily too, if it were not that they have received from the works of Shakspeare, pleasure far beyond what the most perfect poetical compositions of a different character can afford.

Our taste for it is durable as it is universal. Independently of those circumstances which first introduced it, the world would not have long been without it. The progress of society would soon have brought it forth; and men in the whimsical decorations of fancy would have displayed the characters and actions of their heroes, the folly and absurdity of their fellow-citizens, had no Priests of Bacchus ever existed.*

* Though the progress of society would have given us the Drama, independently of the particular cause of its first commencement, the peculiar circumstances connected with its origin, have had considerable influence upon its character and style, in the ages through which it has passed even to our days, and still will continue to affect it. Homer had long preceded the dramatick poets of Greece; poetry was in a high state of cultivation when they began to write; and their style, the construction of their pieces, and the characters of their heroes were different from what they would have been, had theatrical exhibitions been the invention of an earlier age or a ruder people. Their works were represented to an audience, already accustomed to hear long poems rehearsed at their publick games, and the feasts of their gods. A play, with the principal characters of which they were previously acquainted; in which their great men and heroes, in the most beautiful language, complained of their rigorous fate, but piously submitted to the will of the Gods; in which sympathy was chiefly excited by tender and affecting sentiments; in which strong bursts of passion were few; and in which whole scenes frequently passed, without giving the actors any thing to do but to speak, was not too insipid for them. Had the Drama been the invention of a less cultivated nation, more of action and of passion would have been introduced into it. It would have been

In whatever age or country the Drama might have taken its rise, tragedy would have been the first-born of its children. For every nation has its great men, and its great events upon record; and to represent their own forefathers struggling with those difficulties, and braving those dangers, of which they have heard with admiration, and the effects of which they still, perhaps, experience, would certainly have been the most animating subject for the poet, and the most interesting for his audience, even independently of the natural

more irregular, more imperfect, more varied, more interesting. From poor beginnings it would have advanced in a progressive state; and succeeding poets, not having those polished and admired originals to look back upon, would have presented their respective contemporaries with the produce of a free and unbridled imagination. A different class of poets would most likely have been called into existence. The latent powers of men are called forth by contemplating those works in which they find any thing congenial to their own peculiar talents; and if the field, wherein they could have worked, is already enriched with a produce unsuited to their cultivation, they think not of entering it at all. Men, therefore, whose natural turn of mind led them to labour, to reason, to refine and exalt, have caught their animation from the beauties of the Grecian Drama, and they who, perhaps, ought only to have been our Criticks have become our Poets. I mean not, however, in any degree to depreciate the works of the ancients; a great deal we have gained by those beautiful compositions; and what we have lost by them it is impossible to compute. Very strong genius will sometimes break through every disadvantage of circumstances: Shakspeare has arisen in this country, and we ought not to complain.

inclination we all so universally shew for scenes of horrour and distress, of passion and heroick exertion. Tragedy would have been the first child of the Drama, for the same reasons that have made heroick ballad, with all its battles, murders, and disasters, the earliest poetical compositions of every country.

We behold heroes and great men at a distance, unmarked by those small but distinguishing features of the mind, which give a certain individuality to such an infinite variety of similar beings, in the near and familiar intercourse of life. They appear to us from this view like distant mountains, whose dark outlines we trace in the clear horizon, but the varieties of whose roughened sides, shaded with heath and brushwood, and seamed with many a cleft, we perceive not. When accidental anecdote reveals to us any weakness or peculiarity belonging to them, we start upon it like a discovery. They are made known to us in history only, by the great events they are connected with, and the part they have taken in extraordinary or important transactions. Even in poetry and romance, with the exception of some love story interwoven with the main events of their lives, they are seldom more intimately made known to us. To Tragedy it belongs to lead them forward to our nearer regard, in all the distinguishing varieties which nearer inspection discovers; with the passions, the humours, the weaknesses, the prejudices of men. It is for her to present to us the great and magnanimous hero, who appears to our distant view as a superior being, as a God, softened down with those smaller frailties and imperfections which enable us to glory in, and claim kindred to his virtues. It is for her to exhibit to us the daring and ambitious man, planning his dark designs, and executing his bloody purposes, mark'd with those appropriate characteristicks, which distinguish him as an individual of that class; and agitated with those varied passions, which disturb the mind of man when he is engaged in the commission of such deeds. It is for her to point out to us the brave and impetuous warrior struck with those visitations of nature, which, in certain situations, will unnerve the strongest arm, and make the boldest heart tremble. It is for her to shew the tender, gentle, and unassuming mind animated with that fire which, by the provocation of circumstances, will give to the kindest heart the ferocity and keenness of a tiger. It is for her to present to us the great and striking characters that are to be found amongst men, in a way which the poet, the novelist, and the historian can but imperfectly attempt. But above all, to her, and to her only it belongs to unveil to us the human mind under the dominion of those strong and fixed passions,

which, seemingly unprovoked by outward circumstances, will from small beginnings brood
within the breast, till all the better dispositions,
all the fair gifts of nature are borne down before
them. Those passions which conceal themselves
from the observation of men; which cannot
unbosom themselves even to the dearest friend ;
and can, often times, only give their fulness vent
in the lonely desert, or in the darkness of midnight.
For who hath followed the great man into his
secret closet, or stood by the side of his nightly
couch, and heard those exclamations of the soul
which heaven alone may hear, that the historian
should be able to inform us ? and what form of
story, what mode of rehearsed speech will communicate to us those feelings, whose irregular
bursts, abrupt transitions, sudden pauses, and
half-uttered suggestions, scorn all harmony of
measured verse, all method and order of relation?

On the first part of this task her Bards have
eagerly exerted their abilities: and some amongst
them, taught by strong original genius to deal
immediately with human nature and their own
hearts, have laboured in it successfully. But in
presenting to us those views of great characters,
and of the human mind in difficult and trying
situations which peculiarly belong to Tragedy,
the far greater proportion, even of those who may
be considered as respectable dramatick poets,

have very much failed.   From the beauty of those
original dramas to which they have ever looked
back with admiration, they have been tempted
to prefer the embellishments of poetry to faithfully
delineated nature. They have been more occupied
in considering the works of the great Dramatists
who have gone before them, and the effects produced by their writings, than the varieties of
human character which first furnished materials
for those works, or those principles in the mind
of man by means of which such effects were
produced. Neglecting the boundless variety of
nature, certain strong outlines of character,
certain bold features of passion, certain grand
vicissitudes, and striking dramatick situations
have been repeated from one generation to
another ; whilst a pompous and solemn gravity,
which they have supposed to be necessary for
the dignity of tragedy, has excluded almost
entirely from their works those smaller touches
of nature, which so well develope the mind; and
by showing men in their hours of state and
exertion only, they have consequently shewn
them imperfectly. Thus, great and magnanimous
heroes, who bear with majestick equanimity every
vicissitude of fortune ; who in every temptation
and trial stand forth in unshaken virtue, like a
rock buffeted by the waves ; who encompast with
the most terrible evils, in calm possession of

their souls, reason upon the difficulties of their
state ; and, even upon the brink of destruction,
pronounce long eulogiums on virtue, in the most
eloquent and beautiful language, have been held
forth to our view as objects of imitation and
interest ; as though they had entirely forgotten that
it is only from creatures like ourselves that we feel,
and therefore, only from creatures like ourselves
that we receive the instruction of example.* Thus,
passionate and impetuous warriors, who are proud,
irritable, and vindictive, but generous, daring,
and disinterested ; setting their lives at a pin's
fee for the good of others, but incapable of
curbing their own humour of a moment to gain
the whole world for themselves ; who will pluck

---

* To a being perfectly free from all human infirmity our
sympathy refuses to extend. Our Saviour himself, whose
character is so beautiful, and so harmoniously consistent; in
whom, with outward proofs of his mission less strong than those
that are offered to us, I should still be compelled to believe,
from being utterly unable to conceive how the idea of such a
character could enter into the imagination of man, never touches
the heart more nearly than when he says, " Father, let this
cup pass from me." Had he been represented to us in all the
unshaken strength of these tragick heroes, his disciples would
have made fewer converts, and his precepts would have been
listened to coldly. Plays in which heroes of this kind are held
forth, and whose aim is, indeed, honourable and praise-worthy,
have been admired by the cultivated and refined, but the tears
of the simple, the applauses of the young and untaught have
been wanting.

D

the orbs of heaven from their places, and crush
the whole universe in one grasp, are called forth
to kindle in our souls the generous contempt of
every thing abject and base; but with an effect
proportionably feeble, as the hero is made to
exceed in courage and fire what the standard of
humanity will agree to. *   Thus, tender and

---

* In all burlesque imitations of tragedy, those plays in
which this hero is pre-eminent, are always exposed to bear the
great brunt of the ridicule; which proves how popular they
have been, and how many poets, and good ones too, have been
employed upon them. That they have been so popular, however, is not owing to the intrinsick merit of the characters they
represent, but their opposition to those mean and contemptible
qualities belonging to human nature, of which we are most
ashamed. Besides, there is something in the human mind,
independently of its love of applause, which inclines it to boast.
This is ever the attendant of that elasticity of soul, which makes
us bound up from the touch of oppression; and if there is nothing
in the accompanying circumstances to create disgust, or suggest
suspicions of their sincerity, (as in real life is commonly the
case,) we are very apt to be carried along with the boasting of
others. Let us in good earnest believe that a man is capable of
achieving all that human courage can achieve, and we will
suffer him to talk of impossibilities. Amidst all their pomp of
words, therefore, our admiration of such heroes is readily
excited, (for the understanding is more easily deceived than the
heart,) but how stands our sympathy affected? As no caution
nor foresight, on their own account, is ever suffered to occupy the
thoughts of such bold disinterested beings, we are the more
inclined to care for them, and take an interest in their fortune
through the course of the play: yet, as their souls are unappalled

pathetick lovers, full of the most gentle affections, the most amiable dispositions, and the most exquisite feelings ; who present their defenceless bosoms to the storms of this rude world in all the graceful weakness of sensibility, are made to sigh out their sorrows in one unvaried strain of studied pathos, whilst this constant demand upon our feelings makes us absolutely incapable of answering it.* Thus, also, tyrants are represented as monsters of cruelty, unmixed with any feelings of humanity ; and villains as delighting in all manner of treachery and deceit, and acting upon many occasions for the very love of villainy itself; though the perfectly wicked are as ill fitted for the purposes of warning, as the perfectly virtuous are for those of

by any thing ; as pain and death are not at all regarded by them ; and as we have seen them very ready to plunge their own swords into their own bosoms, on no very weighty occasion, perhaps, their death distresses us but little, and they commonly fall unwept.

* Were it not, that in tragedies where these heroes preside, the same soft tones of sorrow are so often repeated in our ears, till we are perfectly tired of it, they are more fitted to interest us than any other : both because in seeing them, we own the ties of kindred between ourselves and the frail mortals we lament ; and sympathize with the weakness of mortality unmixed with any thing to degrade or disgust ; and also, because the misfortunes, which form the story of the play, are frequently of the more familiar and domestick kind. A king driven from his throne, will not move our sympathy so strongly, as a private man torn from the bosom of his family.

example.* This spirit of imitation, and attention
to effect, has likewise confined them very much
in their choice of situations and events to bring
their great characters into action ; rebellions,
conspiracies, contentions for empire, and rivalships
in love have alone been thought worthy of trying
those heroes ; and palaces and dungeons the only
places magnificent or solemn enough for them
to appear in.

They have, indeed, from this regard to the
works of preceding authors, and great attention
to the beauties of composition, and to dignity of
design, enriched their plays with much striking,
and sometimes sublime imagery, lofty thoughts,
and virtuous sentiments ; but in striving so eagerly
to excell in those things that belong to tragedy

---

* I have said nothing here in regard to female character,
though in many tragedies it is brought forward as the principal
one of the piece, because what I have said of the above characters
is likewise applicable to it. I believe there is no man that ever
lived, who has behaved in a certain manner, on a certain occasion,
who has not had amongst women some corresponding spirit, who
on the like occasion, and every way similarly circumstanced,
would have behaved in the like manner. With some degree
of softening and refinement, each class of the tragick heroes I
have mentioned has its corresponding one amongst the heroines.
The tender and pathetick no doubt has the most numerous, but
the great and magnanimous is not without it, and the passionate
and impetuous boasts of one by no means inconsiderable in
numbers, and drawn sometimes to the full as passionate and
impetuous as itself.

in common with many other compositions, they
have very much neglected those that are peculiarly
her own. As far as they have been led aside from
the first labours of a tragick poet by a desire to
communicate more perfect moral instruction,
their motive has been respectable, and they
merit our esteem. But this praise-worthy end
has been injured instead of promoted by their
mode of pursuing it. Every species of moral
writing has its own way of conveying instruction,
which it can never, but with disadvantage,
exchange for any other. The Drama improves
us by the knowledge we acquire of our own
minds, from the natural desire we have to look
into the thoughts, and observe the behaviour of
others. Tragedy brings to our view men placed
in those elevated situations, exposed to those
great trials, and engaged in those extraordinary
transactions, in which few of us are called upon
to act. As examples applicable to ourselves,
therefore, they can but feebly effect us; it is
only from the enlargement of our ideas in regard
to human nature, from that admiration of virtue,
and abhorrence of vice which they excite, that
we can expect to be improved by them. But if
they are not represented to us as real and natural
characters, the lessons we are taught from their
conduct and their sentiments will be no more to
us than those which we receive from the pages of
the poet or the moralist.

But the last part of the task which I have mentioned as peculiarly belonging to tragedy, unveiling the human mind under the dominion of those strong and fixed passions, which seemingly unprovoked by outward circumstances, will from small beginnings brood within the breast, till all the better dispositions, all the fair gifts of nature are borne down before them, her poets in general have entirely neglected, and even her first and greatest have but imperfectly attempted. They have made use of the passions to mark their several characters, and animate their scenes, rather than to open to our view the nature and portraitures of those great disturbers of the human breast, with whom we are all, more or less, called upon to contend.   With their strong and obvious features, therefore, they have been presented to us, stripped almost entirely of those less obtrusive, but not less discriminating traits, which mark them in their actual operation.   To trace them in their rise and progress in the heart, seems but rarely to have been the object of any dramatist. We commonly find the characters of a tragedy affected by the passions in a transient, loose, un-connected manner ; or if they are represented as under the permanent influence of the more powerful ones, they are generally introduced to our notice in the very height of their fury, when all that timidity, irresolution, distrust, and a thou-

sand delicate traits, which make the infancy of
every great passion more interesting, perhaps,
than its full-blown strength, are fled. The impassioned character is generally brought into view
under those irresistible attacks of their power,
which it is impossible to repell ; whilst those gradual steps that led him into this state, in some of
which a stand might have been made against the
foe, are left entirely in the shade. These passions
that may be suddenly excited, and are of short
duration, as anger, fear, and oftentimes jealousy,
may in this manner be fully represented ; but
those great masters of the soul, ambition, hatred,
love, every passion that is permanent in its nature,
and varied in progress, if represented to us but in
one stage of its course, is represented imperfectly.
It is a characteristick of the more powerful passions
that they will encrease and nourish themselves on
very slender aliment ; it is from within that they
are chiefly supplied with what they feed on ; and
it is in contending with opposite passions and affections of the mind that we least discover their
strength, not with events. But in tragedy it is
events more frequently than opposite affections
which are opposed to them ; and those often of
such force and magnitude that the passions themselves are almost obscured by the splendour and
importance of the transactions to which they are
attached. But besides being thus confined and

mutilated, the passions have been, in the greater part of our tragedies, deprived of the very power of making themselves known. Bold and figurative language belongs peculiarly to them. Poets, admiring those bold expressions which a mind, labouring with ideas too strong to be conveyed in the ordinary forms of speech, wildly throws out, taking earth, sea, and sky, every thing great and terrible in nature to image forth the violence of its feelings, borrowed them gladly, to adorn the calm sentiments of their premeditated song. It has therefore been thought that the less animated parts of tragedy might be so embellished and enriched. In doing this, however, the passions have been robbed of their native prerogative ; and in adorning with their strong figures and lofty expressions the calm speeches of the unruffled, it is found that, when they are called upon to raise their voice, the power of distinguishing themselves has been taken away. This is an injury by no means compensated, but very greatly aggravated by embellishing, in return, the speeches of passion with the ingenious conceits, and compleat similies of premeditated thought.* There are many other things

* This, perhaps, more than any thing else has injured the higher scenes of tragedy. For having made such free use of bold hyperbolical language in the inferior parts, the poet when he arrives at the highly impassioned sinks into total inability : or if he will force himself to rise still higher on the wing, he

regarding the manner in which dramatick poets
have generally brought forward the passions in
tragedy, to the great prejudice of that effect
they are naturally fitted to produce upon the
mind, which I forbear to mention, lest they should
too much increase the length of this discourse;
and leave an impression on the mind of my reader,
that I write more on the spirit of criticism, than
becomes one who is about to bring before the
publick a work, with, doubtless, many faults and
imperfections on its head.

From this general view, which I have endeavoured to communicate to my reader, of tragedy,
and those principles in the human mind upon
which the success of her efforts depends, I have
been led to believe, that an attempt to write a
series of tragedies, of simpler construction, less
embellished with poetical decorations, less constrained by that lofty seriousness which has so generally been considered as necessary for the support of tragick dignity, and in which the chief object should be to delineate the progress of the
higher passions in the human breast, each play ex-
hibiting a particular passion, might not be unac-
ceptable to the publick. And I have been the
more readily induced to act upon this idea, because I am confident, that tragedy, written upon

flies beyond nature altogether, into the regions of bombast and
nonsense.

this plan, is fitted to produce stronger moral effect
than upon any other. I have said that tragedy
in representing to us great characters struggling
with difficulties, and placed in situations of emi-
nence and danger, in which few of us have any
chance of being called upon to act, conveys its
moral efficacy to our minds by the enlarged views
which it gives to us of human nature, by the admiration of virtue, and execration of vice which it
excites, and not by the examples it holds up for
our immediate application. But in opening to us
the heart of man under the influence of those passions to which all are liable, this is not the case.
Those strong passions that, with small assistance
from outward circumstances, work their way in the
heart, till they become the tyrannical masters of it,
carry on a similar operation in the breast of the
Monarch, and the man of low degree. It exhibits
to us the mind of man in that state when we are
most curious to look into it, and is equally interesting to all. Discrimination of character is a
turn of mind, tho' more common than we are aware
of, which every body does not possess ; but to the
expressions of passion, particularly strong passion,
the dullest mind is awake ; and its true unsophisticated language the dullest understanding will
not misinterpret. To hold up for our example
those peculiarities in disposition, and modes of
thinking which nature has fixed upon us, or which

long and early habit has incorporated with our original selves, is almost desiring us to remove the everlasting mountains, to take away the native land-marks of the soul; but representing the passions brings before us the operation of a tempest that rages out its time and passes away. We cannot, it is true, amidst its wild uproar, listen to the voice of reason, and save ourselves from destruction; but we can foresee its coming, we can mark its rising signs, we can know the situations that will most expose us to its rage, and we can shelter our heads from the coming blast. To change a certain disposition of mind which makes us view objects in a particular light, and thereby, oftentimes, unknown to ourselves, influences our conduct and manners, is almost impossible; but in checking and subduing those visitations of the soul, whose causes and effects we are aware of, every one may make considerable progress, if he proves not entirely successful. Above all, looking back to the first rise, and tracing the progress of passion, points out to us those stages in the approach of the enemy, when he might have been combated most successfully; and where the suffering him to pass may be considered as occasioning all the misery that ensues.

Comedy presents to us men as we find them in the ordinary intercourse of the world, with all the weaknesses, follies, caprice, prejudices, and absur-

dities which a near and familiar view of them discovers. It is her task to exhibit them engaged in
the busy turmoil of ordinary life, harassing and
perplexing themselves with the endless pursuits
of avarice, vanity, and pleasure ; and engaged
with those smaller trials of the mind, by which
men are most apt to be overcome, and from which
he, who could have supported with honour the
attack of greater occasions, will oftentimes come
off most shamefully foiled. It belongs to her to
shew the varied fashions and manners of the world,
as, from the spirit of vanity, caprice, and imitation,
they go on in swift and endless succession ; and
those disagreeable or absurd peculiarities attached
to particular classes and conditions in society. It
is for her also to represent men under the influence
of the stronger passions ; and to trace the rise and
progress of them in the heart, in such situations,
and attended with such circumstances as take off
their sublimity, and the interest we naturally take
in a perturbed mind. It is hers to exhibit those
terrible tyrants of the soul, whose ungovernable
rage has struck us so often with dismay, like wild
beasts tied to a post, who growl and paw before
us, for our derision and sport. In pourtraying the
characters of men she has this advantage over tragedy, that the smallest traits of nature, with the
smallest circumstances which serve to bring them
forth, may by her be displayed, however ludicrous

and trivial in themselves, without any ceremony. And in developing the passions she enjoys a similar advantage ; for they often most strongly betray themselves when touched by those small and familiar occurrences which cannot, consistently with the effect it is intended to produce, be admitted into tragedy.

As tragedy has been very much cramped in her endeavours to exalt and improve the mind, by that spirit of imitation and confinement in her successive writers, which the beauty of her earliest poets first gave rise to, so comedy has been led aside from her best purposes by a different temptation. Those endless changes in fashions and in manners, which offer such obvious and ever-new subjects of ridicule ; that infinite variety of tricks and manœuvres by which the ludicrous may be produced, and curiosity and laughter excited : the admiration we so generally bestow upon satirical remark, pointed repartee, and whimsical combinations of ideas, have too often led her to forget the warmer interest we feel, and the more profitable lessons we receive from genuine representations of nature. The most interesting and instructive class of comedy, therefore, the real characteristick, has been very much neglected, whilst satirical, witty, sentimental, and, above all, busy or circumstantial comedy have usurped the ex-

ertions of the far greater proportion of Dramatick
Writers.

In Satirical Comedy, sarcastick and severe reflections on the actions and manners of men, introduced with neatness, force, and poignancy of
expression into a lively and well supported dialogue,
of whose gay surface they are the embossed ornaments, make the most important and studied part
of the work : Character is a thing talked of rather
than shewn. The persons of the drama are indebted for the discovery of their peculiarities to
what is said to them, rather than to any thing they
are made to say or do for themselves. Much incident being unfavourable for studied and elegant
dialogue, the plot is commonly simple, and the few
events that compose it neither interesting nor striking. It only affords us that kind of moral instruction which an essay or a poem could as well have
conveyed, and, though amusing in the closet, is but
feebly attractive in the Theatre. *

In what I have termed Witty Comedy, every
thing is light, playful, and easy. Strong decided

---

* These plays are generally the work of men, whose judgement and acute observation, enable them admirably well to ge-
neralize, and apply to classes of men the remarks they have made
upon individuals ; yet know not how to dress up, with any natural congruity, an imaginary individual in the attributes they
have assigned to those classes.

1

condemnation of vice is too weighty and material to dance upon the surface of that stream, whose shallow currents sparkle in perpetual sun-beams, and cast up their bubbles to the light. Two or three persons of quick thought, and whimsical fancy, who perceive instantaneously the various connections of every passing idea, and the significations, natural or artificial, which single expressions, or particular forms of speech can possibly convey, take the lead thro' the whole, and seem to communicate their own peculiar talent to every creature in the play. The plot is most commonly feeble rather than simple, the incidents being numerous enough, but seldom striking or varied. To amuse, and only to amuse, is its aim: it pretends not to interest nor instruct. It pleases when we read, more than when we see it represented; and pleases still more when we take it up by accident, and read but a scene at a time.

Sentimental Comedy treats of those embarrassments, difficulties, and scruples, which, though sufficiently distressing to the delicate minds who entertain them, are not powerful enough to gratify the sympathetick desire we all feel to look into the heart of man in difficult and trying situations, which is the sound basis of tragedy, and are destitute of that seasoning of the lively and ludicrous, which prevents the ordinary transactions of comedy from becoming insipid. In real life, those who,

from the peculiar frame of their minds, feel most
of this refined distress, are not generally communicative upon the subject; and those who do feel
and talk about it at the same time, if any such
there be, seldom find their friends much inclined
to listen to them. It is not to be supposed, then,
long conversations upon the stage about small sentimental niceties, can be generally interesting. I
am afraid plays of this kind, as well as works of a
similar nature, in other departments of literature,
have only tended to encrease amongst us a set of
sentimental hypocrites; who are the same persons
of this age that would have been the religious ones
of another; and are daily doing morality the same
kind of injury, by substituting the particular
excellence which they pretend to possess, for plain
simple uprightness and rectitude.

In Busy or Circumstantial Comedy, all those ingenious contrivances of lovers, guardians, gover-
nantes and chamber-maids; that ambushed bush-
fighting amongst closets, screens, chests, easy-
chairs, and toilet-tables, form a gay varied game of
dexterity and invention; which, to those who have
played at hide-and-seek, who have crouched down,
with beating heart, in a dark corner, whilst the
enemy groped near the spot; who have joined
their busy school-mates in many a deep-laid plan
to deceive, perplex, and torment the unhappy mortals deputed to have the charge of them, cannot be

scen with indifference. Like an old hunter, who pricks up his cars at the sound of the chace, and starts away from the path of his journey, so, leaving all wisdom and criticism behind us, we follow the varied changes of the plot, and stop not for reflection. The studious man who wants a cessation from thought, the indolent man who dislikes it, and all those who, from habit or circumstances, live in a state of divorce from their own minds, are pleased with an amusement in which they have nothing to do but to open their eyes and behold; the moral tendency of it, however, is very faulty. That mockery of age and domestick authority, so constantly held forth, has a very bad effect upon the younger part of an audience; and that continual lying and deceit in the first characters of the piece, which is necessary for conducting the plot, has a most pernicious one.

But Characteristick Comedy, which represents to us this motley world of men and women in which we live, under those circumstances of ordinary and familiar life most favourable for the discovery of the human heart, offers to us a wide field of instruction, adapted to general application. We find in its varied scenes an exercise of the mind analogous to that which we all, less or more, find out for ourselves, amidst the mixed groupes of people whom we meet with in society; and which I have already mentioned as an exercise universally pleasing to

E

man.   As the distinctions which it is its highest
aim to discriminate, are those of nature and not
situation, they are judged of by all ranks of men;
for a peasant will very clearly perceive in the character of a peer, those native peculiarities which
belong to him as a man, though he is entirely at a
loss in all that regards his manners and address as a
nobleman.   It illustrates to us the general remarks
we have made upon men; and in it we behold,
spread before us, plans of those original ground-
works, upon which the general ideas we have been
taught to conceive of mankind, are founded.   It
stands but little in need of busy plot, extraordinary
incidents, witty repartee, or studied sentiments.
It naturally produces for itself all that it requires;
characters who are to speak for themselves, who
are to be known by their own words and actions,
not by the accounts that are given of them by
others, cannot well be developed without considerable variety of judicious incident; a smile that
is raised by some trait of undisguised nature, and
a laugh that is provoked by some ludicrous effect
of passion, or clashing of opposite characters, will
be more pleasing to the generality of men, than
either the one or the other when occasioned by a
play upon words, or a whimsical combination of
ideas; and to behold the operation and effects of
the different propensities and weaknesses of men,
will naturally call up in the mind of the spectator

moral reflections more applicable, and more impressive, than all the high-sounding sentiments,
with which the graver scenes of Satirical and Sentimental Comedy are so frequently interlarded. It
is much to be regretted, however, that the eternal
introduction of love as the grand business of the
Drama, and the consequent necessity for making
the chief persons in it such, in regard to age, appearance, manners, dispositions, and endowments,
as are proper for interesting lovers, has occasioned
so much insipid similarity in the higher characters.
It is chiefly, therefore, on the second and inferiour
characters, that the efforts, even of our best poets,
have been exhausted; and thus we are called
upon to be interested in the fortune of one man,
whilst our chief attention is directed to the character of another, which produces a disunion of
ideas in the mind, injurious to the general effect of
the whole. From this cause, also, those characteristick varieties have been very much neglected,
which men present to us in the middle stages of
life; when they are too old for lovers or the con-
fidents of lovers, and too young to be the fathers,
uncles, and guardians, who are contrasted with
them; but when they are still in full vigour of
mind, eagerly engaged with the world, joining the
activity of youth to the providence of age, and
offer to our attention objects sufficiently interesting
and instructive. It is to be regretted that strong

contrasts of character are too often attempted, instead of those harmonious shades of it, which nature so beautifully varies, and which we so greatly delight in, whenever we clearly distinguish them. It is to be regretted that in place of those characters, which present themselves to the imagination of a writer from his general observations upon mankind, inferiour poets have so often pourtrayed with senseless minuteness the characters of particular individuals. We are pleased with the eccentricities of individuals in real life, and also in history or biography, but in fictitious writings, we regard them with suspicion ; and no representation of nature, that corresponds not with some of our general ideas in regard to it, will either instruct or inform us. When the originals of such characters are known and remembered, the plays in which they are introduced are oftentimes popular ; and their temporary success has induced a still inferiour class of poets to believe, that, by making men strange, and unlike the rest of the world, they have made great discoveries, and mightily enlarged the boundaries of dramatick character. They will, therefore, distinguish one man from another by some strange whim or imagination, which is ever uppermost in his thoughts, and influences every action of his life ; by some singular opinion, perhaps, about politicks, fashions, or the position of the stars ; by some strong unaccountable love for

one thing or aversion from another ; entirely forgetting, that such singularities, if they are to be
found in nature, can no where be sought for, with
such probability of success, as in Bedlam. Above
all it is to be regretted that those adventitious distinctions amongst men, of age, fortune, rank, profession, and country, are so often brought forward
in preference to the great original distinctions of
nature ; and our scenes so often filled with
courtiers, lawyers, citizens, Frenchmen, &c. &c.
With all the characteristicks of their respective
conditions, such as they have been represented
from time immemorial. This has introduced a
great sameness into many of our plays, which all
the changes of new fashions burlesqued, and new
customs turned into ridicule, cannot conceal.

In comedy, the stronger passions, love excepted,
are seldom introduced but in a passing way. We
have short bursts of anger, fits of jealousy and im-
patience ; violent passion of any continuance we
seldom find. When this is attempted, however,
forgetting that mode of exposing the weakness of
the human mind, which peculiarly belongs to her,
it is too frequently done in the serious spirit of
tragedy ; and this has produced so many of those
serious comick plays, which so much divide and
distract our attention.* Yet we all know from

* Such plays, however excellent the parts may be of which
they are composed, can never produce the same strength and

our own experience in real life, that, in certain situations, and under certain circumstances, the stronger passions are fitted to produce scenes more exquisitely comick than any other; and one well-wrought scene of this kind, will have a more powerful effect in repressing similar intemperance

unity of effect upon our minds which we receive from plays of a simpler undivided construction. If the serious and distressing scenes make a deep impression, we do not find ourselves in a humour for the comick ones that succeed; and if the comick scenes enliven us greatly, we feel tardy and unalert in bringing back our minds to a proper tone for the serious. As in tragedy we smile at those native traits of character, or that occasional sprightliness of dialogue, which are sometimes introduced, to animate her less-interesting parts, so may we be moved by comedy; but our tears should be called forth by those gentle strokes of nature, which come at once with kindred kindness on the heart, and are quickly succeeded by smiles. Like a small summer-cloud, whose rain-drops sparkle in the sun, and which swiftly passes away, is the genuine pathetick of comedy: the gathering foreseen storm, that darkens the whole face of the sky, belongs to tragedy alone. It is often observed, I confess, that we are more apt to be affected by those scenes of distress which we meet with in comedy, than the high-wrought woes of tragedy; and I believe it is true. But this arises from the woes of tragedy being so often appropriated to high and mighty personages, and strained beyond the modesty of nature, in order to suit their great dignity; or from the softened griefs of more gentle and familiar characters being rendered feeble and tiresome with too much repetition and whining. It arises from the greater facility with which we enter into the distresses of people, more upon a level with ourselves; and whose sorrows are expressed in less studied and unnatural language.

in the mind of a spectator, than many moral cautions, or even, perhaps, than the terrifick examples of tragedy. There are to be found, no doubt, in the works of our best dramatick writers, comick scenes descriptive of the stronger passions, but it is generally the inferiour characters of the piece who are made the subjects of them, very rarely those in whom we are much interested ; and consequently the useful effect of such scenes upon the mind is very much weakened. This general appropriation of them has tempted our less-skilful Dramatists to exaggerate, and step, in further quest of the ludicrous, so much beyond the bounds of nature, that the very effect they are so anxious to produce is thereby destroyed, and all useful application of it entirely cut off; for we never apply to ourselves a false repre-sentation of nature.

But a complete exhibition of passion, with its varieties and progress in the breast of man has, I believe, scarcely ever been attempted in comedy. Even love, though the chief subject of almost every play, has been pourtrayed in a loose, scattered, and imperfect manner. The story of the lovers is acted over before us, whilst the characteristicks of that passion by which they are actuated, and which is the great master-spring of the whole, are faintly to be discovered. We are generally introduced to a lover after he has

6

long been acquainted with his mistress, and
wants but the consent of some stubborn relation,
relief from some embarrassment of situation, or
the clearing up some mistake or love-quarrel
occasioned by malice or accident, to make him
completely happy. To overcome these difficulties,
he is engaged in a busy train of contrivance and
exertion, in which the spirit, activity and ingenuity of the man is held forth to view, whilst the
lover, comparatively speaking, is kept out of
sight. But even when this is not the case ; when
the lover is not so busied and involved, this stage
of the passion is exactly the one that is least
interesting, and least instructive : not to mention
as I have done already, that one stage of any
passion must shew it imperfectly.

From this view of the Comick Drama I have
been induced to believe, that, as companions to
the forementioned tragedies, a series of comedies
on a similar plan, in which bustle of plot, bril-
liancy of dialogue, and even the bold and striking
in character, should, to the best of the authour's
judgment, be kept in due subordination to nature,
might likewise be acceptable to the publick. I
am confident that comedy upon this plan is
capable of being made as interesting, as enter-
taining, and superiour in moral tendency to any
other. For even in ordinary life, with very slight
cause to excite them, strong passions will foster

themselves within the breast ; and what are all
the evils which vanity, folly, prejudice, or peculiarity of temper lead to, compared with those
which such unquiet inmates produce ?   Were
they confined to the exalted and the mighty, to
those engaged in the great events of the world,
to the inhabitants of palaces and camps, how
happy comparatively would this world be !   But
many a miserable being, whom firm principle,
timidity of character, or the fear of shame keeps
back from the actual commission of crimes, is
tormented in obscurity, under the dominion of
those passions which set the seducer in ambush,
rouse the bold spoiler to wrong, and strengthen
the arm of the murderer.   Though to those with
whom such dangerous enemies have long found
shelter, exposing them in an absurd and ridiculous
light,   may be shooting a finely-pointed arrow
against the hardened rock ; yet to those with
whom they are but new, and less assured guests,
this may prove a more successful mode of attack
than any other.

It was the saying of a sagacious Scotchman,
' let who will make the laws of a nation, if I have
the writing of its ballads.'   Something similar to
this may be said in regard to the Drama.   Its
lessons reach not, indeed, to the lowest classes
of the labouring people, who are the broad
foundation of society, which can never be gene-

rally moved without endangering every thing
that is constructed upon it, and who are our
potent and formidable ballad readers; but they
reach to the classes next in order to them, and
who will always have over them no inconsiderable
influence. The impressions made by it are com-
municated, at the same instant of time, to a
greater number of individuals, than those made
by any other species of writing; and they are
strengthened in every spectator, by observing
their effects upon those who surround him.
From this observation, the mind of my reader
will suggest of itself, what it would be unnecessary,
and, perhaps, improper in me here to enlarge
upon. The theatre is a school in which much
good or evil may be learned. At the beginning
of its career the Drama was employed to mislead
and excite; and were I not unwilling to refer
to transactions of the present times, I might
abundantly confirm what I have said by recent
examples. The authour, therefore, who aims in
any degree to improve the mode of its instruction,
and point to more useful lessons than it is generally employed to dispense, is certainly praise-
worthy, though want of abilities may unhappily
prevent him from being successful in his efforts.

This idea has prompted me to begin a work
in which I am aware of many difficulties. In
plays of this nature the passions must be depicted

not only with their bold and prominent features, but also with those minute and delicate traits which distinguish them in an infant, growing, and repressed state ; which are the most difficult of all to counterfeit, and one of which falsely imagined, will destroy the effect of a whole scene. The characters over whom they are made to usurp dominion, must be powerful and interesting, exercising them with their full measure of opposition and struggle ; for the chief anta-gonists they contend with must be the other passions and propensities of the heart, not outward circumstances and events. Though belonging to such characters, they must still be held to view in their most baleful and unseductive light ; and those qualities in the impassioned which are necessary to interest us in their fate, must not be allowed, by any lustre borrowed from them, to diminish our abhorrence of guilt. The second and even the inferiour persons of each play, as they must be kept perfectly distinct from the great impassioned one, should generally be repre-sented in a calm unagitated state, and therefore more pains is necessary than in other dramatick works, to mark them by appropriate distinctions of character, lest they should appear altogether insipid and insignificant. As the great object here is to trace passion through all its varieties, and in every stage, many of which are marked

by shades so delicate, that in much bustle of
events they would be little attended to, or entirely
overlooked, simplicity of plot is more necessary,
than in those plays where only occasional bursts
of passion are introduced, to distinguish a character, or animate a scene. But where simplicity
of plot is necessary, there is very great danger of
making a piece appear bare and unvaried, and
nothing but great force and truth in the deline-
ations of nature will prevent it from being tiresome.* Soliloquy, or those overflowings of the

---

* To make up for this simplicity of plot, the shew and
decorations of the theatre ought to be allowed, to plays written
upon this plan, in their full extent. How fastidious soever some
poets may be in regard to these matters, it is much better to
relieve our tired-out attention with a battle, a banquet, or a
procession, than an accumulation of incidents. In the latter
case the mind is harassed and confused with those doubts, con-
jectures, and disappointments which multiplied events occasion,
and in a great measure unfitted for attending to the worthier
parts of the piece; but in the former it enjoys a rest, a pleasing
pause in its more serious occupation, from which it can return
again, without any incumberance of foreign intruding ideas.
The shew of a splendid procession will afford to a person of the
best understanding, a pleasure in kind, though not in degree,
with that which a child would receive from it. But when it is
past he thinks no more of it; whereas some confusion of circumstances, some half-explained mistake, which gives him no
pleasure at all when it takes place, may take off his attention
afterwards from the refined beauties of a natural and characteristick
dialogue.

perturbed soul, in which it unburthens itself of
those thoughts which it cannot communicate to
others, and which in certain situations is the only
mode that a Dramatist can employ to open to
us the mind he would display, must necessarily
be often, and to considerable length, introduced.
Here, indeed, as it naturally belongs to passion,
it will not be so offensive as it generally is in
other plays, when a calm unagitated person tells
over to himself all that has befallen him, and all
his future schemes of intrigue or advancement;
yet to make speeches of this kind sufficiently
natural and impressive, to excite no degree of
weariness nor distaste, will be found to be no
easy task. There are, besides these, many other
difficulties peculiarly belonging to this undertaking, too minute and tedious to mention.
If, fully aware of them, I have not shrunk back
from the attempt, it is not from any idea that
my own powers or discernment will at all times
enable me to overcome them; but I am em-
boldened by the confidence I feel in that candour
and indulgence, with which the good and enlight-
ened do ever regard the experimental efforts of
those, who wish in any degree to enlarge the
sources of pleasure and instruction amongst men.

It will now be proper to say something of the
particular plays which compose this volume. But,
in the first place I must observe, that as I pretend

not to have overcome the difficulties attached
to this design, so neither from the errours and
defects, which, in these pages, I have thought
it necessary to point out in the works of others,
do I at all pretend to be blameless. To conceive
the great moral object and outline of a story;
to people it with various characters, under the
influence of various passions; and to strike out
circumstances and situations calculated to call
them into action, is a very different employment
of the mind from calmly considering those propensities of our nature, to which dramatick
writings are most powerfully addressed, and taking
a general view upon those principles of the works
of preceding authours. They are employments
which cannot well occupy it at the same time;
and experience has taught us, that criticks do not
unfrequently write in contradiction to their own
rules. If I should, therefore, sometimes appear
in the foregoing remarks to have provided a stick
wherewith to break mine own pate, I entreat that
my reader will believe I am neither confident
nor boastful, and use it with gentleness.

In the two first plays, where love is the passion
under review, their relation to the general plan
may not be very obvious. Love is the chief
groundwork of almost all our tragedies and
comedies, and so far they are not distinguished
from others. But I have endeavoured in both

to give an unbroken view of the passion from its beginning, and to mark it as I went along, with those peculiar traits which distinguish its different stages of progression. I have in both these pieces grafted this passion not on those open communicative impetuous characters, who have so long occupied the dramatick station of lovers, but on men of a firm, thoughtful, reserved turn of mind, with whom it commonly makes the longest stay, and maintains the hardest struggle. I should be extremely sorry if, from any thing at the conclusion of the tragedy, it should be supposed that I mean to countenance suicide, or condemn those customs whose object is the discouragement of it, by withholding from the body of the self-slain those sacred rites, and marks of respect commonly shewn to the dead. Let it be considered, that whatever I have inserted there, which can at all raise any suspicion of this kind, is put into the mouths of rude uncultivated soldiers, who are roused with the loss of a beloved leader, and indignant at any idea of disgrace being attached to him. If it should seem inconsistent with the nature of this work, that in its companion the comedy, I have made strong moral principle triumph over love, let it be remembered, that without this the whole moral tendency of a play, which must end happily, would have been destroyed; and that it is not my intention to encourage the indulgence of this passion, amiable as it is, but to restrain it. The last play, the subject of which is hatred, will more clearly discover the nature and intention of my design. The rise and progress of this passion I have been obliged to give in retrospect, instead of representing it all along in its actual operation, as I could have wished to have done. But hatred is a passion of slow growth ; and to have exhibited it from its beginnings would have included a longer period, than even those who are least scrupulous about the limitation of dramatick time, would have thought allowable. I could not have introduced my chief characters upon the stage as boys, and then as men. For this passion must be kept distinct from that dislike which we conceive for another when he has greatly offended us, and which is almost the constant companion of anger ; and also from that eager desire to crush, and inflict suffering on him who has injured us, which constitutes revenge. This passion, as I have conceived it, is that rooted and settled aversion, which from opposition of character, aided by circumstances of little importance, grows at last into such antipathy and personal disgust as makes him who entertains it, feel, in the presence of him who is the object of it, a degree of torment and restlesness which is insufferable. It is a passion, I believe less frequent than any other of the stronger passions, but in the breast where it does exist, it creates, perhaps, more misery than any other. To endeavour to interest the mind for a man under the dominion of a passion so baleful, so unamiable, may seem, perhaps, reprehensible. I therefore beg it may be considered that it is the passion and not the man which is held up to our execration; and that this and every other bad passion does more strongly evince its pernicious and dangerous nature, when we see it thus counteracting and destroying the good gifts of heaven, than when it is represented as the suitable associate in the breast of inmates as dark as itself. This remark will likewise be applicable to many of the other plays belonging to my work, that are intended to follow. A decidedly wicked character can never be interesting; and to employ such for the display of any strong passion would very much injure instead of improving the moral effect. In the breast of a bad man passion has comparatively little to combat, how then can it shew its strength? I shall say no more upon this subject, but submit myself to the judgment of my reader.

It may, perhaps, be supposed from my publishing these plays, that I have written them for the closet rather than the stage. If upon perusing them with attention, the reader is disposed to think they are better calculated for the first than the last, let him impute it to want of skill in the authour, and not to any previous design. A play, but of small poetical merit, that is suited to strike and interest the spectator, to catch the attention of him who will not, and of him who cannot read, is a more valuable and useful production than one whose elegant and harmonious pages are admired in the libraries of the tasteful and refined. To have received approbation from an audience of my countrymen, would have been more pleasing to me than any other praise. A few tears from the simple and young would have been, in my eyes, pearls of great price; and the spontaneous, untutored plaudits of the rude and uncultivated would have come to my heart as offerings of no mean value. I should, therefore, have been better pleased to have introduced them to the world from the stage than from the press. I possess, however, no likely channel to the former mode of publick introduction; and upon further reflection it appeared to me that by publishing them in this way, I have an opportunity afforded me of explaining the design of my work, and enabling the publick to judge, not only of each play by itself, but as making a part likewise of the whole; an advantage which, perhaps, does more than over-balance the splendour and effect of theatrical representation.

It may be thought that with this extensive plan before me, I should not have been in a hurry to publish, but have waited to give a larger portion of it to the publick, which would have enabled them to make a truer estimate of its merit. To bring forth only three plays of the whole, and the last without its intended companion, may seem like the haste of those vain people, who as soon as they have written a few pages of a discourse, or a few couplets of a poem, cannot be easy till every body has seen them. I do protest, in honest simplicity! it is distrust and not confidence, that has led me at this early stage of the undertaking, to bring it before the publick. To labour in uncertainty is at all times unpleasant; but to proceed in a long and difficult work with any impression upon your mind that your labour may be in vain; that the opinion you have conceived of your ability to perform it may be a delusion, a false suggestion of self-love, the fantasy of an aspiring temper, is most discouraging and cheerless. I have not proceeded so far, indeed, merely upon the strength of my own judgment; but the friends to whom I have shewn my manuscripts are partial to me, and their approbation which in the case of any indifferent person would be in my mind completely decisive, goes but a little way in relieving me from these apprehensions. To step beyond the

circle of my own immediate friends in quest of
opinion, from the particular temper of my mind
I feel an uncommon repugnance : I can with
less pain to myself bring them before the publick
at once, and submit to its decision.*   It is to
my countrymen at large that I call for assistance.
If this work is fortunate enough to attract their
attention, let their strictures as well as their
praise come to my aid : the one will encourage
me in a long and arduous undertaking, the other
will teach me to improve it as I advance.   For
there are many errours that may be detected, and
improvements that may be suggested in the
prosecution of this work, which from the observations of a great variety of readers are more
likely to be pointed out to me, than from those
of a small number of persons, even of the best
judgment.   I am not possessed of that confidence
in mine own powers, which enables the concealed
genius, under the pressure of present discouragement, to pursue his labours in security,
looking firmly forward to other more enlightened·
times for his reward.   If my own countrymen

---

* The first of these plays, indeed, has been shewn to two
or three Gentlemen whom I have not the honour of reckoning
amongst my friends. One of them, who is a man of distinguished
talents, has honoured it with very flattering approbation; and,
at his suggestion, one or two slight alterations in it have been
made.

with whom I live and converse, who look upon
the same race of men, the same state of society,
the same passing events with myself, receive not
my offering, I presume not to look to posterity.

Before I close this discourse, let me crave the
forbearance of my reader, if he has discovered
in the course of it any unacknowledged use of
the thoughts of other authours, which he thinks
ought to have been noticed ; and let me beg the
same favour, if in reading the following plays,
any similar neglect seems to occur. There are
few writers who have sufficient originality of
thought to strike out for themselves new ideas
upon every occasion. When a thought presents
itself to me, as suited to the purpose I am aiming
at, I would neither be thought proud enough to
reject it, on finding that another has used it
before me, nor mean enough to make use of
it without acknowledging the obligation, when
I can at all guess to whom such acknowledgments
are due. But I am situated where I have no
library to consult ; my reading through the whole
of my life has been of a loose, scattered, unme-
thodical kind, with no determined direction, and
I have not been blessed by nature with the advan-
tages of a retentive or accurate memory. Do
not, however, imagine from this, I at all wish
to insinuate that I ought to be acquitted of every
obligation to preceding authours ; and that when

a palpable similarity of thought and expression is observable between us, it is a similarity produced by accident alone, and with perfect unconsciousness on my part. I am frequently sensible, from the manner in which an idea arises to my imagination, and the readiness with which words, also, present themselves to clothe it in, that I am only making use of some dormant part of that hoard of ideas which the most indifferent memories lay up, and not the native suggestions of mine own mind. Whenever I have suspected myself of doing so, in the course of this work, I have felt a strong inclination to mark that suspicion in a note. But, besides that it might have appeared like an affectation of scrupulousness which I would avoid, there being likewise, most assuredly, many other places in it where I have done the same thing without being conscious of it, a suspicion of wishing to slur them over, and claim all the rest as unreservedly my own, would unavoidably have attached to me. If this volume should appear, to any candid and liberal critick, to merit that he should take the trouble of pointing out to me in what parts of it I seem to have made that use of other authours' writings, which according to the fair laws of literature ought to have been acknowledged, I shall think myself obliged to him. I shall examine the sources he points out as having supplied my own lack of ideas; and if this book should have the good fortune to go through a second edition, I shall not fail to own my obligations to him, and the authours from whom I may have borrowed.

How little credit soever, upon perusing these plays, the reader may think me entitled to in regard to the execution of the work, he will not, I flatter myself, deny me some credit in regard to the plan. I know of no series of plays, in any language, expressly descriptive of the different passions; and I believe there are few plays existing in which the display of one strong passion is the chief business of the drama, so written that they could properly make part of such a series. I do not think that we should, from the works of various authours, be able to make a collection which would give us any thing exactly of the nature of that which is here proposed. If the reader, in perusing it, perceives that the abilities of the authour are not proportioned to the task which is imposed upon them, he will wish in the spirit of kindness rather than of censure, as I most sincerely do, that they had been more adequate to it. However, if I perform it ill, I am still confident that this (pardon me if I call it, noble) design will not be suffered to fall to the ground; some one will arise after me who will do it justice; and there is no poet, possessing genius for such a work, who will not at the same

3

time possess that spirit of justice and of candour, which will lead him to remember me with respect.

I have now only to thank my reader, whoever he may be, who has followed me through the pages of this discourse, for having had the patience to do so. May he, in going through what follows (a wish the sincerity of which he cannot doubt) find more to reward his trouble than I dare venture to promise him ; and for the pains he has already taken, and that which he intends to take for me, I request that he will accept of my grateful acknowledgments.

* Shakspeare, more than any of our poets, gives peculiar and appropriate distinction to the characters of his tragedies. The remarks I have made, in regard to the little variety of character to be met with in tragedy, apply not to him. Neither has he, as other Dramatists generally do, bestowed pains on the chief persons of his drama only, leaving the second and inferiour ones insignificant and spiritless. He never wears out our capacity to feel, by eternally pressing upon it. His tragedies are agreeably chequered with variety of scenes, enriched with good sense, nature, and vivacity, which relieve our minds from the fatigue of continued distress. If he sometimes carries this so far as to break in upon that serious tone of mind, which disposes us to listen with effect to the higher scenes of tragedy, he has done so chiefly in his historical plays, where the distresses set forth are commonly of that publick kind, which does not, at any rate, make much impression upon the feelings.

COUNT BASIL:

A TRAGEDY.

PERSONS OF THE DRAMA.

MEN.

COUNT BASIL, *a General in the Emperour's service.*

COUNT ROSINBERG, *his Friend.*

DUKE OF MANTUA.

GAURICEIO, *his Minister.*

VALTOMER,
FREDERICK, } *Two Officers of* Basil's *Troops.*

GEOFFRY, *an old Soldier, very much maimed in the Wars.*

MIRANDO, *a little Boy, favourite to* Victoria.

WOMEN.

VICTORIA, *Daughter to the* Duke of Mantua.

COUNTESS OF ALBINI, *Friend and Governess to* Victoria.

ISABELLA, *a Lady attending upon* Victoria.

Officers, Soldiers, *and* Attendants, Masks, Dancers, *&c.*

** *The Scene is in* Mantua, *and its environs. Time supposed to be in the Sixteenth Century, when* CHARLES *the Fifth defeated* FRANCIS *the First, at the Battle of* Pavia.

COUNT BASIL.

ACT I.—SCENE I.

An Open Street, crouded with People, who seem to be waiting in expectation of some Show.

Enter a CITIZEN.

First Man. Well friend, what tidings of the
    grand procession?
Cit. I left it passing by the northern gate.
Second Man. I've waited long, I'm glad it comes
    at last.
Young Man. And does the Princess look so
    wondrous fair
As fame reports?
Cit. She is the fairest lady of the train,
And all the fairest beauties of the court
Are in her train.
Old Man. Bears she such off'rings to Saint
    Francis' shrine,
So rich, so marvellous rich as rumour says?
'Twill drain the treasury.
Cit. Since she in all this splendid pomp, returns
Her publick thanks to the good patron Saint,
Who from his sick bed hath restor'd her father,
Thou wouldst not have her go with empty hands?

She loves magnificence.—

    (Discovering among the croud Old Geoffry.*)*

Ha! art thou here, old remnant of the wars ?

Thou art not come to see this courtly show,

Which sets the young agape ?

    Geof. I came not for the show; and yet, methinks,

It were a better jest upon me still,

If thou didst truly know mine errand here.

    Cit. I pri'thee say.

    Geof.   What, must I tell it thee ?

As o'er my ev'ning fire I musing sat

Some few days since, my mind's eye backward
        turn'd

Upon the various changes I have pass'd—

How in my youth with gay attire allur'd,

And all the grand accoutrements of war,

I left my peaceful home : Then my first battles,

When clashing arms, and sights of blood were new:

Then all the after chances of the war ;

Ay, and that field, a well-fought field it was,

When with this arm (I speak not of it oft)

             (Pointing to his empty sleeve.)

Which now thou seest is no arm of mine,

In a straight pass I stopp'd a thousand foes,

And turn'd my flying comrades to the charge ;

For which good service, in his tented court,

My prince bestow'd a mark of favour on me :

Whilst his fair consort, seated by his side,

The fairest lady e'er mine eyes beheld,

Gave me what more than all besides I priz'd,

Methinks I see her still ! a gracious smile;

'Twas a heart-kindling smile,—a smile of praise—
Well, musing thus on all my fortunes past,
A Neighbour drew the latchet of my door,
And full of news from town, in many words
Big with rich names, told of this grand procession.
E'en as he spoke a fancy seiz'd my soul
To see the princess pass, if in her face
I yet might trace some semblance of her mother.
This is the simple truth ; laugh as thou wilt,
I came not for the show.

Enter an OFFICER.

Officer to Geof. Make way, that the procession
          may have room ;
Stand you aside, and let this man have place.
     (Pushing Geof. *and endeavouring to put another*
              in his place.)
     Geof. But that thou art the prince's officer,
I'd give thee back thy push with better blows.
     Officer. What wilt thou not give place ? the
          prince is near,
I will complain to him, and have thee caged.
     Geof. Yes do complain, I pray; and when thou
          dost,
Say that the private of the tenth brigade,
Who sav'd his army on the Danube's bank,
And since that time a private hath remain'd,
Dares, as a citizen, his right maintain
Against thy insolence. Go tell him this,
And ask him then what dungeon of his tower
He'll have me thrust into ?

Cit. to Officer. This is old Geoffry of the tenth
    brigade.

Off. I knew him not : you should have told me
    sooner.   [EXIT, *looking much ashamed.*

Martial Musick heard at a distance.
Cit. Hark, this is musick of a warlike kind.

Enter Second CITIZEN.

To Sec. Cit. What sounds are these, good
    friend, which this way bear ?

Sec. Cit. The Count of Basil is upon his march,
To join the Emp'rour with some chosen troops,
And doth through Mantua pass in right of Allies.

Geof. I have heard a good report of this young
    soldier.

Sec. Cit. 'Tis said he disciplines his men severely,
And acts with them too much the old commander,
Which is ungracious in so young a man.

Geof. I know he loves not ease and revelry ;
He makes them soldiers at no dearer rate
Than he himself hath paid. What, dost thou think
That e'en the very meanest simple craft
May not, but with due diligence, be learn'd,
And yet the noble art of soldiership
May be attain'd by loit'ring in the sun ?
Some men are born to feast, and not to fight ;
Whose sluggish minds, e'en in fair honour's field,
Still on their dinner turn—
Let such pot-boiling varlets stay at home,
And wield a flesh-hook rather than a sword.
In times of easy service, true it is,

An easy, careless chief, all soldiers love ;
But O ! how gladly in the day of battle
Would they their jolly bottle-chief desert,
And follow such a leader as Count Basil.
So gath'ring herds, at pressing dangers' call,
Confess the master Deer.

(*Musick is heard again, and nearer.* Geoffry *walks
up and down with a military triumphant step.*

Cit. What moves thee thus ?

Geof. I've march'd to this same tune in glorious
days.

My very limbs catch motion from the sound,
As they were young again.

Sec. Cit.   But here they come.

Enter Count BASIL, *Officers and Soldiers in Procession, with Colours flying, and martial musick.
When they have marched half way over the Stage,
an Officer of the Duke's enters from the opposite
side, and speaks to Count* BASIL, *upon which he
gives a sign with his hand, and the martial
musick ceases ; soft musick is heard at a little
distance, and* VICTORIA, *with a long procession
of Ladies, enters from the opposite side. The
General, &c. pay obeisance to her, as she passes ;
she stops to return it, and then goes off with her
train. After which the military procession moves
on, and Exeunt.*

Cit. to Geof. What thinkst thou of the princess?
Geof.   She is fair,
But not so fair as her good mother was. [EXEUNT.

SCENE II.

A Publick Walk on the Ramparts of the Town.

Enter Count ROSINBERG, VALTOMER, *and* FRE-
DERICK.—VALTOMER *enters by the opposite side
of the Stage, and meets them.*

Valt. O ! what a jolly town for way-worn
    soldiers !
Rich steaming pots, and smell of dainty fare,
From every house salute you as you pass :
Light fcats and jugglers' tricks attract the eye ;
Frolick, and mirth, musick in ev'ry street ;
Whilst pretty damsels, in their best attire,
Trip on in wanton groups, then look behind,
To spy the fools a-gazing after them.
    Fred. But short will be the season of our ease,
For Basil is of flinty mattcr madc,
And cannot be allur'd—
'Faith Rosenberg, I would thou didst command us;
Thou art his kinsman, of a rank as noble,
Some years his elder too ; how has it been
That he should be preferr'd ? I see not why.
    Ros. Ah! but I see it, and allow it well ;
He is too much my pride to wake my envy.
    Fred. Nay, Count, it is thy foolish admiration
Which raises him to such superiour height ;
And truly thou hast so infected us,
That I have fclt at times an awe before him,
I know not why.   'Tis cursed folly ;

Thou art as brave, of as good parts as he.

Ros. Our talents of a diff'rent nature are ;
Mine for the daily intercourse of life,
And his for higher things.

Fred. Well, praise him as thou wilt ; I see it not;
I'm sure I am as brave a man as he.

Ros. Yes, brave thou art, but 'tis subaltern
     brav'ry,
And doth respect thyself.   Thou'lt bleed as well,
Give, and receive as deep an wound as he.
When Basil fights he wields a thousand swords :
For 'tis their trust in his unshaken mind,
O'erwatching all the changes of the field,
Calm and inventive midst the battle's storm,
Which makes his soldiers bold.——
There have been those, in early manhood slain,
Whose great heroick souls did yet inspire
With such a noble zeal their gen'rous troops,
That to their latest day of bearing arms,
Their grey-hair'd soldiers would all dangers brave
Of desp'rate service, claim'd with boastful pride,
For having fought beneath them in their youth.
Such men have been ; of whom it may be said,
Their spirits conquer'd when their clay was cold.

Valt. Yes, I have seen in the eventful field,
When new occasion mock'd all formed art,
E'en old commanders hold experience cheap,
And look to Basil ere his chin was dark.

Ros. One fault he has, I know but only one ;
His too great love of military fame

G

Destroys his thoughts, and makes him oft appear
Unsocial and severe.

   Fred. Well, feel I not undaunted in the field ?
As much enthusiastick love of glory ?
Why am I not as good a man as he ?

   Ros. He's form'd for great occasions, thou for
     small.

   Valt. But small occasions in the path of life
Lie thickly sown, while great are rarely scatter'd.

   Ros. By which you would infer that men like
     Fred'rick,
Should on the whole a better figure make,
Than men of higher parts ; but 'tis not so,
For some shew well, and fair applauses gain,
Where want of skill in other men is graceful.
But do not frown, good Fred'rick, no offence;
Thou canst not make a great man of thyself,
Yet wisely deign to use thy native pow'rs,
And prove an honour'd courtly gentleman.
But hush ! no more of this, here Basil comes.

   Enter BASIL, *who returns their salute without*
      speaking.

   Ros. What thinkst thou, Valtomer, of Mantua's
     princess ?

   Valt. Fame prais'd her much, but hath not
     prais'd her more
Than on a better proof the eye consents to.
With all that grace and nobleness of mien,
She might do honour to an Emp'rour's throne;

She is too noble for a petty court.
Is it not so, my Lord ?—*(To* Basil, *who only bows
        assent.)*
Nay, she demeans herself with so much grace,
Such easy state, such gay magnificence,
She should be queen of revelry and show.

    Fred. She's charming as the goddess of delight.

    Valt. But after her, she most attracted me
Who wore the yellow scarf and walk'd the last,
For tho' Victoria is a lovely woman—

    Fred. Nay, it is treason but to call her woman;
She's a divinity, and should be worshipp'd.
But on my life, since now we talk of worship,
She worshipp'd Francis with right noble gifts !
They sparkled so with gold and precious gems
Their value must be great; some thousand crowns?

    Ros. I would not rate them at a price so mean;
The cup alone, with precious stones beset,
Would fetch a sum as great.   That olive branch
The princess bore herself, of fretted gold,
Was exquisitely wrought.   I mark'd it more,
Because she held it in so white a hand.

    Basil, in a quick voice. Mark'd you her hand?
        I did not see her hand,
And yet she wav'd it twice.

    Ros. It is a fair one, tho' you mark'd it not.

    Valt. I wish some painter's eye had view'd the
        group,
As she and all her lovely damsels pass'd ;
He would have found wherewith t'enrich his art.

    Ros. I wish so too ; for oft their fancied beauties

Have so much cold perfection in their parts,
'Tis plain they ne'er belong'd to flesh and blood.
This is not truth, and doth not please so well
As the varieties of lib'ral nature,
Where ev'ry kind of beauty charms the eye;
Large and small featur'd, flat, and prominent,
Ay, by the mass! and snub-nos'd beauties too.
'Faith ev'ry woman hath some 'witching charm,
If that she be not proud, or captious.

Valt. Demure, or over-wise, or giv'n to freaks.

Ros. Or giv'n to freaks! hold, hold good
Valtomer!
Thou'lt leave no woman handsome under heav'n.

Valt. But I must leave you for an hour or so,
I mean to view the town if aught worth notice.

Fred. I'll go with thee, my friend.

Ros.   And so will I.
[EXEUNT *Valt. Fred.* and *Ros.*

Re-enter ROSINBERG.

Ros. I have repented me, I will not go;
They will be too long absent.—*(Pauses, and
looks at* Basil, *who remains still musing
without seeing him.)*
What mighty thoughts engage my pensive friend?

Bas. O! it is admirable.

Ros. How runs thy fancy? what is admirable?

Bas. Her form, her face, her motion, ev'rything!

Ros. The princess? yes, have we not prais'd
her much?

Bas. I know you prais'd her, and her off'rings too;

She might have giv'n the treasures of the east
E'er I had known it.
She came again upon my wond'ring sight—
O! didst thou mark her when she first appear'd?
Still distant, slowly moving with her train;
Her robe, and tresses floating on the wind,
Like some light figure in a morning cloud?
Then as she onward to the eye became
The more distinct, the lovelier still she grew.
That graceful bearing of her slender form;
Her roundly-spreading breast, her tow'ring neck,
Her face ting'd sweetly with the bloom of youth—
But when on near approach she tow'rds us turn'd,
Kind mercy! what a countenance was there!
And when to our salute she gently bow'd,
Didst mark that smile rise from her parting lips?
Soft swell'd her glowing cheek, her eyes smil'd too;
O! how they smil'd! 'twas like the beams of
        heav'n!
I felt my roused soul within me start,
Like something wak'd from sleep.
    Ros. Ah! many a slumb'rer heav'n's beams
        do wake
To care and misery!
    Bas. There's something grave and solemn in
        your voice
As you pronounce these words. What dost thou
        mean?
Thou wouldst not sound my knell?
    Ros. No, not for all beneath the vaulted sky!
But to be plain, thus earnest from your lips

Her praise displeases me.   To men like you
If love should come, he proves no easy guest.

    Bas. What dost thou think I am beside myself,
And cannot view the fairness of perfection
With that delight which lovely beauty gives,
Without tormenting me with fruitless wishes ;
Like the poor child who sees its brighten'd face,
And whimpers for the moon ? Thou art not serious?
From early youth, war has my mistress been,
And tho' a rugged one, I'll constant prove,
And not forsake her now.   There may be joys
Which to the strange o'erwhelming of the soul,
Visit the lover's breast beyond all others ;
E'en now, how dearly do I feel there may !
But what of them ? they are not made for me—
The hasty flashes of contending steel
Must serve instead of glances from my love,
And for soft breathing sighs the cannon's roar.

    Ros. taking his hand. Now am I satisfied.   For-
       give me Basil.

    Bas. I'm glad thou art, we'll talk of her no
       more.
Why should I vex my friend ?

    Ros. Thou hast not giv'n orders for the march.

    Bas. I'll do it soon ; thou need'st not be afraid.
To-morrow's sun shall bear us far from hence,
Never perhaps to pass these gates again.

    Ros. With last night's close did you not curse
       this town
That would one single day your troops retard ?
And now, methinks, you talk of leaving it,

As though it were the place that gave you birth;
As tho' you had around these strangers' walls
Your infant gambols play'd.

Bas. The sight of what may be but little priz'd,
Doth cause a solemn sadness in the mind,
When view'd as that we ne'er shall see again.

Ros. No, not a whit to wand'ring men like us,
No, not a whit! what custom hath endear'd
We part with sadly, tho' we prize it not;
But what is new some pow'rful charm must own,
Thus to affect the mind.

Bas. hastily. Yes, what is new, but—No, thou
    art impatient;
We'll let it pass—It hath no consequence.

Ros. I'm not impatient. 'Faith, I only wish
Some other route our destin'd march had been,
That still thou mightst thy glorious course pursue
With an untroubled mind.

Bas. O! wish it, wish it not! bless'd be that
    route!
What we have seen to-day I must remember—
I should be brutish if I could forget it.
Oft in the watchful post, or weary march,
Oft in the nightly silence of my tent,
My fixed mind shall gaze upon it still;
But it will pass before my fancy's eye,
Like some delightful vision of the soul,
To soothe, not trouble it.

Ros. What, midst the dangers of eventful war,
Still let thy mind be haunted by a woman?
Who would, perhaps, hear of thy fall in battle,

    3

As Dutchmen read of earthquakes in Calabria,
And never stop to cry alack-a-day!
For me there is but one of all the sex,
Who still shall hold her station in my breast,
Midst all the changes of inconstant fortune;
Because I'm passing sure she loves me well,
And for my sake a sleepless pillow finds
When rumour tells bad tidings of the war;
Because I know her love will never change,
Nor make me prove uneasy jealousy.

    Bas. Happy art thou! who is this wond'rous
        woman?

    Ros. It is mine own good mother, faith and truth!

    Bas. smiling. Give me thy hand; I love her
        dearly too.

Rivals we are not, though our love is one.

    Ros. And yet I might be jealous of her love,
For she bestows too much of it on thee,
Who hast no claim but to a nephew's share.

    Bas. going. I'll meet thee some time hence. I
        must to Court.

    Ros. A private conf'rence will not stay thee long.
I'll wait thy coming near the palace gate.

    Bas. 'Tis to the publick Court I mean to go.

    Ros. I thought you had determin'd otherwise.

    Bas. Yes, but on farther thought it did appear
As though it would be failing in respect
At such a time—That look doth wrong me,
        Rosinberg!
For on my life, I had determin'd thus
Ere I beheld—Before we enter'd Mantua.

But wilt thou change that soldier's dusty garb,
And go with me thyself?

 Ros.   Yes, I will go.

 (As they are going Ros. *stops, and looks at* Basil.*)*

 Bas. Why dost thou stop?

 Ros.   'Tis for my wonted caution,
Which first thou gav'st me, I shall ne'er forget it.
'Twas at Vienna, on a publick day,
Thou but a youth, I then a man full form'd;
Thy stripling's brow grac'd with its first cockade,
Thy mighty bosom swell'd with mighty thoughts;
Thou'rt for the court, dear Rosinberg, quoth thou;
Now pray thee be not caught with some gay dame,
To laugh and ogle, and befool thyself;
It is offensive in the publick eye,
And suits not with a man of thy endowments.
So said your serious lordship to me then,
And have on like occasions often since,
In other terms repeated—
But I must go to-day without my caution.

 Bas. Nay Rosinberg, I am impatient now.
Did I not say we'd talk of her no more.

 Ros. Well, my good friend, God grant we keep
  our word!

         [Exeunt.

END OF THE FIRST ACT.

ACT II.—SCENE I.

A Room of State.   The DUKE *of* MANTUA, BASIL,
ROSINBERG, *and a number of Courtiers, Attendants,* &c. *The* DUKE *and* BASIL *appear talking
together on the front of the Stage.*

Duke. But our opinions differ widely there ;
From the position of the rival armies,
I cannot think they'll join in battle soon.
  Bas. I am indeed beholden to your highness,
But tho' unwillingly, we must depart.
The foes are near, the time is critical ;
A soldier's reputation is too fine
To be expos'd e'en to the smallest cloud.
  Duke. An untried soldier's is ; but yours, my
          lord,
Nurs'd with the bloody show'rs of many a field,
And brightest sunshine of successful fortune,
A plant of such a hardy stem hath grown,
E'en Envy's sharpest blasts assail it not.
But after all, by the bless'd holy Cross !
I feel too warm an interest in the cause
To stay your progress here a single hour,
Did I not know your soldiers are fatigu'd,
And two days' rest would but renew their strength.
  Bas. Your highness will be pleas'd to pardon me ;
My troops are not o'ermarch'd, and one day's rest
Is all our needs require.
  Duke.   Ah ! hadst thou come

Unfetter'd with the duties of command,
I then had well retain'd thee for my guest,
With claims too strong, too sacred for denial;
Thy noble sire my fellow-soldier was,
Together many a rough campaign we serv'd;
I lov'd him well, and much it pleases me
A son of his beneath my roof to see.

 Bas. Were I indeed free master of myself,
Strong inclination would detain me here;
No other tie were wanting.
These gracious tokens of your princely favour
I'll treasure with my best rememb'rances;
For he who shews them for my father's sake,
Doth something sacred in his kindness bear,
As tho' he shed a blessing on my head.

 Duke. Well, bear my greetings to the brave
  Piscaro,
And say how warmly I embrace the cause.
Your third day's march will to his presence bring
Your valiant troops: said you not so, my lord?

Enter VICTORIA, *the* Countess *of* ALBINI,
 ISABELLA, and *Ladies.*

 Bas. (who changes countenance upon seeing them.)
Yes, I believe—I think—I know not well—
Yes, please your grace, we march by break of day.

 Duke. Nay, that I know. I ask'd you, noble
  count,
When you expect th'Imperial force to join.

 Bas. When it shall please your grace—I crave
  your pardon—

I somewhat have mistaken of your words.

    Duke. You are not well? your colour changes,
        Count,

What is the matter?

    Bas. A dizzy mist that swims before my sight—

A ringing in mine ears—'tis strange enough—

'Tis slight—'tis nothing worth—'tis gone already.

    Duke. I'm glad it is. Look to your friend,
        Count Rosinberg,

It may return again.—*(To* Rosinberg, *who stands
at a little distance, looking earnestly at* Basil.
—Duke *leaves them, and joins* Victoria's *party.)*

    Ros. Good heavens! Basil, is it thus with thee!

Thy hand shakes too! *(taking his hand)* Would
        we were far from hence.

    Bas. I'm well again, thou need'st not be afraid.

'Tis like enough my frame is indispos'd

With some slight weakness from our weary march.

Nay, look not on me thus, it is unkindly—

I cannot bear thine eyes.

The DUKE, *with* VICTORIA *and her Ladies, advance
to the front of the Stage, to* BASIL.

    Duke. Victoria, welcome here the brave Count
        Basil.

His kinsman too, the gallant Rosinberg.

May you, and these fair ladies so prevail,

Such gentle suitors cannot plead in vain,

To make them grace my court another day.

I shall not be offended when I see

Your power surpasses mine.

Vict. Our feeble efforts will presumptuous seem
In what your highness fails.

    Duke. There's honour in th'attempt ; good
       success to ye.—*(Duke retires, and mixes with
       the Courtiers at the bottom of the Stage.)*

    Vict. I fear we incommoded you, my Lord,
With the slow tedious length of our procession.
E'en as I pass'd, against my heart it went
To stop your weary soldiers on their way
So long a time.—

    Bas.   Ah ! Madam, all too short !
Time never bears such moments on his wing,
But when he flies too swiftly to be mark'd.

    Vict. Ah ! surely then you make too good
       amends
By marking now his after-progress well.
To-day must seem a weary length to him
Who is so eager to be gone to-morrow.

    Ros. They must not linger who would quit
       these walls ;
For if they do, a thousand masked foes,
Some under show of rich luxurious feasts,
Gay, sprightly pastime, and high-zested game ;—
Nay, some, my gentle ladies, true it is,
The very worst and fellest of the crew,
In fair alluring shape of beauteous dames,
Do such a barrier form t'oppose their way,
As few men may o'ercome.

    Isab. From this last wicked foe should we infer
Yourself have suffer'd much ?

    Albin. No, Isabella, these are common words,

To please you with false notions of your pow'r.
So all men talk of ladies and of love.

Vict. 'Tis even so.   If love a tyrant be,
How dare his humble chained votaries,
To tell such rude and wicked tales of him ?

Bas. Because they most of lover's ills complain,
Who but affect it as a courtly grace,
Whilst he who feels is silent.

Ros. But there you wrong me ; I have felt it oft.
Oft has it made me sigh at ladies' feet,
Soft ditties sing, and dismal sonnets scrawl.

Albin. In all its strange effects, most worthy
        Rosinberg,
Has it e'er made thee in a corner sit,
Sad, lonely, moping sit. and hold thy tongue?

Ros. No, 'faith, it never has.

Albin. Ha, ha, ha, ha! then thou hast never lov'd.

Ros. Nay, but I have, and felt its bondage too.

Vict. O! it is pedantry to call it bondage !
Love-marring wisdom, reason full of bars,
Deserve, methinks, that appellation more.
Is it not so, my Lord ?—*(To Basil.)*

Bas.   O ! surely Madam ;
That is not bondage which the soul enthrall'd
So gladly bears, and quits not but with anguish.
Stern honour's laws, the fair report of men,
These are the fetters that enchain the mind,
But such as must not, cannot be unloos'd.

Vict. No, not unloos'd, but yet one day relax'd,
To grant a lady's suit, unus'd to sue.

Ros. Your highness deals severely with us now,

And proves indeed our freedom is but small,
Who are constrain'd, when such a lady sues,
To say it cannot be.

    Vict. It cannot be ! Count Basil says not so.

    Ros. For that I am his friend, to save him pain
I take th'ungracious office on myself.

    Vict. How ill thy face is suited to thine office !

    Ros. smiling. Would I could suit mine office
         ˋ to my face,
If that would please your highness.

    Vict. No, you are obstinate and perverse all,
And would not grant it if you had the pow'r.
Albini I'll retire ; come Isabella.

    Bas. aside to Ros. Ah! Rosinberg, thou hast
        too far presum'd ;
She is offended with us.

    Ros.   No, she is not—
What dost thou fear ? be firm and let us go.

    *Vict. (pointing to a door leading to other apartments,
        by which she is ready to go out.)*
These are apartments strangers love to see ;
Some famous paintings do their walls adorn.
It leads you also to the palace court
As quickly as the way by which you came.

    [Exit Vict. *led out by* Ros. *and followed by* Isab.

    Bas. (aside, looking after them.) O! what a fool
        am I! where fled my thoughts?
I might as well as he, now by her side
Have held her precious hand enclos'd in mine ;
As well as he, who cares not for it neither.
O! damn it, but he does! that were impossible!

Albin. You stay behind, my Lord.

Bas. Your pardon Madam ; honour me so far—
                    [EXEUNT, *handing out* Albini.

SCENE II.

A Gallery hung with Pictures. VICTORIA *discovered in conversation with* ROSINBERG, BASIL, ALBINI, *and* ISABELLA.

Vict. to Ros. It is indeed a work of wond'rous
    art.

To Isab. You call'd Francisco here?

Isab.   He comes even now.

Enter ATTENDANT.

Vict. to Ros. He will conduct you to the nor-
    thern gall'ry ;

Its striking shades will call upon the eye,

To point its place no guide is wanted there.
                    [EXEUNT *Ros.* and *Attendant.*

To Bas. Loves not Count Basil too this charm-
    ing art?

It is an ancient painting much admir'd.

Bas. Ah! do not banish me these few short
    moments ;

Too soon they will be gone! for ever gone!

Vict. If they are precious to you say not so,

But add to them another precious day.

A Lady asks it.

Bas. Ah, Madam! ask the life-blood from my
    heart!

Ask all but what a soldier may not give.

 Vict. 'Tis ever thus when favours are denied,
All had been granted but the thing we beg;
And still some great unlikely substitute,
Your life, your soul, your all of earthly good,
Is proffer'd in the room of one small boon.
So keep your life-blood, gen'rous, valiant lord,
And may it long your noble heart enrich,
Until I. wish it shed.

  Bas. (attempts to speak.) Nay, frame no new excuse; I will not hear it:
   [*She puts out her hand as if she would shut his
   mouth, but at a distance from it*; Bas. *runs
   eagerly up to her and presses it to his lips.*]
  Bas. Let this sweet hand indeed its threat perform,
And make it heav'n to be for ever dumb!

   (VICT. *looks stately and offended*—Basil
   kneels.)

O! pardon me, I know not what I do.
Frown not, reduce me not to wretchedness,
But only grant—

 Vict.   What should I grant to him
Who has so oft my earnest suit deny'd?

 Bas. By heav'n I'll grant it! I'll do any thing,
Say but thou art no more offended with me.

  Vict. (raising him.) Well Basil, this good pro-
  mise is thy pardon.
I will not wait your noble friend's return
Since we shall meet again.—
You will perform your word!

Bas. I will perform it.

Vict. Farewell, my lord.

[EXEUNT, *with her Ladies.*

Bas. alone. " Farewell, my lord," O! what de-
lightful sweetness
The musick of that voice dwells on the ear!
" Farewell, my lord!"—Ay, and then look'd she
    so—
The slightest glance of her bewitching eye,
Those dark blue eyes, command the inmost soul.
Well, there is yet one day of life before me,
And whatsoe'er betides I will enjoy it.
Tho' but a partial sunshine in my lot
I will converse with her, gaze on her still,
If all behind were pain and misery.
Pain! were it not the easing of all pain,
E'en in the dismal gloom of after years,
Such dear rememb'rance on the mind to wear?
Like silv'ry moon-beams on the 'nighted deep,
When heav'n's blest sun is gone!
Kind mercy! how my heart within me beat
When she so sweetly pled the cause of love!
Can she have lov'd? why shrink I at the thought?
Why should she not? no, no, it cannot be—
No man on earth is worthy of her love.
Ah! if she could, how blest a man were he!
Where rove my giddy thoughts? it must not be.
Yet might she well some gentle kindness bear;
Think of him oft, his absent fate enquire,
And, should he fall in battle, mourn his fall.

Yes, she would mourn—such love might she
    bestow ;
And poor of soul the man who would exchange it
For warmest love of the most loving dame.
But here comes Rosinberg—have I done well ?
He will not say I have.

Enter ROSINBERG.

  Ros. Where is the princess ?
I'm sorry I return'd not ere she went.
  Bas. You'll see her still.
  Ros.   What, comes she forth again ?
  Bas. She does to-morrow.
  Ros.   Thou hast yielded then.
  Bas. Come, Rosinberg, I'll tell thee as we go :
It was impossible I should not yield.
  Ros. And has the first look of a stranger's face
So far bewitched thee ?
  Bas.   A stranger's face !
Long has she been the inmate of my breast !
The smiling angel of my nightly dreams.
  Ros. What mean you now ? Your mind is
    raving, Basil.
  Bas. I speak in sober earnest. Two years since,
When marching on the confines of this state,
We heard the distant musick of the chace,
And trampling horses near, I turn'd to look,
And saw the loveliest sight of woman's form
That ever blest mine eyes. Her fiery steed,
Struck with the strange accoutrements of war,
Became unruly, and despis'd the rein.

I gently led him with his lovely charge
Past all the ranks: she thank'd me courteously;
Then, with the few companions of her sport,
Took to the woods again.   I, with my men,
Our route pursued, and met with her no more.
——————————Her name and state I knew not;
Yet, like a beauteous vision from the blest,
Her form has oft upon my mind return'd;
And tho' this day the sight had ne'er restor'd,
It ne'er had been forgotten.   Gentle Rosinberg!
Be not displeas'd!   I would have told thee this,
When first to-day we talk'd of Mantua's princess,
But thou wert griev'd and jealous of me then,
And so I shut my breast and said no more.

    Ros. O Basil! thou art weaker than a child.

    Bas. Yes, yes, my friend, but 'tis a noble weak-
        ness ;

A weakness which hath greater things atchiev'd
Than all the firm, determin'd strength of reason.
By heav'n! I feel a new-born pow'r within me
Shall make me twenty-fold the man I've been
Before this fated day.

    Ros. Fated indeed! but an ill-fated day,
That makes thee other than thy former self.
Yet let it work its will; it cannot change thee
To ought I shall not love.

    Bas. Thanks, Rosinberg! thou art a noble
        heart!

I would not be the man thou couldst not love
For an Imperial Crown.

                        [EXEUNT.

SCENE III.

A Small Apartment in the Palace.

Enter DUKE *and* GAURIECIO.

Duke. The point is gain'd; my daughter is successful,
And Basil is detain'd another day.

Gaur. But does the princess know your secret aim?

Duke. No, that had marr'd the whole : she is a woman;
Her mind, as suits the sex, too weak and narrow
To relish deep-laid schemes of policy.
Besides, so far unlike a child of mine,
She holds its subtle arts in high derision,
And will not serve us but with bandag'd eyes.
Gauriecio, could I hasty servants find,
Experienc'd, crafty, close, and unrestrain'd
By silly superstitious child-learnt fears,
What might I not effect?

Gaur. O! any thing ;
The deep and piercing genius of your highness,
So ably serv'd, might e'en atchieve the empire.

Duke. No, no, my friend, thou dost o'erprize my parts.
Yet mighty things might be—deep subtle wits
In truth are master-spirits in the world.
The brave man's courage, and the student's lore,
Are but as tools his secret ends to work,
Who hath the skill to use them.

This brave Count Basil, dost thou know him well?
Much have we gain'd but for a single day
At such a time to hold his troops detain'd;
When by that secret message of our spy,
The rival pow'rs are on the brink of action:
But might we more effect? Know'st thou this
     Basil?
Might he be tamper'd with?
    Gaur.   That were most dang'rous—
He is a man, whose sense of right and wrong
To such a high romantic pitch is wound,
And all so hot and fiery in his nature,
The slightest hint, as tho' you did suppose
Baseness and treach'ry in him, so he'll deem it,
Would be to rouse a flame that might destroy.
    Duke. But int'rest, int'rest; man's all-ruling
     pow'r,
Will tame the hottest spirit to your service,
And skilfully applied, mean service too.
E'en as there is an element in nature
Which when subdu'd, will on your hearth fulfil
The lowest uses of domestick wants.
    Gaur. Earth-kindled fire, which from a little
     spark
On hidden fuel feeds its growing strength,
Till o'er the lofty fabrick it aspires
And rages out it's pow'r, may be subdu'd,
And in your base domestick service bound;
But who would madly in its wild career
The fire of heav'n arrest to boil his pot?
No, Basil will not serve your secret schemes,
1

Tho' you had all to give ambition strives for.
We must beware of him.

   Duke. His father was my friend, I wish'd to gain
       him,
But since fantastick fancies bind him thus,
The sin be on his head, I stand acquitted,
And must deceive him, even to his ruin.

   Gaur. I have prepar'd Bernardo for your service;
To-night he will depart for th' Austrian camp,
And should he find them on the eve of battle,
I've bid him wait the issue of the field.
If that our secret friends victorious prove,
With th' arrow's speed he will return again;
But should fair Fortune crown Piscaro's arms,
Then shall your soothing message greet his ears;
For till our friends some sound advantage gain,
Our actions still must wear an Austrian face.

   Duke. Well hast thou school'd him.   Did'st
      thou add withal,
That 'tis my will he garnish well his speech,
With honied words of the most dear regard,
And friendly love I bear him.   This is needful;
And lest my slowness in the promis'd aid
Awake suspicion, bid him e'en rehearse
The many favours on my house bestow'd
By his Imperial master, as a theme
On which my gratitude delights to dwell.

   Gaur. I have, an' please your highness.
   Duke.   Then 'tis well.
   Gaur. But for the yielding up that little fort
There could be no suspicion.

Duke. My Governor I have severely punish'd
As a most daring traitor to my orders.
He cannot from his darksome dungeon tell,
Why then should they suspect?

    Gaur. He must not live if Charles should prove
       victorious.

    Duke. He's done, me service, say not so
       Gauriecio.

    Gaur. A traitor's name he will not calmly bear,
He'll tell his tale aloud—he must not live.

    Duke. Well, if it must—we'll talk of this again.

    Gaur. But while with anxious care and crafty
       wiles,
You would enlarge the limits of your state,
Your highness must beware lest inward broils
Bring danger near at hand: your northern subjects
E'en now are discontented and unquiet.

    Duke. What, dare the ungrateful miscreants
       thus return
The many favours of my princely grace?
'Tis ever thus indulgence spoils the base,
Raising up pride, and lawless turbulence,
Like noxious vapours from the fulsome marsh
When morning shines upon it—
Did I not lately, with parental care,
When dire invaders their destruction threaten'd,
Provide them all with means of their defence?
Did I not, as a mark of gracious trust,
A body of their vagrant youth select
To guard my sacred person? Till that day
An honour never yet allow'd their race.
Did I not suffer them upon their suit

T'establish manufactures in their towns?
And after all some chosen soldiers spare
To guard the blessings of interiour peace?
   Gaur. Nay, please your highness, they do well
      allow
That when your enemies, in fell revenge,
Your former inroads threaten'd to repay,
Their ancient arms you did to them restore,
With kind permission to defend themselves.
That so far have they felt your princely grace
In drafting from their fields their goodliest youth
To be your servants. That you did vouchsafe,
On paying of a large and heavy fine,
Leave to apply the labour of their hands
As best might profit to the country's weal;
And to encourage well their infant trade
Quarter'd your troops upon them—please your
      grace,
All this they do most readily allow.
   Duke. They do allow it then, ungrateful varlets;
What would they have? what would they have,
      Gauriecio?
   Gaur. Some mitigation of their grievous burdens,
Which, like an iron weight around their necks,
Do bend their care-worn faces to the earth,
Like creatures form'd upon its soil to creep,
Not stand erect, and view the sun of heav'n.
   Duke. But they beyond their proper sphere
      would rise;
Let them their lot fulfil as we do ours;
Society of various parts is form'd;

6

They are its grounds, its mud, its sediment,
And we the mantling top which crowns the whole.
Calm, steady labour is their greatest bliss,
To aim at higher things beseems them not.
To let them work in peace my care shall be,
To slacken labour is to nourish pride.
Methinks thou art a pleader for these fools;
What may this mean Gauriecio?

    Gaur. They were resolv'd to lay their cause
      before you,
And would have found some other advocate
Less pleasing to your Grace, had I refus'd.

    Duke. Well, let them know some more con-
      venient season
I'll think of this, and do for them as much
As suits the honour of my princely state;
Their prince's honour should be ever dear
To worthy subjects as their precious lives.

    Gaur. I fear, unless you give some special pro-
      mise,
They will be violent still—

    Duke. Then do it, if the wretches are so bold;
We can retract it when the times allow
'Tis of small consequence. Go see Bernardo,
And come to me again.

                [EXEUNT.

    Gaur. solus. O! happy people! whose indul-
      gent lord
From ev'ry care, with which increasing wealth,
With all its hopes and fears, doth ever move
The human bosom, would most kindly free,

And kindly leave ye nought to do but toil !
This creature now, with all his reptile cunning,
Writhing and turning thro' a maze of wiles,
Believes his genius form'd to rule mankind,
And calls his sordid wish for territory,
That noblest passion of the soul, ambition :
Born had he been to follow some low trade,
A petty tradesman still he had remain'd,
And us'd the arts with which he rules a state,
To circumvent his brothers of the craft,
Or cheat the buyers of his paltry ware.
And yet he thinks, ha, ha, ha, ha, ha, ha !
I am the tool and servant of his will.
Well, let it be ; thro' all the maze of trouble
His plots and base oppression must create,
I'll shape myself a way to higher things,
And who will say 'tis wrong ?
A sordid being who expects no faith
But as self-interest binds, who would not trust
The strongest ties of nature on the soul,
Deserves no faithful service.   Perverse fate !
Were I like him I would despise this dealing ;
But being as I am, born low in fortune,
Yet with a mind aspiring to be great,
I must not scorn the steps which lead to it :
And if they are not right, no saint am I ;
I follow nature's passion in my breast,
Which urges me to rise, in spite of fortune.

[EXIT.

SCENE IV.

An Apartment in the Palace; VICTORIA *and*
ISABELLA *are discovered playing at Chess; the*
Countess ALBINI *sitting by them, reading to herself.*

Vict. Away with it, I will not play again ;
May men no more look foolish in my presence
If thou art not a cheat, an errant cheat.

Isab. To swear that I am false by such an oath,
Should prove me honest, since its forfeiture
Would bring your highness gain.

Vict. Thou 'rt wrong, my Isabella, simple maid,
For in the very forfeit of this oath,
There's death to all the dearest pride of women.
May man no more look foolish in my presence !

Isab. And does your grace, hail'd by applauding
          crouds,
In all the graceful eloquence address'd
Of most accomplish'd, noble, courtly youths,
Prais'd in the songs of heav'n-inspired bards ;
Those awkward proofs of admiration prize,
The rustick swain his village fair-one pays ?

Vict. O! love will master all the pow'r of art,
Ay all ! and she who never has beheld
The polish'd courtier, or the tuneful sage,
Before the glances of her conq'ring eye,
A very native simple swain become,
Has only vulgar charms.
To make the cunning artless, tame the rude,
Subdue the haughty, shake th'undaunted soul ;

Yea, put a bridle in the lion's mouth,
And lead him forth as a domestick cur,
These are the triumphs of all-pow'rful beauty !
Did nought but flatt'ring words and tuneful praise,
Sighs, tender glances, and obsequious service,
Attend her presence, it were nothing worth.
I'd put a white coif o'er my braided locks,
And be a plain, good, simple, fire-side dame.

    Alb. (raising her head from her book) And is,
        indeed, a plain domestick dame,
Who fills the duties of an useful state,
A being of less dignity, than she
Who vainly on her transient beauty builds
A little poor ideal tyranny ?

    Isab. Ideal too !

    Alb.   Yes, most unreal pow'r ;
For she who only finds her self-esteem
In others admiration, begs an alms,
Depends on others for her daily food,
And is the very servant of her slaves ;
Tho' oftentimes, in a fantastick hour,
O'er men she may a childish pow'r exert,
Which not ennobles, but degrades her state.

    Vict. You are severe, Albini, most severe :
Were human passions plac'd within the breast
But to be curb'd, subdu'd, pluck'd by the roots ?
All heav'n's gifts to some good end were giv'n.

    Alb. Yes, for a noble, for a gen'rous end.

    Vict. Am I ungen'rous then ?

    Alb.   O ! most ungen'rous,
Who for the pleasure of a little pow'r

Would give most unavailing pain to those
Whose love you ne'er can recompense again.
E'en now, to-day, O! was it not ungen'rous
To fetter Basil with a foolish tie,
Against his will, perhaps against his duty?

Vict. What, dost thou think against his will,
        my friend?

Alb. Full sure I am against his reason's will.

Vict. Ah! but indeed thou must excuse me here,
For duller than a shelled crab were she,
Who could suspect her pow'r in such a mind,
And calmly leave it doubtful and unprov'd.
But wherefore dost thou look so gravely on me?
Ah! well I read those looks! methinks they say,
Your mother did not so.

Alb. Your highness reads them true, she did
        not so.
If foolish vanity e'er soil'd her thoughts
She kept it low, withheld its aliment;
Not pamper'd it with ev'ry motley food,
From the fond tribute of a noble heart,
To the lisp'd flatt'ry of a cunning child.

Vict. Nay, speak not thus Albini, speak not thus
Of little blue-ey'd, sweet, fair-hair'd Mirando.
He is the orphan of a hapless pair,
A loving, beautiful, but hapless pair,
Whose story is so pleasing, and so sad,
The swains have turn'd it to a plaintive lay,
And sing it as they tend their mountain sheep.

To Isab. Besides I am the guardian of his choice,
When first I saw him dost not thou remember?

Isab. 'Twas in the publick garden.

Vict.   Even so;
Perch'd in his nurse's arms, a roughsome quean,
Ill suited to the lovely charge she bore.
How steadfastly he fix'd his looks upon me,
His dark eyes shining thro' forgotten tears !
Then stretch'd his little arms, and call'd me mam!
What could I do ! I took the bantling home—
I could not tell the imp he had no mam!

> *Alb.* Ah ! there my child, thou hast indeed no
> blame.

Vict. Ay, this is kindly said, thanks sweet Albini!
Still call me child, and chide me as thou wilt.
O ! would that I were such as thou couldst love !
Couldst dearly love ! as thou didst love my mother.

> *Alb.* (*pressing her to her breast.*) And do I not?
> all perfect as she was,

I know not that she went so near my heart
As thou, with all thy faults.

> *Vict.* And sayst thou so ? would I had sooner
> known!

I had done any thing to give thee pleasure.

> *Alb.* Then do so now, and put away thy faults.
>
> *Vict.* No, say not faults; the freaks of thought-
> less youth.
>
> *Alb.* Nay, very faults they must indeed be call'd.
>
> *Vict.* O ! say but foibles ! youthful foibles only!
>
> *Alb.* Faults, faults, real faults you must confess
> they are.
>
> *Vict.* In truth, I cannot do your sense the wrong

To think so poorly of the one you love.

Alb. I must be gone; thou hast o'ercome me now,
Another time I will not yield it so.   ' [Exit.

Isab. The Countess is severe, she's too severe;
She once was young, tho' now advanc'd in years.

Vict. No, I deserve it all; she is most worthy.
Unlike those faded beauties of the court,
But now the wither'd stems of former flow'rs,
With all their blossoms shed; her nobler mind
Procures to her the privilege of man,
Ne'er to be old till nature's strength decays.
Some few years hence, if I should live so long,
I'd be Albini rather than myself.

Isab. Here comes your little pet.

Vict. I am not in the humour for him now.

Enter MIRANDO, *running up to* VICTORIA, *and
taking hold of her gown, but she takes no notice
of him, while he holds up his mouth to be kissed.*

Isab. to Mir. Thou seest the princess ca'nt be
    troubled with thee.

Mir. O! but she will! I'll scramble up her robe,
As naughty boys do when they climb for apples.

Isab. Come here, sweet child; I'll kiss thee in
    her stead.

Mir. Nay, but I will not have a kiss of thee.
Would I were tall! O! were I but so tall!

Isab. And how tall wouldst thou be?

Mir.   Thou dost not know?
Just tall enough to reach Victoria's lips.

Vict. (embracing him.) O! I must bend to this,
    thou little urchin.

Who taught thee all this wit, this childish wit ?
Who does Mirando love ? *(embraces him again.)*

Mir.　　　　　　　　He loves Victoria.

Vict. And wherefore loves he her ?

Mir.　　　　　　　　Because she's pretty.

Isab. Hast thou no little prate to-day Mirando ?
No tale to earn a sugar-plumb withal ?

Mir. Ay, that I have ; I know who loves her
　　grace.

Vict. Who is it pray ? thou shalt have comfits
　　for it.

Mir. (looking slily at her.) It is—it is—it is the
　　count of Maldo.

Vict. Away thou little chit, that tale is old,
And was not worth a sugar-plumb when new.

Mir. Well then, I know who loves her highness
　　well.

Vict. Who is it then ?

Isab.　　　　　　　Who is it naughty boy ?

Mir. It is the handsome marquis of Carlatzi.

Vict. No, no, Mirando, thou art naughty still ;
Thou'st twice had comfits for that tale already.

Mir. Well then, indeed, I know who loves
　　Victoria.

Vict. And who is he ?

Mir.　　　　　　　　It is Mirando's self.

Vict. Thou little imp ! this story is not new,
But thou shalt have thy comfits. Let us go.
Go run before us, Boy.

Mir. Nay, but I'll shew you how Count Wolvar
　　did,

I

When he conducted Isabel from Court.

 Vict. How did he do?

 Mir. Give me your hand : he held his body thus,
  (putting himself in a ridiculous bowing posture.)
And then he whisper'd softly ; then look'd so;
    (ogling with his eyes affectedly.)
Then she look'd so, and smil'd to him again.
    (throwing down his eyes affectedly.)
 Isab. Thou art a little knave, and must be whipp'd.
 [EXEUNT. Mirando *leading out* Victoria *affectedly.*

ACT III.—SCENE I.

An Open Street, or Square.

Enter ROSINBERG *and* FREDERICK, *by opposite
sides of the Stage.*

 Fred. So Basil, from the pressing calls of war,
Another day to rest and pastime gives.
How is it now? methinks thou art not pleas'd.

 Ros. It matters little if I am or not.

 Fred. Now pray thee do confess thou art asham'd.
Thou, who art wisely wont to set at nought
The noble fire of individual courage,
And call calm prudence the superiour virtue,
What sayst thou now, my candid Rosinberg?
When thy great captain, in a time like this,
Denies his weary troops one day of rest
Before the exertions of approaching battle,
Yet grants it to a pretty lady's suit?

 Ros. Who told thee this? it was no friendly tale,

And no one else besides a trusty friend,
Could know his motives. Then thou wrongst me too,
For I admire, as much as thou dost Fred'rick,
The fire of valour, e'en rash heedless valour;
But not like thee do I depreciate
That far superiour; yea that god-like talent,
Which doth direct that fire, because indeed
It is a talent nature has denied me.

 Fred. Well, well, and greatly he may boast his
   virtue,
Who risks perhaps th'Imperial army's fate,
To please a lady's freaks—

 Ros.   Go, go, thou'rt prejudic'd :
A passion, which I do not chuse to name,
Has warp'd thy judgement.

 Fred.   No, by heav'n thou wrongst me !
I do, with most enthusiastick warmth,
True valour love; wherever he is found,
I love the hero too; but hate to see
The praises due to him so cheaply earn'd.

 Ros. Then mayst thou now these gen'rous
   feelings prove.
Behold the man whose short and grizzly hair
In clust'ring locks, his dark brown face o'ershades;
Where now the scars of former sabre wounds,
In hon'rable companionship are seen
With the deep lines of age ; whose piercing eye,
Beneath its shading eye-brow keenly darts
Its yet unquenched beams, as tho' in age
Its youthful fire had been again renew'd,
To be the guardian of its darken'd mate.

See with what vig'rous steps his upright form
He onward bears; nay, e'en that vacant sleeve,
Which droops so sadly by his better side,
Suits not ungracefully the vet'ran's mien.
This is the man, whose glorious acts in battle
We heard to-day related o'er our wine.
I go to tell the Gen'ral he is come.
Enjoy the gen'rous feelings of thy breast,
And make an old man happy.   [EXIT.

Enter GEOFFRY.

Fred. Brave soldier, let me profit by the chance
That led me here; I've heard of thy exploits.

Geof. Ah! then you have but heard an ancient
        tale,
Which has been long forgotten.

Fred. But true it is, and should not be forgotten;
Tho' Gen'rals, jealous of their soldiers' fame,
May dash it with neglect.

Geof. There are, perhaps, who may be so
        ungen'rous.

Fred. Perhaps, sayst thou? in very truth there are;
How art thou else rewarded with neglect,
Whilst many a paltry fellow in thy corps
Has been promoted? it is ever thus.
Serv'd not Mardini in your company?
He was, tho' honour'd with a valiant name,
To those who knew him well, a paltry soldier.

Geof. Your pardon, Sir, we did esteem him much,
Although inferiour to his gallant friend,
The brave Sebastian.

Fred.   The brave Sebastian !
He was, as I am told, a learnèd coxcomb,
And lov'd a goose-quill better than a sword.
What, dost thou call him brave ?
Thou, who dost bear about that war-worn trunk,
Like an old target, hack'd and rough with wounds,
Whilst, after all his mighty battles, he
Was with a smooth skin in his coffin laid,
Unblemish'd with a scar.

    Geof. His duty call'd not to such desp'rate
       service ;
For I have fought where few alive remain'd,
And none unscath'd ; where but a few remain'd,
Thus marr'd, and mangl'd. *(Shewing his wounds.)*
       As belike you've seen,
O'summer nights, around th'evening lamp,
Some wretched moths, wingless, and half-consum'd,
Just feebly crawling o'er their heaps of dead—
In Savoy, on a small, tho' desp'rate post,
Of full three hundred goodly, chosen men,
But twelve were left, and right dear friends were we
Forever after.   They are all dead now,
I'm old and lonely—we were valiant hearts—
Fred'rick Dewalter would have stopp'd a breach
Against the devil himself.   I'm lonely now.

    Fred. I'm sorry for thee. Hang ungrateful
       chiefs !
Why art thou not promoted ?

    Geof. After that battle, where my happy fate
Had led me to fulfil a glorious part,
Chaf'd with the gibing insults of a slave,

The worthless fav'rite of a great man's fav'rite,
I rashly did affront ; our cautious prince,
With narrow policy dependant made,
Dar'd not, as I am told, promote me then,
And now he is asham'd, or has forgot it.

   Fred. Fye, fye upon it ! let him be asham'd !
Here is a trifle for thee—*(offering him money)*

   Geof.   No, good sir,
I have enough to live as poor men do.
When I'm in want I'll thankfully receive
Because I'm poor, but not because I'm brave.

   Fred. You're proud, old soldier—

   Geof.   No, I am not proud ;
For if I were, methinks I'd be morose,
And willing to depreciate other men.

Enter ROSINBERG.

   Ros. (clapping Geof. *on the shoulder.)* How goes
       it with thee now, my good Field-marshal ?

   Geof. The better that I see your honour well,
And in the humour to be merry with me.

   Ros. 'Faith, by my sword, I've rightly nam'd
       thee too ;
What is a good Field-marshal, but a man
Whose gen'rous courage and undaunted mind,
Doth marshal others on in glory's way ?
Thou art not one by princely favour dubb'd,
But one of nature's making.

   Geof. You shew, my lord, such pleasant courtesy,
I know not how—

   Ros.   But see, the Gen'ral comes.

Enter Basil.

Ros. *(pointing to* Geof.) Behold the worthy
      vet'ran.

Bas. *(taking him by the hand.)* Brave, hon'rable
      man, your worth I know,
And greet it with a brother-soldier's love.

Geof. *(taking away his hand in confusion.)* My
      Gen'ral, this is too much, too much honour.

Bas. *(taking his hand again.)* No valiant soldier,
      I must have it so.

Geof. My humble state agrees not with such
      honour.

Bas. Confound thy state ! it is no part of thee:
Let mean souls, highly rank'd, look down on thee ;
As the poor dwarf, perch'd on a pedestal,
O'erlooks the giant.   'Tis not worth a thought.
Art thou not Geoffry of the tenth brigade,
Whose warlike feats child, maid, and matron know ?
And oft, cross-elbow'd, o'er his nightly bowl,
The jolly toper to his comrade tells.
Whose glorious feats of war, by cottage door,
The ancient soldier tracing in the sand
The many movements of the varied field,
In warlike terms to list'ning swains relate ;
Whose bosoms glowing at the wond'rous tale,
First learn to scorn the hind's inglorious life.
Shame seize me if I would not rather be
The man thou art, than court-created chief,
Known only by the dates of his promotion.

Geof. Ah! would I were, would I were young
  again,
To fight beneath your standard, noble gen'ral !
Methinks what I have done were but a jest,
Ay, but a jest to what I now should do,
Were I again the man that I have been.
O ! I could fight !
 Bas.   And wouldst thou fight for me?
 Geof. Ay, to the death !
 Bas. Then come brave man, and be my cham-
  pion still ;
The sight of thee will fire my soldiers' breasts.
Come, noble vet'ran, thou shalt fight for me.
      [Exit *with* Geoffry.
 Fred. What does he mean to do ?
 Ros.   We'll know ere long.
 Fred. Our gen'ral bears it with a careless face
For one so wise.
 Ros.   A careless face ! on what ?
 Fred. Now feign not ignorance, we know it all,
News which have spread in whispers from the court,
Since last night's messenger arriv'd from Milan.
 Ros. As I'm an honest man I know it not!
 Fred. 'Tis said the rival armies are so near,
A battle must immediately ensue.
 Ros. It cannot be. Our gen'ral knows it not.
The Duke is of our side, an ally sworn,
And had such messenger to Mantua come,
He would have been appriz'd upon the instant.
It cannot be, it is some idle tale.
 Fred. So may it prove till we have join'd them too,

Then heaven grant they may be nearer still;
For O! my soul for war and danger pants,
As doth the noble lion for his prey.
My soul delights in battle.

 Ros. Upon my simple word, I'd rather see
A score of friendly fellows shaking hands,
Than all the world in arms.   Hast thou no fear?

 Fred. What dost thou mean?

 Ros.   Hast thou no fear of death?

 Fred. Fear is a name for something in the mind,
But what, from inward sense I cannot tell.
I could as little anxious march to battle,
As when a boy to childish games I ran.

 Ros. Then as much virtue hast thou in thy
   valour,
As when a child thou hadst in childish play.
The brave man is not he who feels no fear,
For that were stupid and irrational,
But he, whose noble soul its fear subdues,
And bravely dares the danger nature shrinks from.
As for your youth, whom blood and blows delight,
Away with them! there is not in the crew
One valiant spirit.—Ha! what sound is this?

      (shouting is heard without.)

 Fred. The soldiers shout; I'll run and learn
   the cause.

 Ros. But tell me first, how didst thou love the
   vet'ran?

 Fred. He is too proud; he was displeas'd with me
Because I offer'd him a little sum.

 Ros. What money! O! most gen'rous noble spirit!

Noble rewarder of superiour worth !
A halfpenny for Bellisarius !
But hark ! they shout again—here comes Valtomer.
(*Shouting heard without.*)

Enter VALTOMER.

What docs this shouting mean ?
  Valt. O ! I have seen a sight, a glorious sight!
Thou wouldst have smil'd to see it.
  Ros. How smile ? methinks thine eyes are wet
    with tears.
  Valt. (*passing the back of his hand across his eyes.*)
    'Faith so they are; well, well, but I smil'd too,
You heard the shouting.
  Ros. and Fred.   Yes.
  Valt. O ! had you seen it !
Drawn out in goodly ranks, there stood our troops;
Here, in the graceful state of manly youth,
His dark face brighten'd with a gen'rous smile,
Which to his eyes such flashing lustre gave,
As tho' his soul, like an unsheathed sword,
Had thro' them gleam'd, our noble gen'ral stood ;
And to his soldiers, with heart-moving words,
The vet'ran shewing, his brave deeds rehears'd ;
Who by his side stood like a storm-scath'd oak,
Beneath the shelter of some noble tree,
In the green honours of its youthful prime.
  Ros. How look'd the vet'ran ?
  Valt.   O! I cannot tell thee !
At first he bore it up with chearful looks,
As one who fain would wear his honours bravely,

And greet the soldiers with a comrade's face;
But when Count Basil, in such moving speech
Told o'er his actions past, and bad his troops
Great deeds to emulate, his count'nance chang'd;
High-heav'd his manly breast, as it had been
By inward strong emotion half convuls'd;
Trembled his neither lip; he shed some tears.
The gen'ral paus'd, the soldiers shouted loud;
Then hastily he brush'd the drops away,
And wav'd his hand, and clear'd his tear-chok'd
    voice,
As tho' he would some grateful answer make;
When back with double force the whelming tide
Of passion came; high o'er his hoary head
His arm he toss'd, and heedless of respect,
In Basil's bosom hid his aged face,
Sobbing aloud.   From the admiring ranks
A cry arose; still louder shouts resound.
I felt a sudden tightness grasp my throat
As it would strangle me; such as I felt,
I knew it well, some twenty years ago,
When my good father shed his blessing on me.
I hate to weep, and so I came away.
   Ros. (giving Valt. his hand.) And there, take
    thou my blessing for the tale.
Hark! how they shout again! 'tis nearer now.
This way they march.
*Martial Musick heard. Enter Soldiers marching in
  order, bearing* GEOFFRY *in triumph on their
  shoulders. After them enter* BASIL; *the whole
  preceded by a band of musick. They cross over
  the Stage, are joined by* Ros. &c. *and* EXEUNT.

SCENE II.

Enter Gauriecio *and a* Gentleman, *talking as they enter.*

Gaur. So slight a tie as this we cannot trust.
One day her influence may detain him here,
But love a feeble agent will be found
With the ambitious.

Gent. And so you think this boyish odd conceit
Of bearing home in triumph with his troops
That aged soldier, will your purpose serve?

Gaur. Yes, I will make it serve; for tho' my
    prince
Is little scrupulous of right and wrong,
I have possess'd his mind, as tho' it were
A flagrant insult on his princely state
To honour thus the man he has neglected;
Which makes him relish, with a keener taste,
My purpos'd scheme. Come let us fall to work,
With all their warm heroick feelings rous'd,
We'll spirit up his troops to mutiny,
Which must retard, perhaps undo him quite.
Thanks to his childish love, which has so well
Procur'd us time to tamper with the fools.

Gent. Ah! but those feelings he has wak'd
    within them,
Are gen'rous feelings, and endear himself.

Gaur It matters not; tho' gen'rous in their
    nature,
They yet may serve a most ungen'rous end;

2

And he who teaches men to think, tho' nobly,
Doth raise within their minds a busy judge
To scan his actions.   Send thine agents forth,
And sound it in their ears how much Count Basil
Affects all difficult and desp'rate service,
To raise his fortunes by some daring stroke ;
And to the Emp'rour hath pledg'd his word,
To make his troops all dreadful hazards brave ;
For which intent he fills their simple minds
With idle tales of glory and renown ;
Using their warm attachment to himself
For most unworthy ends.
This is the busy time, go forth my friend ;
Mix with the soldiers now in jolly groups,
Around their ev'ning cups. There, spare no cost,
                              (gives him a purse.)
Observe their words, see how the poison takes,
And then return again.

  Gent.   I will, my lord.

       Exeunt *severally.*

SCENE III.

*A Suite of grand Apartments, with their wide
doors thrown open; lighted up with lamps, and
filled with company in masks. Enter several
masks, and pass through the first apartment to
the other rooms.   Then enter* BASIL *in the disguise
of a wounded soldier.*

  Bas. alone. Now am I in the region of delight !
Within the blessed compass of these walls
She is ; the gay light of those blazing lamps

Doth shine upon her, and this painted floor
Is with her footsteps press'd.   E'en now perhaps
Amidst that motley rout she plays her part.
There will I go ; she cannot be conceal'd,
For but the flowing of her graceful robe
Will soon betray the lovely form that wears it,
Tho' in a thousand masks.   Ye homely weeds,——
                              (looking at his habit.)
Which half conceal, and half declare my state,
Beneath your kind disguise, O ! let me prosper,
And boldly take the privilege ye give.
Follow her mazy steps, croud by her side ;
Thus, near her face my list'ning ear incline,
And feel her soft breath fan my glowing cheek ;
Her fair hand seize, yea press it closely too;
May it not be e'en so ? by heav'n it shall !
This once, O ! serve me well, and ever after
Ye shall be treasur'd like a monarch's robes ;
Lodg'd in my chamber, near my pillow kept ;
And oft with midnight lamp I'll visit ye,
And gazing wistfully, this night recall,
With all its past delights.—But yonder moves
A slender form, dress'd in an azure robe ;
It moves not like the rest—it must be she.

(*Goes hastily into another apartment, and mixes
        with the masks.)*

Enter ROSINBERG *fantastically dressed, with a
    willow upon his head, and scraps of sonnets, and
    torn letters fluttering round his neck ; pursued
    by a group of masks from one of the inner*

*apartments, who hoot at him, and push him about
as he enters.*

1st Mask. Away, thou art a saucy jeering knave,
And fain wouldst make a jest of all true love.

Ros. Nay, gentle ladies, do not buffet me;
I am a right true servant of the fair; ·
And as this woeful chaplet on my brow,
And these tear-blotted sonnets would denote,
A poor abandon'd lover out of place;
With any mistress ready to engage,
Who will enlist me in her loving service.
Of a convenient kind my talents are,
And to all various humours may be shap'd.

2d Mask. What canst thou do?

3d Mask.　　　　Ay, what besides offending?

Ros. O! I can sigh so deeply, look so sad;
Pale out a piteous tale on bended knee;
Groan like a ghost, so very wretched be,
As would delight a tender lady's heart
But to behold.

1st Mask.　　Poo, poo, insipid fool!

Ros. But should my lady brisker mettle own,
And tire of all those gentle dear delights,
Such pretty little quarrels I'd invent—
As whether such a fair-one (some dear friend!)
Whose squirrel's tail was pinch'd, or the soft maid,
With fav'rite lap-dog of a surfeit sick,
Have greatest cause of delicate distress:
Or whether—

1st Mask.　　Go, thou art too bad indeed!
(aside.) How could he know I quarrell'd with the
　　　　Count?

2d Mask. Wilt thou do nothing for thy lady's
    fame ?

Ros. Yes, lovely shepherdess, on ev'ry tree,
I'll carve her name, with true-love garlands bound.
Write madrigals upon her roseate cheeks,
Odes to her eye, 'faith ev'ry wart and mole
That spots her snowy skin, shall have its sonnet !
I'll make love-posies for her thimble's edge,
Rather than please her not.

    3d Mask. But for her sake what dangers wilt
    thou brave ?

Ros. In truth, fair Nun, I stomach dangers less
Than other service, and were something loth
To storm a convent's walls for one dear glance ;
But if she'll wisely manage this alone,
As maids have done, come o'er the wall herself,
And meet me fairly on the open plain,
I will engage her tender steps to aid
In all annoyance of rude briar or stone,
Or crossing rill, some half-foot wide, or so,
Which that fair lady should unaided pass,
Ye gracious powers forbid ! I will defend
Against each hideous fly, whose dreadful buz—

    4th Mask. Such paltry service suits thee best
    indeed.
What maid of spirit would not spurn thee from
    her ?

Ros. Yes, to recall me soon, sublime Sultana !
For I can stand the burst of female passion,
Each change of humour and affected storm ;
Be scolded, frown'd upon, to exile sent,

ecall'd, caress'd, chid and disgrac'd again ;

nd say what maid of spirit would forego

he bliss of one to exercise it thus ?

! I can bear ill treatment like a lamb ;

4th Mask, beating him. Well, bear it then, thou
  hæst deserv'd it well.

Ros. 'Zounds, lady ! do not give such heavy
  blows ;

ι not your husband, as belike you guess.

5th Mask. Come lover, I enlist thee for my
  swain,

ιercfore good lady, do forbear your blows,

ɔr thus assume my rights.

Ros. Agreed.   Wilt thou a gracious mistress
  prove ?

5th Mask. Such as thou wouldst, such as thy
  genius suits ;

r since of universal scope it is

 women's humour shalt thou find in me.

 gently soothe thee with such winning smiles—

 nothing sink thee with a scornful frown ;

ize thee with peevish and affected fricks,

:ess thee, love thee, hate thee, break thy pate ;

t still between the whiles I'll careful be,

ïeigned admiration of thy parts,

y shape, thy manners, or thy graceful mien,

 bind thy giddy soul with flatt'ry's charm :

· well thou knowst that flatt'ry ever is

ɔ tickling spice, the pungent seas'ning,

ιich makes this motley dish of monstrous scraps

pleasing to the dainty lover's taste.

Thou canst not leave, tho' violent in extreme,
And most vexatious in her teazing moods,
Thou canst not leave the fond admiring soul
Who did declare, when calmer reason rul'd,
Thou hadst a pretty leg.

    Ros. Marry, thou hast the better of me there.

    5th Mask. And more, I'll pledge to thee my
        honest word,

That when your noble swainship shall bestow
More faithful homage on the simple maid,
Who loves you with sincerity and truth,
Than on the changeful and capricious tyrant
Who mocking leads you like a trammell'd ass,
My studied woman's wiles I'll lay aside,
And such a one become.

    Ros. Well spoke, brave lady, I will follow thee.

          (follows her to the corner of the stage.)

Now on my life, these ears of mine I'd give,
To have but one look of that little face,
Where such a biting tongue doth hold its court
To keep the fools in awe. Nay, nay, unmask ;
I'm sure thou hast a pair of wicked eyes,
A short and saucy nose ; now prithee do.

                (unmasking.)

    Alb. (unmasking) Well hast thou guess'd me
        right ?

    Ros. (bowing low.) Wild freedom chang'd to
        most profound respect

Doth make an aukward booby of me now.

    Alb. I've join'd your frolick with a good intent,
For much I wish'd to gain your private ear.

The time is precious, and I must be short.

    Ros. On me your slightest word more pow'r
      will have,

Most honour'd lady, than a conn'd oration.

Thou art the only one of all thy sex,

Who wearst thy years with such a winning grace,

Thou art the more admir'd the more thou fadst.

    Alb. I thank your lordship for these courteous
      words,

But to my purpose. You are Basil's friend ;

Be friendly to him then, and warn him well

This court to leave, nor be allur'd to stay,

For if he does, there's mischief waits him here

May prove the bane of all his future days.

Remember this, I must no longer stay.

God bless your friend and you ; I love you both.

                               [Exit.

    Ros. alone. What may this warning mean ? I
      had my fears.

There's something hatching which I know not of.

I've lost all spirit for this masking now.

      (throwing away his papers and his willow.)

Away ye scraps ! I have no need of you.

I would I knew what garment Basil wears ;

I watch'd him but he did escape my sight ;

But I must search again and find him out. [Exit.

Enter BASIL *much agitated, with his mask in his
      hand.*

    Bas. In vain I've sought her, follow'd ev'ry
      form

Where aught appear'd of dignity or grace;
I've listen'd to the tone of ev'ry voice;
I've watch'd the entrance of each female mask;
My flutt'ring heart rous'd like a startled hare,
With the imagin'd rustling of her robes,
At ev'ry dame's approach.   Deceitful night,
How art thou spent? where are thy promis'd joys?
How much of thee is spent! O! spiteful fate!
And yet within the compass of these walls
Somewhere she is, altho' to me she is not.
Some other eye doth gaze upon her form,
Some other ear doth listen to her voice;
Some happy fav'rite doth enjoy the bliss
My spiteful stars deny.
Disturber of my soul! what veil conceals thee?
What dev'lish spell is o'er this cursed hour?
O! heav'ns and earth, where art thou?

Enter Mask in the dress of a female conjuror.

Mask. Methinks thou art impatient, valiant
    soldier,
Thy wound doth gall thee sorely; is it so?
Bas. Away, away, I cannot fool with thee.
Mask. I have some potent drugs may ease thy
    smart.
Where is thy wound? is't here?
                    (pointing to the bandage on his arm.)
Bas.   Poo, poo, begone!
Thou canst do nought—'tis in my head, my
    heart—
'Tis ev'ry where, where med'cine cannot cure.

Mask. If woundcd in thc heart, it is a wound
Which some ungrateful fair-one hath inflicted,
And I may conjure something for thy good.

    Bas. Ah! if thou couldst! what must I fool
        with thee?

    Mask. Thou must awhile, and be examin'd too.
What kind of woman did the wicked deed?

    Bas. I cannot tell thee.   In her presence still
My mind in such a wild delight hath been,
I could not pause to picture out her beauty;
Yet nought of woman e'er was form'd so fair.

    Mask. Art thou a soldier, and no weapon
        bear'st
To send her wound for wound?

    Bas. Alas! she shoots from such a hopeless
        height,
No dart of mine hath plume to mount so far.
None but a prince may dare.

    Mask. But if thou hast no hope, thou hast no
        love.

    Bas. I love, and yet in truth I had no hope,
But that she might at least with some good will,
Some gentle pure regard, some secret kindness,
Within her dear remembrance give me place.
This was my all of hope, but it is flown,
For she regards me not; despises, scorns me;
Scorns, I must say it too, a noble heart,
That would have bled for her.

    (Mask, discovering herself to be Victoria, by speak-
        ing in her true voice.) O! no, she does not.
                  [EXIT *hastily in confusion.*

Bas. (stands for a moment rivetted to the spot,
    then holds up both his hands in an extacy.)
It is herself! it is her blessed self!   .
O ! what a fool am I that had no power
To follow her, and urge th'advantage on.
Be gone unmanly fears ! I must be bold.
                               [EXIT *after her.*

A Dance of Masks.

Enter DUKE *and* GAURIECIO, *unmasked.*

Duke. This revelry, methinks, goes gaily on.
The hour is late, and yet your friend returns not.
  Gaur. He will return ere long—nay, there he
    comes.

Enter GENTLEMAN.

  Duke. Does all go well ? *(going close up to him.)*
  Gent.   All as your grace could wish.
For now the poison works, and the stung soldiers
Rage o'er their cups, and with fire-kindled eyes
Swear vengeance on the chief who would betray
    them.
That Frederick too, the discontented man
Of whom your highness was so lately told,
Swallows the bait, and does his part most bravely.
Gauriecio counsel'd well to keep him blind,
Nor with a bribe attempt him. On my soul !
He is so fiery he had spurn'd us else,
And ruin'd all the plot.
  Duke. Speak softly, friend—I'll hear it all in
    private.
A gay and careless face we uow assume.

Duke, Gaur. *and* Gen. *retire into the inner partment, appearing to laugh and talk gaily to the ifferent masks as they pass them.*

Re-enter Victoria *followed by* Basil.

Vict. Forbear, my lord, these words offend mine
    ear.

Bas. Yet let me but this once, this once offend,
Nor thus with thy displeasure punish me ;
And if my words against all prudence sin,
O ! hear them, as the good of heart do list
To the wild ravings of a soul distraught.

Vict. If I indeed should listen to thy words,
They must not talk of love.

Bas. To be with thee, to speak, to hear thee
    speak,
To claim the soft attention of thine eye,
I'd be content to talk of any thing,
If it were possible to be with thee,
And think of ought but love.

Vict. I fear, my lord, you have too much pre-
    sum'd,
On those unguarded words, which were in truth
Utter'd at unawares, with little heed,
And urge their meaning far beyond the night.

Bas. I thought, indeed, that they were kindly
    meant,
As tho' thy gentle breast did kindly feel
Some secret pity for my hopeless pain,
And would not pierce with scorn, ungen'rous scorn,
A heart so deeply stricken.

Vict. So far thou'st read it well.

Bas.   Ha! have I well?
Thou dost not hate me then?

Vict.   My father comes;
He were displeas'd if he should see thee thus.

Bas. Thou dost not hate me, then?

Vict. Away, he'll be displeas'd—I cannot say—

Bas. Well, let him come, it is thyself I fear;
For did destruction thunder o'er my head,
By the dread pow'r of heav'n I would not stir
Till thou hadst answer'd my impatient soul!
Thou dost not hate me?

Vict. Nay, nay, let go thy hold—I cannot hate
         thee.   *(breaks from him and exit.)*

Bas. alone. Thou canst not hate me! no, thou
         canst not hate me!
For I love thee so well, so passing well,
With such o'erflowing heart, so very dearly,
That it were sinful not to pay me back
Some small, some kind return.

         Enter MIRANDO, *dressed like* Cupid.

Mir. Bless thee, brave soldier.

Bas. What sayst thou, pretty child? what play-
         ful fair
Has deck'd thee out in this fantastick guise?

Mir. It was Victoria's self; it was the princess.

Bas. Thou art her fav'rite then?

Mir.   They say I am;
And now, between ourselves, I'll tell thee, soldier,
I think in very truth she loves me well.

Such merry little songs she teaches me—
Sly riddles too, and when I'm laid to rest
Oft times on tip-toe near my couch she steals,
And lifts the cov'ring so, to look upon me.
And often times I feign as tho' I slept ;
For then her warm lips to my cheek she lays,
And pats me softly with her fair white hands ;
And then I laugh, and thro' mine eye-lids peep,
And then she tickles me, and calls me cheat ;
And then we do so laugh, ha, ha, ha, ha !

 Bas. What, does she even so, thou happiest
  child ?
And have those rosy cheeks been press'd so
 dearly ?
Delicious urchin ! I will kiss thee too.

   (Takes him eagerly up in his arms, and
    kisses him.)

 Mir. No, let me down, thy kisses are so rough,
So furious rough—she doth not kiss me so.

 Bas. Sweet boy, where is thy chamber ? by
  Victoria's ?

 Mir. Hard by her own.

 Bas. Then will I come beneath thy window
  soon,
And, if I could, some pretty song I'd sing
To lull thee to thy rest.

 Mir. O ! no, thou must not ; 'tis a frightful
  place,
It is the church-yard of the neighb'ring dome.
The princess loves it for the lofty trees,

Whose spreading branches shade her chamber
    walls ;
So do not I ; for when 'tis dark o'nights
Goblins howl there, and ghosts rise thro' the
    ground.
I hear them many a time when I'm a bed,
And hide beneath the cloaths my cow'ring head.
O ! is it not a frightful thing, my lord,
To sleep alone i' the dark ?
    Bas. Poor harmless child ! thy prate is won-
    drous sweet.

Enter a group of Masks.

    1st Mask. What dost thou here, thou little
    truant boy ?
Come play thy part with us.

Masks *place* MIRANDO *in the middle, and range
themselves round him.*

S O N G,—A GLEE.

Child, with many a childish wile,
Timid look, and blushing smile,
Downy wings to steal thy way,
Gilded bow, and quiver gay,
Who in thy simple mien would trace
The tyrant of the human race ?

Who is he whose flinty heart
Hath not felt thy flying dart ?
Who is he that from the wound
Hath not pain and pleasure found ?
Who is he that hath not shed
Curse and blessing on thy head?

Ah Love! our weal, our woe, our bliss, our bane,
A restless life have they who wear thy chain!
Ah Love! our weal, our woe, our bliss, our bane,
More hapless still are they who never felt thy pain.

*All the masks dance round Cupid.   Then enter a
band of satyrs, who frighten away Love and his
votaries, and conclude the scene, dancing in a
grotesque manner.*

ACT IV.—SCENE I.

The Street before BASIL's *Lodging.*

Enter ROSINBERG *and two Officers.*

Ros. speaking as he enters. Unless we find him
    quickly, all is lost.
1*st. Off.* His very guards, methinks, have left
    their post
To join the mutiny.
    Ros. (knocking very loud.) Holla! who's there
    within? confound this door!
It will not ope. O! for a Giant's strength.
Holla, holla, within! will no one hear?

Enter a Porter from the house.
    Ros. eagerly to the Porter. Is he return'd, is he
    return'd? not yet!
Thy face doth tell me so.
    Port.   Not yet, my lord.
    Ros. Then let him ne'er return——

Tumult, disgrace, and ruin have their way !
I'll search for him no more.

Port. He hath been absent all the night, my lord.

Ros. I know he hath.

2d Off.   And yet 'tis possible
He may have enter'd by the secret door;
And now, perhaps, in deepest sleep entranc'd,
Is dead to ev'ry sound.

(*Ros. without speaking, rushes into the
house, and the rest follow him.*)

Enter BASIL.

Bas. The blue air of the morning pinches
keenly.
Beneath her window all the chilly night
I felt it not. Ah! night has been my day,
And the pale lamp which from her chamber
gleam'd,
Has to the breeze a warmer temper lent
Than the red burning east.

Re-enter ROSINBERG, *&c. from the house.*

Ros. Himself! himself! He's here, he's here !
O ! Basil,
What fiend at such a time could lead thee forth ?

Bas. What is the matter which disturbs you
thus?

Ros. Matter that would a wiser man disturb.
Treason's abroad, thy men have mutinied.

Bas. It is not so ; thy wits have mutinied,
And left their sober station in thy brain.

1st. Off. Indeed, my Lord, he speaks in sober
 earnest.
Some secret enemies have been employ'd
To fill your troops with strange imaginations;
As tho' their gen'ral would, for selfish gain,
Their gen'rous valour urge to desp'rate deeds.
All to a man, assembled on the ramparts,
Now threaten vengeance, and refuse to march.

 Bas. What! think they vilely of me? threaten
 too!
O! most ungen'rous, most unmanly thought!
Didst thou attempt *(to Ros.)* to reason with their
 folly?
Folly it is; baseness it cannot be!

 Ros. Yes, truly, did I reason's pow'r essay,
But as well might I reason with the storm,
And bid it cease to rage———
Their eyes look fire on him who questions them;
The hollow murmurs of their mutter'd wrath
Sound dreadful thro' the dark extended ranks,
Like subterraneous grumblings of an earthquake.
————————————The vengeful hurricane
Does not with such fantastick writhings toss
The woods green boughs, as does convulsive rage
Their forms with frantick gesture agitate.
Around the chief of hell such legions throng'd,
To bring back curse and discord on creation.

 Bas. Nay, they are men, altho' impassion'd
 ones.
I'll go to them—

 Ros.   And we will stand by thee.

This sword is thine against ten thousand strong,
If it should come to this.

    Bas.   No, never, never !
There is no mean.   I with my soldiers must
Or their commander or their victim prove.
But are my officers all staunch and faithful ?

    Ros. All but that devil, Fred'rick——
He, disappointed, left his former corps,
Where he, in truth, had been too long neglected,
Thinking he should all on the sudden rise,
From Basil's well-known love of valiant men ;
And now, because it still must be deferr'd,
He thinks you seek from envy to depress him,
And burns to be reveng'd.

    Bas. Well, well——This grieves me too——
    But let us go.   [Exeunt.

SCENE II.

*The ramparts of the Town.   The Soldiers are dis-
covered drawn up in disorderly manner, hollaing
and speaking big, and clashing their arms tumul-
tuously.*

    1st Sol. No, comrade, no, hell gape and swallow
        me !
If I do budge for such most dev'lish orders.

    2d Sol. Huzza, brave comrades ! Who says
        otherwise ?

    3d Sol. No one, huzza! confound all treach'rous
        leaders !
        (The Soldiers huzza and clash their arms.)

5th Sol. Heav'n dart its fiery light'ning on his
    head !

We're men, we're not cattle to be slaughter'd !

2d Sol. They who do long to caper high in air,
Into a thousand bloody fragments blown,
May follow our brave gen'ral.

1st Sol.   Curse his name !
I've fought for him till my strain'd nerves have
    crack'd !

2d Sol. We will command ourselves; for Milan,
    comrades.

5th Sol. Ay, ay, for Milan, valiant hearts,
    huzza !

               *(All the Soldiers cast up their caps
                in the air, and huzza.)*

2d Sol. Yes, comrades, tempting booty waits
    us there,
And easy service: keep good hearts, my soldiers!
The gen'ral comes, good hearts ! no flinching,
    boys !
Look bold and fiercely ; we're the masters now.

*(They all clash their arms, and put on a fierce
threatening aspect to receive their General, who
now enters, followed by* Rosinberg *and Officers.*
Basil *walks close along the front ranks of the Soldiers, looking at them very steadfastly ; then retires a few paces back, and raising his arm, speaks
with a very full loud voice.)*

Bas. How is it, soldiers, that I see you thus,
Assembled here, unsummon'd by command ?

*(A confused murmur is heard amongst
      the Soldiers; some of them call out)*

But we command ourselves; we wait no orders.

*(A confused noise of voices is heard, and
      one louder than the rest calls out)*

Must we be butcher'd, for that we are brave?

*(A loud clamour and clashing of arms,
      then several voices call out)*

Damn hidden treach'ry! we defy thy orders.
Fred'rick shall lead us now————————

(Other voices call out)

We'll march where'er we list, for Milan march.

(Basil, *waving his hand, and beckoning them to be
      silent, speaks with a very loud voice)*

Yes, march where'er ye list, for Milan march.
    Sol. Hear him, hear him!

(The murmur ceases—a short pause.)

    Bas. Yes, march where'er ye list, for Milan
        march,
But as banditti, not as soldiers go;
For on this spot of earth I will disband,
And take from you the rank and name of soldiers.

*(A great clamour amongst the ranks————
      some call out)*

What wear we arms for?

(Others call out)

No, he dares not do it.

(One voice very loud)

Disband us at thy peril, treach'rous Basil!

(Several of the Soldiers brandish their arms, and

3

threaten to attack him ; the Officers gather round
Basil, *and draw their swords to defend him.)*

Bas. Put up your swords, my friends, it must
    not be.

thank your zeal, I'll deal with them alone.

Ros. What, shall we calmly stand and see thee
    butcher'd ?

Bas. (very earnestly.) Put up, my friends.

(Officers still persit.) What are you rebels too ?

ill no one here his gen'ral's voice obey?

lo command you to put up your swords.

etire, and at a distance wait th' event.

bey, or henceforth be no friends of mine.

(Officers retire, very unwillingly. Basil *waves them*
    off with his hand till they are all gone, then
    walks up to the front of his Soldiers, who still
    hold themselves in a threatening posture.)

ldiers, we've fought together in the field,

nd bravely fought ; i' the face of horrid death

: honour's call I've led you dauntless on;

or do I know the man of all your bands,

at ever poorly from the trial shrunk,

: yielded to the foe contended space.

n I the meanest then of all my troops,

at thus ye think, with base unmanly threats,

ɔ move me now ? Put up those paltry weapons;

ney edgeless are to him who fears them not :

ocks have been shaken from the solid base ;

ıt what shall move a firm and dauntless mind ?

ıt up your swords, or dare the threaten'd deed—

bey, or murder me————

L

(A confused murmur—some of the soldiers
    call out)

March us to Milan, and we will obey thee.

                (Others call out)

Ay, march us there, and be our leader still.

  Bas. Nay, if I am your leader, I'll command
      ye ;

And where I do command, there shall you go,

But not to Milan. No, nor shall you deviate

E'en half a furlong from your destin'd way,

To seize the golden booty of the east.

Think not to gain, or temporize with me,

For should I this day's mutiny survive,

Much as I've lov'd you, soldiers, ye shall find me

Still more relentless in pursuit of vengeance ;

Tremendous, cruel, military vengeance.

There is no mean—a desp'rate game ye play,

Therefore I say, obey, or murder me.

Do as ye will, but do it manfully.

He is a coward who doth threaten me,

The man who slays me, but an angry soldier,

Acting in passion, like the frantick son,

Who struck his sire, and wept.

  (Soldier's call out.) It was thyself who sought to
      murder us.

  1st. Sol. You have unto the Emp'ror pledg'd
      your faith,

To lead us foremost in all desp'rate service;

You have agreed to sell your soldiers' blood,

And we have shed our dearest blood for you.

  Bas. Hear me, my soldiers——

2d Sol. No, hear him not, he means to cozen
     you.
·ed'rick will do you right————
     (Endeavouring to stir up a noise and confusion
       amongst them.)
Bas. What cursed fiend art thou, cast out
     from hell
ɔ spirit up rebellion ? damned villain !
(Seizes upon 2d soldier, drags him out from the
     ranks, and wrests his arms from him; then takes
     a pistol from his side, and holds it to his head)
and there, damn'd, meddling villain, and be
     silent ;
ɔr if thou utt'rest but a single word,
 cough, or hem, to cross me in my speech,
 l send thy cursed spirit from the earth,
ɔ bellow with the damn'd !
     (The soldiers keep a dead silence—after a pause,
       Basil resumes his speech.)
sten to me, my soldiers————
ɔu say that I am to the Emp'ror pledg'd
ɔ lead you foremost in all desp'rate service,
ɔr now you call it not the path of glory,
nd if in this I have offended you,
 do indeed repent me of the crime.
ɹt new from battles, where my native troops
 ɩ bravely fought ; I felt me proud at heart,
nd boasted of you, boasted foolishly.
 said fair glory's palm ye would not yield
o e'er the bravest legion train'd to arms.
ɹwore the meanest man of all my troops

Would never shrink before an armed host,
If honour bade him stand.   My royal master,
Smil'd at the ardour of my heedless words,
And promis'd, when occasion claim'd our arms,
To put them to the proof.
But ye do peace, and ease, and booty love,
Safe and ignoble service—be it so—
Forgive me that I did mistake you thus,
But do not earn with savage mutiny,
Your own destruction.   We'll for Pavia march,
To join the royal army near its walls;
And there with blushing forehead will I plead,
That ye are men with warlike service worn,
Requiring ease and rest.   Some other chief,
Whose cold blood boils not at the trumpet's sound,
Will in your rearward station head you then,
And so, my friends, we'll part.   As for myself,
A volunteer, unheeded in the ranks,
I'll rather fight, with brave men for my fellows,
Than be the leader of a sordid band.

    (A great murmur rises amongst the ranks, sol-
      diers call out)

We will not part, no, no, we will not part.

                  (All call out together)

We will not part, be thou our gen'ral still.

   Bas. How can I be your gen'ral? ye obey
As caprice moves you; I must be obey'd
As honest men against themselves perform
A sacred oath.—
Some other chief will more indulgent prove—
You're weary grown—I've been too hard a master.

Soldiers. Thyself, and only thee, will we obey.

Bas. But if you follow me, yourselves ye pledge
nto no easy service:—hardships, toils,
he hotest dangers of most dreadful fight,
Vill be your portion; and when all is o'er,
ach, like his gen'ral, must contented be
nbootied to return, a poor brave soldier.
ow say ye now? I spread no tempting lure—
better fate than this, I promise none.

Soldiers. We'll follow Basil.

Bas. What token of obedience will ye give ?

(A deep pause.)

oldiers, lay down your arms.

(They all lay down their arms.)

' any here are weary of the service,
ow let them quit the ranks, and they shall have
. free discharge, and passport to their homes ;
nd from my scanty fortune I'll make good
he well-earn'd pay their royal master owes them.
et those who follow me their arms resume.

(They all resume their arms.)

Basil Holding up his hands.) High heaven be
prais'd!
had been griev'd to part with you, my soldiers.
[ere is a letter from my gracious master,
Vith offer of preferment in the north,
Tost high preferment, which I did refuse,
'or that I would not leave my gallant troops.

*(Takes out a letter, and throws it amongst
them.)*

6

*(A great commotion amongst the soldiers ; many
of them quit their ranks, and croud about
him, calling out,)*

Our gallant gen'ral!

(Others call out)

We'll spend our heart's blood for thee, noble Basil!

Bas. And so you thought me false? this bites
    to th' quick!

My soldiers thought me false!

*(They all quit their ranks, and croud eagerly
around him. Basil waving them off with his
hands.)*

Away, away, you have disgusted me.

(Soldiers retire to their ranks.)

'Tis well—retire, and hold yourselves prepar'd
To march upon command; nor meet again
Till you are summon'd by the beat of drum.
Some secret enemy has tamper'd with you,
For yet I will not think that in these ranks,
There moves a man who wears a traitor's heart.

*(The soldiers begin to march off, and musick
strikes up.)*

Basil holding up his hand.) Cease, cease trium-
    phant sounds,

Which our brave fathers, men without reproach,
Rais'd in the hour of triumph ; but this hour
To us no glory brings—
Then silent be your march—ere that again
Our steps to glorious strains like these shall move
A day of battle o'er our heads must pass,

\nd blood be shed to wash out this day's stain.
                [Exeunt *soldiers, silent and dejected.)*

\:nter FREDERICK, *who starts back on seeing* BASIL
                        alone.

  Bas. Advance, lieutenant; wherefore shrink ye
      back ?
ve ever seen you bear your head erect,
\nd front your man, tho' arm'd with frowning
      death.
ave you done ought the valiant should not do ?
fear you have.   (Fred. *looks confused.)*
\7ith secret art, and false insinuation,
he simple untaught soldiers to seduce
:om their sworn duty, might become the base,
\:come the coward well; but oh ! what villain
ad the curs'd pow'r t'engage thy valiant worth
  such a work as this ?
  Fred. Is Basil, then, so lavish of his praise
n a neglected pitiful subaltern ?
were a libel on his royal master ;
foul reproach upon fair fortune cast,
\) call me valiant :
\d surely he has been too much their debtor
\) mean them this rebuke.
  Bas. Is nature than so sparing of her gifts,
\lat it is wonderful when they are found
\here fortune smiles not ?
\lou art by nature brave, and so am I,
\lt in those distant ranks moves there not one
                      (Pointing off the stage.)

Of high ennobled soul, by nature form'd
A hero and commander, who will, yet,
In his untrophied grave forgotten lie
With meaner men ? I dare be sworn there does.

   Fred. What need of words ? I crave of thee no
      favour.
I have offended against armed law,
And shrink not from my doom.

   Bas. I know thee well, I know thou fear'st not
      death ;
On scaffold or in field with dauntless breast
Thou wilt engage him : and if thy proud soul,
In sullen obstinacy scorns all grace
E'en be it so.   But if with manly gratitude
Thou truly canst receive a brave man's pardon,
Thou hast it freely.

   Fred. It must not be. I've been thine enemy—
I've been unjust to thee—

   Bas.   I know thou hast ;
But thou art brave, and I forgive thee all.

   Fred. My lord ! my gen'ral ! Oh ! I cannot
      speak !
I cannot live and be the wretch I am !

   Bas. But thou canst live, and be an honest man
From errour turn'd,—canst live and be my friend.
         (Raising Fred. *from the ground.)*
Forbear, forbear ! see where our friends advance,
They must not think thee suing for a pardon ;
That would disgrace us both.   Yet, ere they come,
Tell me, if that thou may'st with honour tell,
What did seduce thee from thy loyal faith ?

Fred. No cunning traitor did my faith attempt,
For then I had withstood him : but of late,
I know not how—a bad and restless spirit
Has work'd within my breast, and made me
    wretched.
I've lent mine ear to foolish idle tales,
Of very zealous, tho' but new-made friends.
    Bas. Softly, our friends approach—of this again.
                        [EXEUNT.

SCENE III.

An Apartment in BASIL's *lodgings.* *Enter* BASIL
and ROSINBERG.

    Ros. Thank heaven I am now alone with thee,
Last night I sought thee with an anxious mind,
And curs'd thine ill-tim'd absence—
There's treason in this most deceitful court,
Against thee plotting, and this morning's tumult
Hath been its damn'd effect.
    Bas.   Poo, poo, my friend ;
The nature of man's mind too well thou know'st,
To judge as vulgar hood-wink'd statesmen do ;
Who ever with their own poor wiles misled,
Believe each popular tumult or commotion,
Must be the work of deep-laid policy.
Poor, mean, mechanick souls, who little know
A few short words of energetick force,
Some pow'rful passion on the sudden rous'd,
The animating sight of something noble,
Some fond trait of the mem'ry finely wak'd,

A sound, a simple song without design,
In revolutions, tumults, wars, rebellions,
All grand events, have oft effected more
Than deepest cunning of their paltry art.
Some drunken soldier, eloquent with wine,
Who loves not fighting, hath harangu'd his mates,
For they in truth some hardships have endur'd.
Wherefore in this should we suspect the court?

   Ros. Ah! there is something, friend, in Man-
      tua's court,
Will make the blackest trait of bare-fac'd treason
Seem fair and guiltless to thy partial eye.

   Bas. Nay, 'tis a weakness in thee, Rosinberg,
Which makes thy mind so jealous and distrustful,
Why should the duke be false?

   Ros. Because he is a double, crafty prince—
Because I've heard it rumour'd secretly,
That he in some dark treaty is engag'd,
E'en with our master's enemy the Frank.

   Bas. And so thou think'st—

   Ros.   Nay, hear me to the end,
Last night that good and honourable dame,
Noble Albini, with most friendly art,
From the gay clam'rous throng my steps beguil'd,
Unmask'd before me, and with earnest grace,
Entreated me, if I were Basil's friend,
To tell him hidden danger waits him here,
And warn him well fair Mantua's court to leave.
She said she lov'd thee much, and hadst thou seen
How anxiously she urg'd—

   Bas. (interrupting him)   By heav'n and earth,

ıere is a ray of light breaks thro' thy tale,
ıd I could leap like madmen in their fricks,
 blessed is the gleam! Ah! no, no, no!
cannot be, alas! it cannot be,
ıt didst thou say she urg'd it earnestly?
e is a woman, who avoids all share
 secret politicks; one only charge
ır int'rest claims, Victoria's guardian friend—
ıd she would have me hence—it must be so.
  would it were; how saidst thou, gentle Ro-
     sinberg?
e urg'd it earnestly—how did she urge it?
ıy, pri'thee, do not stare upon me thus,
ıt tell me all her words—what said she else?
Ros. O Basil! I could laugh to see thy folly,
ıt that thy weakness doth provoke me so.
ɔst admirable, brave, determin'd man!
 well, so lately try'd, what art thou now?
vain deceitful thought transports thee thus.
ıinkst thou——
Bas.   I will not tell thee what I think.
Ros. But I can guess it well, and it deceives
     thee.
ave this detested place, this fatal court,
here damn'd deceitful cunning plots thy ruin.
soldier's duty calls thee loudly hence.
ıe time is critical. How wilt thou feel
 hen they shall tell these tidings in thine ear,
ıat brave Piscaro, and his royal troops,
ır valiant fellows, have the en'my fought,
 hilst we, so near at hand, lay loit'ring here?

Bas. Thou dost disturb thy brain with fancied
    fears.
Our fortunes rest not on a point so nice
That one short day should be of all this moment;
And yet this one short day will be to me
Worth years of other time.

Ros.   Nay, rather say,
A day to darken all thy days beside.
Confound the fatal beauty of that woman,
Which has bewitch'd thee so!

Bas.   'Tis most ungen'rous
To push me thus with rough unsparing hand,
Where but the slightest touch is felt so dearly.
It is unfriendly.

Ros. God knows my heart! I would not give
    thee pain;
But it disturbs me, Basil, vexes me,
To see thee so enthralled by a woman.
If she is fair, others are fair as she.
Some other face will like emotions raise,
When thou canst better play a lover's part:
But for the present, fye upon it, Basil!

Bas. What, is it possible thou hast beheld,
Hast tarried by her too, her converse shar'd,
Yet talkst as tho' she were a common fair-one,
Such as a man may fancy and forget?
Thou art not, sure, so dull and brutish grown;
It is not so, thou dost belie thy thoughts,
And vainly try'st to gain me with the cheat.

Ros. So thinks each lover of the maid he loves,
Yet in their lives some many maidens love.

Curse on it! leave this town, and be a soldier!

    Bas. Have done, have done! why dost thou
        bait me thus?

Thy words become disgusting to me, Rosinberg.

What claim hast thou mine actions to controul?

I'll Mantua leave, when it is fit I should.

    Ros. Then, 'faith! 'tis fitting thou shouldst leave
        it now;

Ay, on the instant. Is't not desperation

To stay, and hazard ruin on thy fame,

Tho' yet uncheer'd e'en by that tempting lure,

No lover breathes without? thou hast no hope.

    Bas. What dost thou mean? curse on the paltry
        thought.

That I should count and bargain with my heart,

Upon the chances of unstinted favour,

As little souls their base-bred fancies feed?

O! were I conscious that within her breast

I held some portion of her dear regard,

Tho' pent for life within a prison's walls,

Where thro' my grate I yet might sometimes see

E'en but her shadow sporting in the sun;

Tho' plac'd by fate where some obstructing bound.

Some deep impassable, between us roll'd,

And I might yet from some high tow'ring cliff,

Perceive her distant mansion from afar,

Or mark its blue smoke rising eve and morn;

Nay, tho' within the circle of the moon

Some spell did fix her, never to return,

And I might wander in the hours of night,

And upward turn mine ever-gazing eye,

Fondly to mark upon its varied disk,
Some little spot that might her dwelling be;
My fond, my fixed heart would still adore
And own no other Love.   Away, away!
How canst thou say to one who loves like me,
Thou hast no hope?

    Ros. But with such hope, my friend, how
        stand thy fears?
Are they so well refin'd? How wilt thou bear
Ere long to hear that some high, favour'd prince
Has won her heart, her hand, has married her?
Tho' now unshackled, will it always be?

    Bas. By heav'n thou dost contrive but to tor-
        ment!
And hast a pleasure in the pain thou giv'st.
There is malignity in what thou say'st.

    Ros. No, not malignity, but kindness, Basil,
That fain would save thee from the yawning gulph,
To which blind passion guides thy heedless steps.

    Bas. Go, rather save thyself
From the weak passion which has seiz'd thy breast,
T' assume authority with sage-like brow,
And shape my actions by thine own caprice.
I can direct myself—

    Ros.   Yes, do thyself,
And let no artful woman do it for thee.

    Bas. I scorn thy thought: it is beneath my
        scorn;
It is of meanness sprung—an artful woman!
O! she has all the loveliness of heav'n,
And all its goodness too!

Ros. I mean not to impute dishonest arts.
nean not to impute—
Bas.   No, 'faith, thou canst not.
Ros. What, can I not? their arts all women have.
it now of this no more ; it moves thee greatly.
:t once again, as a most loving friend,
:t me conjure thee, if thou prizest honour,
 soldier's fair repute, a hero's fame,
 hat noble spirits love; and well I know
ill dearly dost thou prize them, leave this place,
id give thy soldiers orders for the march.
Bas. Nay, since thou must assume it o'er me
          thus,
: gen'ral, and command my soldiers too.
Ros. What hath this passion in so short a space,
! curses on it! so far chang'd thee, Basil ?
iat thou dost take with such ungentle warmth,
ie kindly freedom of thine ancient friend.
.ethinks the beauty of a thousand maids
'ould not have mov'd me thus to treat my friend,
[y best, mine earliest friend !
Bas. Say kinsman rather, chance has link'd us so,
ur blood is near, our hearts are sever'd far ;
o act of choice did e'er unite our souls.
[en most unlike we are; our thoughts unlike;
[y breast disowns thee—thou'rt no friend of mine.
Ros. Ah! have I then so long, so dearly lov'd
          thee ;
o often, with an elder brother's care,
'hy childish rambles tended, shar'd thy sports;
ill'd up by stealth thy weary school-boy's task ;

Taught thy young arms thine earliest feats of
     strength ;
With boastful pride thine early rise beheld
In glory's paths, contented then to fill
A second place, so I might serve with thee;
And say'st thou now, I am no friend of thine?
Well, be it so ; I am thy kinsman still,
And by that title will I save thy name
From danger of disgrace.   Indulge thy will;
I'll lay me down and feign that I am sick,
And yet I shall not feign—I shall not feign,
For thy unkindness makes me sick indeed ;
It will be said that Basil tarried here
To save his friend, for so they'll call me still ;
Nor will dishonour fall upon thy name
For such a kindly deed.—

     (Basil *walks up and down in great agitation,*
       then stops, covers his face with his hands,
       and seems to be overcome. Rosinberg *looks*
       at him earnestly.)

Ros.   O ! blessed heav'n, he weeps !
    (Runs up to him, and catches him in his arms.)
O Basil! I have been too hard upon thee.
And is it possible I've mov'd thee thus?

   Bas. (in a convulsed broken voice.) I will re-
     nounce—I'll leave—

   Ros.   What says my Basil?

   Bas. I'll Mantua leave—I'll leave this seat of
     bliss—
This lovely woman—tear my heart in twain—

st off at once my little span of joy—
wretched—miserable—whate'er thou wilt—
ıst thou forgive me ?

Ros.   O my friend! my friend!
ıve thee now more than I ever lov'd thee.
ıust be cruel to thee to be kind,
ːh pang I see thee feel strikes thro' my heart ;
en spare us both, call up thy noble spirit,
d meet the blow at once—thy troops are ready—
ː us depart, nor lose another hour.

> (Basil *shrinks from his arms, and looks at
> him with somewhat of an upbraiding, at
> the same time of a sorrowful look.)*

Bas. Nay, put me not to death upon the
  instant ;
see her once again, and then depart.

Ros. See her but once again, and thou art ruin'd.
 nust not be—if thou regard'st me—

Bas. Well then, it shall not be.   Thou hast no
  mercy !

Ros. Ah! thou wilt bless me all thine after-life
ˈwhat, to thee, seems now so merciless.

Bas. (sitting down very dejectedly.) Mine after
  life ! what is mine after life?
ˈday is clos'd! the gloom of night is come !
ιopeless darkness settles o'er my fate.
ı seen the last look of her heav'nly eyes,
ː heard the last sounds of her blessed voice,
ː seen her fair form from my sight depart ;
ˈdoom is clos'd !

M

Ros. (Hanging over him with pity and affection.)
Alas! my friend!

Bas. In all her lovely grace she disappear'd,
Ah! little thought I never to return.

Ros. Why so desponding? think of warlike
    glory.
The fields of fair renown are still before thee;
Who would not burn such noble fame to earn?

Bas. What now are arms, or fair renown to me?
Strive for it those who will—and yet a while
Welcome rough war, with all thy scenes of blood,
                    (Starting from his seat.)
Thy roaring thunders, and thy clashing steel,
Welcome once more! what have I now to do
But play the brave man o'er again, and die?

Enter ISABELLA.

Isab. to Bas. My princess bids me greet you,
    noble count.

Bas. (starting.) What dost thou say?

Ros.   D—n this untimely message!

Isab. The princess bids me greet you, noble
    count;
In the cool grove, hard by the southern gate,
She with her train—

Bas.   What, she indeed herself?

Isab. Herself, my lord, and she requests to see
    you.

Bas. Thank heav'n for this; I will be there
    anon.

Ros. (taking hold of him.) Stay, stay, and do not
    be a madman still.

Bas. Let go thy hold; what, must I be a brute,
A very brute to please thee ? no, by heav'n!
             (Breaks from him, and EXIT.*)*

Ros. (striking his forehead.) All lost again! black
    curses light upon her!
             (Turning eagerly to Isab.)
And so thy virtuous mistress sends thee here
To make appointments, hon'rable dame ?

Isab. Not so, my lord, you must not call it so;
The court will hunt to-morrow, and Victoria
Would have your noble gen'ral of her train.

Ros. Confound these women, and their artful
    snares,
Since men will be such fools !

Isab. Yes, grumble at our empire as you will—

Ros. What, boast ye of it? empire do ye call it?
It is your shame ! a short liv'd tyranny
That ends at last in hatred and contempt.

Isab. Nay, but some women do so wisely rule,
Their subjects never from the yoke escape.

Ros. Some women do, but they are rarely found.
There is not one in all your paltry court
Hath wit enough for the ungen'rous task.
'Faith! of you all, not one, but brave Albini,
And she disdains it.—Good be with you, lady !
             (Going.)

Isab. O! would I could but touch that stub-
    born heart,

M 2

How dearly should he pay for this hour's storm!

[EXEUNT *severally.*

SCENE IV.

A Summer Apartment in the Country, the windows of which look to a forest. Enter VICTORIA *in a hunting dress, followed by* ALBINI *and* ISA-BELLA, *speaking as they enter.*

Vict. to Alb. And so you will not share our sport to-day?

Alb. My days of frolick should ere this be o'er,
But thou, my charge, hast kept me youthful still.
I should most gladly go, but since the dawn
A heavy sickness hangs upon my heart,
I cannot hunt to-day.

Vict. I'll stay at home and nurse thee, dear Albini,

Alb. No, no, thou shalt not stay.

Vict.   Nay, but I will.
I cannot follow to the cheerful horn
Whilst thou art sick at home.

Alb.   Not very sick.
Rather than thou shouldst stay, my gentle child,
I'll mount my horse, and go e'en as I am.

Vict. Nay, then I'll go, and soon return again.
Meanwhile, do thou be careful of thyself.

Isab. Hark, hark! the shrill horn calls us to the field,
Your highness hears it?   *(musick without.)*

Vict.   Yes, my Isabella,

I hear it, and methinks e'en at the sound
I vault already on my leathern seat,
And feel the fiery steed beneath me shake
His mantled sides, and paw the fretted earth ;
Whilst I aloft, with gay equestrian grace,
The low salute of gallant lords return ;
Who waiting round with eager watchful eye,
And reined steeds, the happy moment seize.
O! didst thou never hear, my Isabell,
How nobly Basil in the field becomes
His fiery courser's back ?

  Isab.   They say most gracefully.

  Alb. What, is the valiant count not yet departed ?

  Vict. You would not have our gallant Basil go
When I have bade him stay ? not so, Albini.

  Alb. Fye! reigns that spirit still so strong with-
   in thee,
Which vainly covets all men's admiration,
And is to others cause of cruel pain ?
O! would thou couldst subdue it!

  Vict. My gentle friend, thou shouldst not be
   severe ;
For now in truth I love not admiration
As I was wont to do ; in truth I do not!
But yet, this once my woman's heart excuse,
For there is something strange in this man's love,
I never met before, and I must prove it.

  Alb. Well, prove it then, be stricter to thyself,
And bid sweet peace of mind a sad farewell.

Vict. O no! that will not be! 'twill peace re-
    store ;
For after this, all folly of the kind
Will quite insipid and disgusting be ;
And so I shall become a prudent maid,
And passing wise at last.   *(musick heard without.)*
Hark, hark! again!
All good be with you! I'll return ere long.
           [Exeunt Victoria *and* Isabella.
Alb. (solus.) Ay, go, and ev'ry blessing with
    thee go,
My most tormenting, and most pleasing charge !
Like vapour, from the mountain stream art thou,
Which highly rises on the morning air,
And shifts its fleeting form with ev'ry breeze,
For ever varying, and for ever graceful.
Endearing, gen'rous, bountiful and kind ;
Vain, fanciful, and fond of worthless praise ;
Courteous and gentle, proud and magnificent ;
And yet these adverse qualities in thee,
No striking contrast, nor dissonance make ;
For still thy good and amiable gifts
The sober dignity of virtue wear not,
And such a 'witching mien thy follies shew,
They make a very idiot of reproof,
And smile it to disgrace—
What shall I do with thee ?—it grieves me much
To hear count Basil is not yet departed.
When from the chace he comes, I'll watch his
    steps,
And speak to him myself—

O! I could hate her for that poor ambition
Which silly adoration only claims,
But that I well remember, in my youth
I felt the like—I did not feel it long;
I tore it soon, indignant from my breast,
As that which did degrade a noble mind. [Exit.

SCENE V.

*A very beautiful Grove in the forest. Musick and
horns heard afar off, whilst huntsmen and dogs
appear passing over the stage, at a great distance. Enter* VICTORIA *and* BASIL, *as if just
alighted from their horses.*

 Vict. (speaking to attendants without.) Lead on
   our horses to the further grove,
And wait us there—
(to Bas.) This spot so pleasing, and so fragrant is,
'Twere sacrilege with horses hoofs to wear
Its velvet turf, where little elfins dance,
And fairies sport beneath the summer's moon :
I love to tread upon it.
 Bas. O! I would quit the chariot of a god
For such delightful footing!
 Vict.   I love this spot.
 Bas. It is a spot where one would live and die.
 Vict. See, thro' the twisted boughs of those
   high elms,
The sun-beams on the bright'ning foliage play,
And tinge the scaled bark with ruddy brown.
Is it not beautiful ?

Bas.   'Tis passing beautiful
To see the sun-beams on the foliage play,
                         (In a soft voice.)
And tinge the scaled bark with ruddy brown.

Vict. And here I've stood full often, and ad-
    mir'd
The graceful bending, o'er that shady pool,
Of yon green willow, whose fair sweepy boughs
So kiss their image on the glassy plain,
And bathe their leafy tresses in the stream.

Bas. And I too love to see its drooping boughs
So kiss their image on the glassy plain,
And bathe their leafy tresses in the stream.

Vict. My lord, it is uncivil in you thus
My very words with mock'ry to repeat.

Bas. Nay, pardon me, did I indeed repeat?
I meant it not; but when I hear thee speak,
So sweetly dwells thy voice upon mine ear,
My tongue e'en unawares assumes the tone;
As mothers on their lisping infants gaze,
And catch their broken words.   I pri'thee pardon!

Vict. But we must leave this grove, the birds
    fly low,
This should forbode a storm, and yet o'erhead
The sky, bespread with little downy clouds
Of purest white, would seem to promise peace.
How beautiful those pretty snowy clouds!

Bas. Of a most dazzling brightness!

Vict. Nay, nay, a veil that tempers heaven's
    brightness,
Of softest, purest white.

Bas. As tho' an angel, in his upward flight,
Had left his mantle floating in mid-air.

   Vict. Still most unlike a garment, small and
     sever'd,
    (Turning round, and perceiving that he is gaz-
    ing at her.)
But thou regard'st them not.

   Bas. Ah! what should I regard, where should
    I gaze?
For in that far-shot glance, so keenly wak'd
That sweetly rising smile of admiration,
Far better do I learn how fair heav'n is,
Than if I gaz'd upon the blue serene.

   Vict. Remember you have promis'd, gentle
    count,
No more to vex me with such foolish words.

   Bas. Ah! wherefore should my tongue alone
    be mute?
When every look and every motion tell,
So plainly tell, and will not be forbid,
That I adore thee, love thee, worship thee!
     (Victoria looks haughty and displeased.)
Ah! pardon me, I know not what I say.
Ah! frown not thus! I cannot see thee frown.
I'll do whate'er thou wilt, I will be silent;
But O! a reined tongue, and bursting heart,
Are hard at once to bear! will thou forgive me?

   Vict. We'll think no more of it; we'll quit this
    spot;
I do repent me that I led thee here,
But 'twas the fav'rite path of a dear friend.

Here, many a time we wander'd, arm in arm ;
We lov'd this grove, and now that he is absent,
I love to haunt it still.   (Basil *starts.*)

    Bas. His fav'rite path—a friend—here arm in
        arm—

      (Clasping his hands, and raising them to his
      head.)

Then there is such an one !

      (Drooping his head, and looking distractedly
      upon the ground.)

                  I dream'd not of it.

    Vict. (pretending not to see him.) That little lane,
      with woodbine all o'ergrown,

He lov'd so well!—it is a fragrant path,
Is it not, count ?

    Bas.   It is a gloomy one !

    Vict. I have, my lord, been wont to think it
      cheerful.

    Bas. I thought your highness meant to leave
      this spot.

    Vict. I do, and by this lane we'll take our way;
For here he often walk'd with saunt'ring pace,
And listen'd to the wood-lark's ev'ning song ;

    Bas. What, must I on his very footsteps go?
Accursed be the ground on which he's trod !

    Vict. And is Count Basil so uncourtly grown,
That he would curse my brother to my face ?

    Bas. Your brother! gracious god! is it your
      brother ?

That dear, that loving friend of whom you spoke,
Is he indeed your brother?

Vict. He is indeed, my lord.

Bas. Then heav'n bless him ! all good angels
    bless him !

I could weep o'er him now, shed blood for him !

I could—O! What a foolish heart have I !

    (*Walks up and down with a hurried step,*
      tossing about his arms in transport ; then
      stops short, and runs up to Victoria.)

Is it indeed your brother?

    Vict. It is indeed : what thoughts disturb'd
    thee so ?

    Bas. I will not tell thee ; foolish thoughts they
    were.

Heav'n bless your brother!

    Vict. Ay, heav'n bless him too !

I have but he ; would I had two brave brothers,

And thou wert one of them.

    Bas. I would fly from thee to earth's utmost
    bounds,

Were I thy brother—

And yet, methinks, I would I had a sister.

    Vict. And wherefore would ye ?

    Bas. To place her near thee,

The soft companion of thy hours to prove,

And, when far distant, sometimes talk of me.

Thou couldst not chide a gentle sister's cares.

Perhaps, when rumour from the distant war,

Uncertain tales of dreadful slaughter bore,

Thou'dst see the tear hang on her pale wan cheek.

And kindly say, how does it fare with Basil ?

Vict. No more of this—indeed there must no
　　more.

A friend's remembrance I will ever bear thee.
But see where Isabella this way comes,
I had a wish to speak with her alone.
Attend us here, for soon will we return,
And then take horse again.　　　　　[Exit.

　　Bas. (looking after her for some time.) See with
　　　　what graceful steps she moves along,
Her lovely form in ev'ry action lovely.
If but the wind her ruffl'd garment raise,
It twists it into some light pretty fold,
Which adds new grace.　Or should some small
　　mishap,
Some tangling branch, her fair attire derange,
What would in others strange, or aukward seem,
But lends to her some wild bewitching charm.
See, yonder does she raise her lovely arm
To pluck the dangling hedge-flow'r as she goes;
And now she turns her head, as tho' she view'd
The distant landscape; now methinks she walks
With doubtful ling'ring steps—will she look back?
Ah no! yon thicket hides her from my sight.
Bless'd are the eyes that may behold her still,
Nor dread that ev'ry look shall be the last!
And yet she said she would remember me.
I will believe it; Ah! I must believe it,
Or be the saddest soul that sees the light!
But lo! a messenger, and from the army ;
He brings me tidings; grant they may be good!
Till now I never fear'd what man might utter;

　　　　　　　　2

I dread his tale, God grant it may be good!

Enter MESSENGER.

From the army?

 Mess.   Yes, my lord.

 Bas.   What tidings brings't thou?

 Mess. Th' imperial army, under brave Piscaro,
Have beat the enemy near Pavia's walls.

 Bas. Ha! have they fought? and is the battle o'er?

 Mess. Yes, conquer'd; ta'en the French king
   prisoner,
Who, like a noble, gallant gentleman,
Fought to the last, nor yielded up his sword
Till, being one amidst surrounding foes,
His arm could do no more.

 Bas. What dost thou say? who is made prisoner?
What king did fight so well?

 Mess.   The king of France;

 Bas. Thou saidst—thy words do ring so in mine
   ears,
I cannot catch their sense—the battle's o'er?

 Mess. It is, my lord. Piscaro staid your coming,
But could no longer stay.　His troops were bold,
Occasion press'd him, and they bravely fought—
They bravely fought, my lord.

 Bas.   I hear, I hear thee.
Accurs'd am I, that it should wring my heart
To hear they bravely fought.—
They bravely fought, whilst we lay ling'ring here;
O! what a fated blow to strike me thus!
Perdition! shame! disgrace! a damned blow!

Mess. Ten thousand of the enemy are slain;
We too have lost full many a gallant soul.
I view'd the closing armies from afar;
Their close pick'd ranks in goodly order spread,
Which seem'd alas! when that the fight was o'er,
Like the wild marshes' crop of stately reeds,
Laid with the passing storm. But woe is me !
When to the field I came, what dismal sights !
What waste of life! what heaps of bleeding slain !

Bas. Would I were laid a red, disfigur'd corse,
Amid those heaps! they fought, and we were
    absent !
      (Walks about distractedly, then stops short.)
Who sent thee here?

Mess. Piscaro sent me to inform Count Basil
He needs not now his aid, and gives him leave
To march his tardy troops to distant quarters.

Bas. He says so, does he? well it shall be so.
        (Tossing his arms distractedly)
I will to quarters, narrow quarters go,
Where voice of war shall rouse me forth no more,
                [EXIT.

Mess. I'll follow after him, he is distracted ;
And yet he looks so wild I dare not do it.

Enter VICTORIA *as if frightened, followed by*
            ISABELLA.

Vict. to Isab. Didst thou not mark him as he
    pass'd thee too?

Isab. I saw him pass, but with such hasty steps,
I had no time.

Vict. I met him with a wild disorder'd air,
In furious haste ; he stopp'd distractedly,
And gaz'd upon me with a mournful look,
But pass'd away, and spoke not.   Who art thou ?
(*To the Messenger.*)
I fear thou art a bearer of bad tidings.
    Mess. No, rather good as I should deem it,
        madam,
Altho' unwelcome tidings to Count Basil.
Our army hath a glorious battle won ;
Ten thousand French are slain, their monarch
        captive.
    Vict. to Mess. Ah there it is ! he was not in
        the fight.
Run after him I pray—nay, do not so—
Run to his kinsman, good Count Rosinberg,
And bid him follow him—I pray thee run !
    Mess. Nay, lady, by your leave, you seem not
        well,
I will conduct you hence, and then I'll go.
    Vict. No, no, I'm well enough, I'm very well,
Go, hie thee hence, and do thine errand swiftly.
[Exit *Messenger.*
O ! what a wretch am I ! I am to blame !
I only am to blame !
    Isab.   Nay, wherefore say so ?
What have you done that others would not do ?
    Vict. What have I done ? I've fool'd a noble
        heart—
I've wreck'd a brave man's honour !
[Exit, *leaning upon* Isabella.

ACT V.—SCENE I.

*A dark night; no moon, but a few stars glimmering;
the stage represents (as much as can be discovered
for the darkness) a church-yard with part of a
chapel, and a wing of the ducal palace adjoining to
it. Enter* BASIL, *with his hat off, his hair and
his dress in disorder, stepping slowly, and stopping
several times to listen, as if he was afraid of
meeting any one.*

Bas. No sound is here; man is at rest, and I
May near his habitations venture forth,
Like some unblessed creature of the night,
Who dares not meet his face.—Her window's dark;
No streaming light doth from her chamber beam,
That I once more may on her dwelling gaze,
And bless her still.   All now is dark for me!
     (Pauses for some time, and looks upon the graves)
How happy are the dead, who quietly rest
Beneath these stones ! each by his kindred laid,
Still in a hallow'd neighbourship with those,
Who when alive his social converse shar'd:
And now, perhaps, some dear surviving friend,
Doth here at times the grateful visit pay,
Read with sad eyes his short memorial o'er,
And bless his mem'ry still !—
But I, like a vile outcast of my kind,
In some lone spot must lay my unburied corse,
To rot above the earth; where, if perchance

The steps of human wand'rer e'er approach,
He'll stand aghast, and flee the horrid place,
With dark imaginations frightful made,
The haunt of damned sprites.   O! cursed wretch!
I' the fair and honour'd field shouldst thou have
      died,
Where brave friends, proudly smiling thro' their
      tears,
Had pointed out the spot where Basil lay!
         (A light seen in VICTORIA's *window.)*
But ha! the wonted, welcome light appears.
How bright within I see her chamber wall,
Athwart it too, a dark'ning shadow moves,
A slender woman's form; it is herself!
What means that motion of its clasped hands?
That drooping head? alas! is she in sorrow?
Alas! thou sweet enchantress of the mind,
Whose voice was gladness, and whose presence
      bliss,
Art thou unhappy too? I've brought thee woe;
It is for me thou weep'st! Ah! were it so,
Fall'n as I am, I yet could life endure,
In some dark den from human sight conceal'd,
So, that I sometimes from my haunt might steal,
To see and love thee still.   No, no, poor wretch!
She weeps thy shame, she weeps, and scorns thee
      too.
She moves again; e'en darkly imag'd thus,
How lovely is that form!
         (Pauses, still looking at the window.)
To be so near thee, and for ever parted!

N

For ever lost! what art thou now to me?
Shall the departed gaze on thee again?
Shall I glide past thee in the midnight hour,
Whilst thou perceiv'st it not, and thinkst perhaps
'Tis but the mournful breeze that passes by?

(*Pauses again, and gazes at the window,
till the light disappears.*)

'Tis gone, 'tis gone! these eyes have seen their
        last!
The last impression of her heavenly form!
The last sight of those walls wherein she lives,
The last blest ray of light from human dwelling!
I am no more a being of this world,
Farewell! farewell! all now is dark for me!
Come fated deed! come horrour and despair!
Here lies my dreadful way.

Enter GEOFFRY, *from behind a tomb.*

Geof. O! stay, my general!
Bas.   What art thou, from the grave?
Geof. O! my brave gen'ral! do you know me
        not?
I am old Geoffry, the old maimed soldier
You did so nobly honour.
Bas. Then go thy way, for thou art honourable;
Thou hast no shame, thou needst not seek the
        dark
Like fallen, fameless men.   I pray thee go!
Geof. Nay, speak not thus, my noble general!
Ah! speak not thus! thou'rt brave, thou'rt
        honour'd still.

Thy soldier's fame is far too surely rais'd
To be o'erthrown with one unhappy chance.
I've heard of thy brave deeds with swelling heart,
And yet shall live to cast my cap in air
At glorious tales of thee—

    Bas. Forbear, forbear! thy words but wring
      my soul.

    Geof. O! pardon me! I am old maimed
      Geoffry.

O! do not go! I've but one hand to hold thee.

    (Laying hold of Basil *as he attempts to go away.*
    Basil *stops, and looks round upon him with*
    softness.)

    Bas. Two would not hold so well, old honour'd
      vet'ran!

What wouldst thou have me do?

    Geof. Return, my lord, for love of blessed hea-
      ven,

Seek not such desp'rate ways! where would you
    go?

    Bas. Does Geoffry ask? where should a soldier
      go?

To hide disgrace? there is no place but one.

                      (Struggling to get free.)

Let go thy foolish hold, and force me not
To do some violence to thy hoary head—
What, wilt thou not? nay, then it must be so:

         (Breaks violently from him, and EXIT.*)*

    Geof. Curs'd, feeble hand! he's gone to seek
      perdition!

I cannot run. O! curse that stupid hand,

He should have met me here! holla, Fernando!

Enter FERNANDO.

We've lost him, he is gone! he's broke from me!
Did I not bid thee meet me early here,
For that he has been known to haunt this place?
  Fer. Which way has he gone?
  Geof. Towards the forest, if I guess it right;
But do thou run with speed to Rosinberg,
And he will follow him: run swiftly, man!
                       [EXEUNT.

SCENE II.

*A Wood, wild and savage; an entry to a cave, very
much tangled with brushwood, is seen in the back-
ground. The time represents the dawn of morning.
BASIL is discovered standing near the front of the
stage in a thoughtful posture, with a couple of pistols laid by him, on a piece of projecting rock; he
pauses for some time.*

  Bas. alone. What shall I be a few short moments
      hence?
Why ask I now? who from the dead will rise
To tell me of that awful state unknown?
But be it what it may, or bliss, or torment,
Annihilation, dark and endless rest,
Or some dread thing, man's wildest range of
      thought
Hath never yet conceiv'd, that change I'll dare
Which makes me any thing but what I am.

I can bear scorpions' stings, tread fields of fire,
In frozen gulphs of cold eternal lie;
Be toss'd aloft through tracks of endless void,
But cannot live in shame—*(Pauses.)* O! impious
       thought!
Will the great God of mercy, mercy have
On all but those who are most miserable?
Will he not punish with a pitying hand
The poor fall'n, froward child? *(Pauses.)*
And shall I then against his will offend,
Because he is most good and merciful?
O! horrid baseness! what, what shall I do?
I'll think no more—it turns my dizzy brain—
It is too late to think—what must be, must be—
I cannot live, therefore I needs must die.
      (Takes up the pistols, and walks up and down,
       looking wildly around him, then discovering
       the cave's mouth.)
Here is an entry to some darksome cave,
Where an uncoffin'd corse may rest in peace,
And hide its foul corruption from the earth.
The threshold is unmark'd by mortal foot,
I'll do it here.
      (Enters the cave and EXIT: *a deep silence; then*
       the report of a pistol is heard from the cave,
       and soon after, Enter Rosinberg, Valtomer,
       two Officers *and* Soldiers, *almost at the same*
       moment, by different sides of the stage.)
Ros. This way the sound did come.
Valt. How came ye, soldiers? heard ye that
      report?

1st Sol. We heard it, and it seem'd to come from hence,
Which made us this way hie.

Ros. A horrid fancy darts across my mind.
(A groan heard from the cave.)
(to Valt.) Ha! heardst thou that?

Valt. Methinks it is the groan of one in pain.
(A second groan.)

Ros. Ha! there again!

Valt. From this cave's mouth, so dark and choak'd with weeds,
It seems to come.

Ros.   I'll enter first.

1st Off. My Lord, the way is tangled o'er with briers;
Hard by, a few short paces to the left,
There is another mouth of easier access;
I pass'd it even now.

Ros.   Then shew the way. [EXEUNT.

SCENE III.

The Inside of the Cave; BASIL *discovered lying on the ground, with his head raised a little upon a few stones and earth; the pistols lying beside him, and blood upon his breast. Enter* ROSINBERG, VALTOMER, *and* OFFICERS. Rosinberg, *upon seeing* Basil, *stops short with horrour, and remains motionless for some time.*

Valt. Great God of heav'n! what a sight is this?
*(*Rosinberg *runs to* Basil, *and stoops down by his side.)*

Ros. O Basil! O my friend! what hast thou
    done?

Bas. (*Covering his face with his hand.*) Why art
    thou come? I thought to die in peace.

Ros. Thou knowst me not—I am thy Rosin-
    berg,
Thy dearest, truest friend, thy loving kinsman;
Thou dost not say to me, Why art thou come?

    Bas. Shame knows no kindred; I am fall'n, dis-
    grac'd;
My fame is gone, I cannot look upon thee.

    Ros. My Basil, noble spirit! talk not thus!
The greatest mind untoward fate may prove:
Thou art our gen'rous, valiant leader still,
Fall'n as thou art—and yet thou art not fall'n;
Who says thou art, must put his harness on,
And prove his words in blood.

    Bas. Ah Rosinberg! this is no time to boast!
I once had hopes a glorious name to gain;
Too proud of heart, I did too much aspire;
The hour of trial came, and found me wanting.
Talk not of me, but let me be forgotten;—
And O! my friend! something upbraids me here,
               (*Laying his hand on his breast.*)
For that I now remember, how oft-times,
I have usurp'd it o'er thy better worth,
Most vainly teaching where I should have learnt;
But thou wilt pardon me—

    Ros. (*Taking* Basil's *hand, and pressing it to his*
    breast.*) Rend not my heart in twain! O!
    talk not thus!

2

I knew thou wert superiour to myself,
And to all men beside : thou wert my pride;
I paid thee def'rence with a willing heart.

Bas. It was delusion, all delusion, Rosinberg!
I feel my weakness now, I own my pride.
Give me thy hand, my time is near the close;
Do this for me; thou know'st my love, Victoria—

Ros. O! curse that woman! she it is alone,
She has undone us all!

Bas. It doubles unto me the stroke of death
To hear thee name her thus.   O ! curse her not!
The fault is mine; she's gentle, good and blame-
        less.—
Thou wilt not then my dying wish fulfil?

Ros. I will! I will! what wouldst thou have
        me do?

Bas. See her when I am gone; be gentle with
        her,
And tell her that I bless'd her in my death,
E'en in mine agonies I lov'd and bless'd her.
Wilt thou do this?—

Ros.   I'll do what thou desir'st.

Bas. I thank thee Rosinberg; my time draws
        near.

(Raising his head a little and perceiving Officers.)
Is there not some one here? are we alone?

Ros. (making a sign for the Officers to retire)   'Tis
        but a sentry, to prevent intrusion.

Bas. Thou know'st this desp'rate deed from
        sacred rights
Hath shut me out; I am unbless'd of men,

And what I am in sight of th' awful God,
I dare not think : wilt thou, when I am gone,
A good man's prayers to gracious heav'n up send,
For an offending spirit ?—Pray for me.
What thinkst thou? altho' an outcast here,
May not some heavenly mercy still be found?
   Ros. Thou wilt find mercy—O ! my lov'd
      Basil—
It cannot be that thou shouldst be rejected.
I will with bended knee—I will implore—
It choaks mine utt'rance—I will pray for thee—
   Bas. This comforts me—thou art a loving friend.
                  (A noise without.)
   Ros. (to Off. without.) What noise is that ?

Enter VALTOMER.

   Valt. to Ros. My lord, the soldiers all insist to
      enter ;
What shall I do? they will not be denied ;
They say that they will see their noble gen'ral.
   Bas. Ah, my brave fellows! do they call me so?
   Ros. Then let them come.
      (Enter soldiers, who gather round Basil, *and
      look mournfully upon him; he holds out his
      hand to them with a faint smile.)*
   Bas. My gen'rous soldiers, this is kindly meant.
'm low i'the dust; God bless you all, brave hearts!
   1st Sol. And God bless you, my noble, noble
      gen'ral !
Ve'll never follow such a leader more.

2d Sol. Ah! had you staid with us, my noble
    gen'ral,
We would have died for you.

    *(3d Soldier endeavours next to speak, but can-
    not ; and kneeling down by* Basil, *covers his
    face with his cloak.* Rosinberg *turns his
    face to the wall and weeps.)*

Bas. (In a very faint, broken voice.) Where art
    thou ?—do not leave me, Rosinberg—
Come near to me—these fellows make me weep—
I have no power to weep—give me thy hand—
I love to feel thy grasp—my heart beats strangely—
It beats as tho' its breathings would be few—
Remember—

Ros.   Is there aught thou wouldst desire ?

Bas. Nought but a little earth to cover me,
And lay the smooth sod even with the ground—
Let no stone mark the spot—give no offence
I fain would say—what can I say to thee?

    (A deep pause; after a feeble struggle, Basil
    expires.)

1st Sol. That motion was his last.

2d Sol.   His spirit's fled.

1st Sol. God grant it peace ! it was a noble
    spirit !

4th Sol. The trumpet's sound did never rouse a
    braver.

1st Sol. Alas! no trumpet e'er shall rouse him
    more.
Until the dreadful blast that wakes the dead ;

2d Sol. And when that sounds it will not wake
    a braver.

3d Sol. How pleasantly he shar'd our hardest
    toil ;

Our coarsest food the daintiest fare he made.

4th Sol. Ay, many a time i'the cold damp plains
    has he

With cheerful count'nance cried, good rest my
    hearts !

Then wrapp'd him in his cloak, and laid him down

E'en like the meanest soldier in the field.

    (Rosinberg *all this time continues hanging over*
      the body, and gazing upon it. Valtomer
      now endeavours to draw him away.)

Valt. This is too sad, my lord.

Ros. There, seest thou how he lies ? so fix'd,
    so pale ?

Ah! what an end is this! thus lost! thus fall'n!

To be thus taken in his middle course,

Where he so nobly strove; till cursed passion

Came like a sun-stroke on his mid-day toil,

And cut the strong man down. O Basil ! Basil !

Valt. Forbear, my friend, we must not sorrow
    here.

Ros. He was the younger brother of my soul.

Valt. Indeed, my lord, it is too sad a sight.

Time calls us, let the body be remov'd.

Ros. He was—O! he was like no other man !

Valt. (Still endeavouring to draw him away.)
    Nay now forbear.

Ros.   I lov'd him from his birth !·

Valt. Time presses, let the body be remov'd.

Ros. What sayst thou?

Valt.   Shall we not remove him hence?

Ros. He has forbid it, and has charg'd me well
To leave his grave unknown; for that the church
All sacred rights to the self-slain denies.
He would not give offence.

 1st Sol. What! shall our gen'ral, like a very
   wretch,
Be laid unhonour'd in the common ground?
No last salute to bid his soul farewell?
No warlike honours paid? it shall not be.

 2d Sol. Laid thus? no, by the blessed light of
   heav'n!
In the most holy spot in Mantua's walls,
He shall be laid; in face of day be laid;
And tho' black priests should curse us in the teeth,
We will fire o'er him whilst our hands have power
To grasp a musket.

 Several soldiers. Let those who dare forbid it.

 Ros. My brave companions, be it as you will.
  *(Spreading out his arms as if he would em-
  brace the soldiers.—They prepare to remove
  the body.)*

Valt. Nay, stop a while, we will not move it
   now,
For see a mournful visitor appears,
And must not be denied.

   Enter VICTORIA *and* ISABELLA.

 Vict. I thought to find him here, where has he
   fled?

(Rosinberg *points to the body without speaking*;
 Victoria *shrieks out, and falls into the arms
 of* Isabella.)

Isab. Ah, my sweet gentle mistress! this will
 kill thee.

Vict. (recovering.) Unloose thy hold, and let me
 look upon him.

)! horrid, horrid sight! my ruin'd Basil!

s this the sad reward of all thy love?

)! I have murder'd thee!

   (Kneels down by the body, and bends over it.)

These wasted streams of life! this bloody wound!

     (Laying her hand upon his heart.)

Is there no breathing here? all still! all cold!

Open thine eyes, speak, be thyself again,

And I will love thee, serve thee, follow thee,

In spite of all reproach.   Alas! alas!

A lifeless corse art thou for ever laid,

And dost not hear my call—

 Ros. No, madam; now your pity comes too late.

 Vict. Dost thou upbraid me? O! I have deserv'd it?

 Ros. No, madam, no, I will not now upbraid;

But woman's grief is like a summer storm,

Short as it violent is; in gayer scenes,

Where soon thou shalt in giddy circles blaze,

And play the airy goddess of the day,

Thine eye, perchance, amidst the observing crowd,

Shall mark th' indignant face of Basil's friend,

And then it will upbraid.

 Vict. No, never, never? thus it shall not be.

To the dark, shaded cloister wilt thou go,
Where sad and lonely, thro' the dismal grate
Thou'lt spy my wasted form, and then upbraid me.

    Ros. Forgive me, heed me not; I'm griev'd at
        heart;
I'm fretted, gall'd, all things are hateful to me.
If thou didst love my friend, I will forgive thee;
I must forgive thee; with his dying breath
He bade me tell thee, that his latest thoughts
Were love to thee; in death he lov'd and blessed
        thee.

        {Victoria *goes to throw herself upon the body,*
        but is prevented by Valtomer *and* Isabella,
        who support her in their arms, and endea-
        vour to draw her away from it.)

    Vict. Oh! force me not away! by his cold corse
Let me lie down and weep. O! Basil, Basil!
The gallant and the brave! how hast thou lov'd
        me!
If there is any holy kindness in you
                   (To Isab. *and* Valt.)
Tear me not hence.
For he lov'd me in thoughtless folly lost,
With all my faults, most worthless of his love;
And I'll love him in the low bed of death,
In horrour and decay.—
Near his lone tomb I'll spend my wretched days
In humble pray'r for his departed spirit:
Cold as his grave shall be my earthy bed,
As dark my cheerless cell. Force me not hence.

I will not go, for grief hath made me strong.
                    (Struggling to get loose.)
Ros. Do not withhold her, leave her sorrow free.
*(They let her go, and she throws herself upon
    the body in an agony of grief.)*
It doth subdue the sternness of my grief
To see her mourn him thus.—Yet I must curse.—
Heav'n's curses light upon her damned father,
Whose crooked policy has wrought this wreck.

   Isab. If he has done it, you are well reveng'd,
For his dark plots have been detected all.
Gauriceio, for some int'rest of his own,
His master's secret dealings with the foe
Has to Lanoy betray'd; who straight hath sent,
On the behalf of his imperial lord,
A message full of dreadful threats to Mantua.
His discontented subjects aid him not;
He must submit to the degrading terms
A haughty conq'ring power will now impose.

   Ros. And art thou sure of this?
   Isab.   I am, my lord.
   Ros. Give me thy hand, I'm glad on't, O! I'm
     glad on't!
It should be so! how like a hateful ape
Detected, grinning 'midst his pilfer'd hoard
A cunning man appears, whose secret frauds
Are open'd to the day! scorn'd, hooted, mock'd!
Scorn'd by the very fools who most admir'd
His worthless art.   But when a great mind falls,
The noble nature of man's gen'rous heart
Doth bear him up against the shame of ruin;

With gentle censure using but his faults
As modest means to introduce his praise;
For pity like a dewy twilight comes
To close th' oppressive splendour of his day;
And they who but admir'd him in his height,
His alter'd state lament, and love him fall'n.

[EXEUNT.

END OF COUNT BASIL.

THE TRYAL:

A COMEDY.

PERSONS OF THE DRAMA.

MEN.

Mr. Withrington.
Mr. Harwood.
Sir Loftus Prettyman.
Mr. Opal.
Mr. Royston.
Humphry.
Jonathan.
Thomas.
Servants, &c.

WOMEN.

Agnes,
Mariane, } *Nieces to* Withrington.
Miss Eston.
Mrs. Betty, *Maid to* Agnes.

*** *Scene in* Bath, *and in* Mr. Withrington's *house, in the environs of* Bath.

THE TRYAL.

ACT I.—SCENE I.

MR. WITHRINGTON'S *house : Enter* WITHRING-
TON *and his two Nieces hanging upon his arms,
coaxing him in a playful manner as they advance
towards the front of the Stage.*

With. Poo, poo, get along, young gipsies, and
dont teaze me any more.

Ag. So we will, my good sir, when you have
granted our suit.

Mar. Do, dear uncle, it will be so pleasant!

With. Get along, get along. Dont think to
wheedle me into it. It would be very pleasant,
truly, to see an old fellow, with a wig upon his
bald pate, making one in a holy-day mummery
with a couple of mad caps.

Ag. Nay, dont lay the fault upon the wig, good
sir, for it is as youthful, and as sly, and as saucy
looking as the best head of hair in the county.
As for your old wig indeed, there was so much
curmudgeon-like austerity about it, that young
people fled from before it, as, I dare say, the birds
do at present, for I am sure that it is stuck up in
some cherry orchard, by this time, to frighten
the sparrows.

o 2

With. You are mistaken, young mistress, it is up stairs in my wig-box.

Ag. Well I am glad it is any where but upon your pate, uncle. *(Turning his face towards* Mariane.) Look at him, pray! is he not ten years younger since he wore it? Is there one bit of an old grumbler to be seen about him now?

Mar. He is no more like the man he was than I am like my god-mother. *(Clapping his shoulder.)* You must even do as we have bid you, sir, for this excuse will never bring you off.

With. Poo, poo, it is a foolish girl's whimsy: I'll have nothing to do with it.

Ag. It is a reasonable woman's desire, gentle guardian, and you must consent to it. For if I am to marry at all, I am resolved to have a respectable man, and a man who is attached to me, and to find out such a one, in my present situation, is impossible. I am provoked beyond all patience with your old greedy lords, and match-making aunts, introducing their poor noodle heirs-apparent to me, like so many dolts dressed out for a race ball. Your ambitious esquires, and proud obsequious baronets are intolerable, and your rakish younger brothers are nauseous: such creatures only surround me, whilst men of sense keep at a distance, and think me as foolish as the company I keep. One would swear I were made of amber, to attract all the dust and chaff of the community.

With. There is some truth in this 'faith.

Ag. You see how it is with me: so my dear

2

loving good uncle *(Coaxing him)* do let Mariane take my place for a little while. We are newly come to Bath, no body knows us: we have been but at one ball, and as I went in plain dress, and Mariane looks so much better than me, she has already been mistaken for the heiress, and I for her portionless cousin: I have told you how we shall manage it, do lend us your assistance !

With. So in the disguise of a portionless spinster, you are to captivate some man of sense, I suppose.

Ag. I would fain have it so.

With. Go, go, thou art a fool, Agnes ! who will fall in love with a little ordinary girl like thee ? why there is not one feature in thy face that a man would give a farthing for.

Mar. You are very saucy, uncle.

Ag. I should despair of my beauty to be sure, since I am reckoned so much like you, my dear uncle ; yet old nurse told me that a rich lady, a great lady, and the prettiest lady that ever wore silk, fell in love, once on a time, with Mr. Anthony, and would have followed him to the world's end too, if it had not been for an old hunks of a father, who deserved to be drubed for his pains. Don't you think he did, sir ?

With. (endeavouring to look angry.) Old nurse is a fool, and you are an impudent hussy. I'll hear no more of this nonsense. *(Breaks from them and goes towards the door: they run after him, and draw him back again.)*

Ag. Nay, good sir, we have not quite done with you yet : grant our request, and then scamper off as you please.

Mar. I'll hold both your arms till you grant it.

With. to Mar. And what makes you so eager about it, young lady ? you expect, I suppose, to get a husband by the trick. O fy, fy! the poorest girl in England would blush at such a thought, who calls herself an honest one.

Ag. And Mariane would reject the richest man in England who could harbour such a suspicion. But give yourself no uneasiness about this, sir, she need not go a husband-hunting, for she is already engaged.—(Mariane *looks frightened, and makes signs to* Agnes *over her uncle's shoulder, which she answers with a smile of encouragement.*)

With. Engaged ! she is very good, truly, to manage all this matter herself, being afraid to give me any trouble, I suppose. And pray what fool has she picked out from the herd, to enter into this precious engagement with !

Ag. A foolish enough fellow to be sure, your favourite nephew, cousin Edward.

With. Hang, the silly booby ! how could he be such an ideot ? but it can't be, it shan't be,—it is folly to put myself into a passion about it. *(To* Mariane, *who puts her hand on his shoulder to soothe him.)* Hold off your hands, ma'am. This is news indeed to amuse me with of a morning.

Ag. Yes, uncle, and I can tell you more news;

for they are not only engaged, but as soon as he returns from abroad they are to be married.

With. Well, well, let them marry, in the devil's name, and go a begging if they please..

Ag. No, gentle guardian, they need not go a begging; they will have a good fortune to support them.

With. Yes, yes, they will get a prize in the lottery, or find out the philosopher's stone, and coin their old shoes into guineas.

Ag. No, sir, it is not that way the fortune is to come.

With. No ; he has been following some knight-errant then, I suppose, and will have an island in the South Sea for his pains.

Ag. No, you have not guessed it yet. *(Stroaking his hand gently.)* Did you never hear of a good, kind, rich uncle of theirs, the generous Mr. Withrington ? he is to settle a handsome provision upon them as soon as they are married, and leave them his fortune at last.

With. (lifting up his hands.) Well, I must say thou art the impudentest little jade in the kingdom. But did you never hear that this worthy uncle of theirs, having got a new wig, which makes him ten years younger than he was, is resolved to embrace the opportunity, and seek out a wife for himself ?

Ag. O ! that is nothing to the purpose ; for what I have said about the fortune must happen, though he should seek out a score of wives.

With. Must happen! but I say it shall not happen. Whether should you or I know best?

Ag. Why me, to be sure.

With. Ha, ha, ha! how so baggage?

Ag. (resting her arm on his shoulder, looking archly in his face.) You don't know perhaps, that when I went to Scotland last summer, I travelled far, and far, as the tale says, and farther than I can tell, till I came to the Isle of Sky, where every body has the second sight, and has nothing to do but tear a little hole in a tartan plaidy, and peering through it, in this manner, sees every thing past, present, and to come. Now, you must know, I gave an old woman half a crown and a roll of tobacco for a peep or two through her plaid, and what do you think I saw, uncle;

With. The devil dancing a hornpipe, I suppose.

Ag. There was somebody dancing to be sure, but it was not the devil though. Who do you think it was now?

With. Poo, poo!

Ag. It was uncle himself, at Mariane's wedding, leading down the first dance, with the bride. I saw a sheet of parchment in a corner too, signed with his own blessed hand, and a very handsome settlement it was. So he led down the first dance himself, and we all followed after him, as merry as so many hay-makers.

With. Thou hast had a sharp sight, faith!

Ag. And I took a second peep through the plaidy, and what do you think I saw then, sir?

With. Nay, prate on as thou wilt.

Ag. A genteel family house, where Edward and Mariane dwelt, and several little brats running up and down in it. Some of them so tall, and so tall, and some of them no taller than this. And there came good uncle amongst them, and they all flocked about him so merrily! every body was so glad to see him, the very scullions from the kitchen were glad; and methought he looked as well pleased himself as any of them. Don't you think he did, sir?

With. Have done with thy prating.

Ag. I have not done yet, good sir; for I took another peep still, and then I saw a most dismal changed family indeed.. There was a melancholy sick bed set out, in the best chamber, every face was sad, and all the children were weeping. There was one dark eyed rogue amongst them, called little Anthony, and he threw away his bread and butter, and roared like a young bull, for woe's me! old uncle was dying. *(Observing* Withrington *affected.)* But old uncle recovered though, and looked as stout as a veteran again. So I gave the old woman her plaidy, and would not look through any more.

With. Thou art the wildest little witch in the world, and wilt never be at rest till thou hast got every thing thine own way, I believe.

Ag. I thank you, I thank you, dear uncle! *(leaping round his neck,)* it shall be even so, and I shall have my own little boon into the bargain.

With. I did not say so.

Ag. But I know it will be so, and many thanks to you, my dear good uncle! (Mariane *ventures to come from behind,*—Withrington *looks gently to her, she holds out her hand, he hesitates, and* Agnes *joins their hands together, giving them a hearty shake.)*

With. Come, come, let me get away from you now: you are a couple of insinuating gipsies.

[EXIT, *hastily.*

Mar. (embracing Agnes.) Well, heaven bless thee, my sweet Agnes! thou hast done marvels for me. You gave me a fright though; I thought we were ruined.

Ag. O! I knew I should get the better of him some way or other. What a good worthy heart he has! you dont know how dearly I love this old uncle of ours.

Mar. I wonder how it is. I used to think him severe and unreasonable, with his fiddle faddle fancies about delicacy and decorum; but since you came amongst us, Agnes, you have so coaxed him, and laughed at him, and played with him, that he has become almost as frolicksome as ourselves.

Ag. Let us set about our project immediately. No body knows us here but lady Fade and Miss Eston: We must let them both into the secret: Lady Fade is confined with bad health, and though Miss Eston, I believe, would rather tell a secret than hold her tongue, yet as long as there are streets and carriages, and balls and ribbons, and parlours and pantries to talk of, there can be no great danger from her.

Mar. O! we shall do very well. How I long to frolick it away, in all the rich trappings of heirship, amongst those sneaking wretches the fortune-hunters! They have neglected me as a poor girl, but I will play the deuce amongst them as a rich one.

Ag. You will acquit yourself very handsomely, I dare say, and find no lack of admirers.

Mar. I have two or three in my eye just now, but of all men living I have set my heart upon humbling Sir Loftus. He insulted a friend of mine last winter, to ingratiate himself with an envious woman of quality, but I will be revenged upon him, O! how I will scorn him, and toss up my nose at him! I hate him like a toad.

Ag. That is not the way to be revenged upon him, silly girl! He is haughty and reserved in his manners; and though not altogether without understanding, has never suffered a higher idea to get footing in his noddle than that of appearing a man of consequence and fashion, and though he has no happiness but in being admired as a fine gentleman, and no existence but at an assembly, he appears there with all the haughty gravity, and careless indifference of a person superiour to such paltry amusements. Such a man as this must be laughed at, not scorned, familiarity and contempt must be his portion.

Mar. He shall have it then. And as for his

admirer and imitator, Jack Opal, who has for these ten years past, so successfully performed every kind of fine gentlemanship, which every new fool brought into fashion, any kind of bad treatment, I suppose, that happens to come into my head will be good enough for him.

Ag. Quite good enough. You have set him down for one of your admirers too?

Mar. Yes, truly, and a great many more besides.

Ag. Did you observe in the ball-room last night, a genteel young man, with a dark grey eye, and a sensible countenance, but with so little of the foppery of the fashion about him, that one took him at a distance for a much older man?

Mar. Wore he not a plain brownish coat? and stood he not very near us great part of the evening?

Ag. Yes, the very same. Pray endeavour to attract him, Mariane.

Mar. If you are very desirous to see him in my train, I'll try him.

Ag. No, not desirous, neither.

Mar. Then wherefore should I try?

Ag. Because I would have you try every art to win him, and I would not have him to be won.

Mar. O! I comprehend it now! This is the sensible man we are in quest of.

Ag. I shall not be sorry if it proves so. I have enquired who he is, as I shall tell you by and by, and what I have learned of him I like. Is not his appearance prepossessing, cousin Mariane?

Mar. I dot know, he is too grave and dignified for such a girl as thou art; I fear we shall waste our labour upon him.

Ag. But he does not look always so. He kept very near me, if it did not look vain I should say followed me all the evening, and many a varied expression his countenance assumed. But when I went away arm in arm with my uncle, in our usual good humoured way, I shall never forget the look of pleasant approbation with which he followed me. I had learnt but a little while before the mistake which the company made in regard to us, and at that moment the idea of this project came across my mind like a flash of lightning.

Mar. Very well, gentle cousin; the task you assign me is pleasing to my humour; and the idea of promoting your happiness at the same time will make it delightful. Let me see, how many lovers shall I have, one, two, three. (*Counting on her fingers.*)

Ag. I can tell you of one lover more than you wot of.

Mar. Pray who is he?

Ag. Our distant cousin the great 'squire, and man of business, from ——shire, he writes to my uncle that he will be in Bath to-day, upon business of the greatest importance, which he explains to him in three pages of close written paper; but whether it is to court me for himself, or for his son, or to solicit a great man, who is here, for a place, no mortal on earth can discover.

Mar. Well, let him come, I shall manage them all. O! if my Edward were here just how, how he would laugh at us!

Enter SERVANT.

Ser. Miss Eston.

Mar. Let us run out of her way, and say we are not at home. She will sit and talk these two hours.

Ag. But you forgot we have something to say to her. *(To the servant.)* Shew her up stairs to my dressing-room.

[EXIT *servant.*

Mar. Pray let us run up stairs before her, or she will arrest us here with her chat.

[EXEUNT.

Miss Eston (without.) And it is a very bad thing for all that; I never could abide it. I wonder your master don't stop *(Enters walking straight across the stage, still speaking)* up those nasty chinks, there is such a wind in the hall, 'tis enough to give one a hoarseness. Bye the bye Mrs. Mumblecake is sadly to-day; has your lady sent to enquire for her William? I wonder if her *(EXIT, still talking without)* old coachman has left her; I saw a new face on the, &c. &c.

SCENE II.

The fields before MR. WITHRINGTON's *house.*
Enter AGNES, MARIANE, *and* MISS ESTON, *who
seems still busy talking, from the house, and passing
over the Stage arm in arm,* Exeunt. *Enter, by
the same side by which they went out,* SIR LOF-
TUS PRETTYMAN, *and* HARWOOD, *who stands
looking behind him, as if he followed something
with his eyes very eagerly.*

*Sir Loft. (Advancing to the front of the stage,
and speaking to himself.)* How cursedly unlucky
this is now! if she had come out but a few moments sooner, I should have passed her walking
arm in arm with a British peer. How provokingly
these things always happen with me; *(observing
Harwood.)* What! is he staring after her too?
(aloud) What are you looking at, Harwood? does
she walk well?

Har. I can't tell how she walks, but I could stand
and gaze after her till the sun went down upon me.

Sir Loft. She is a fine woman, I grant you.

Har. (vastly pleased.) I knew she would please,
it is impossible she should not! There is something so delightful in the play of her countenance,
it would even make a plain woman beautiful.

Sir Loft. She is a fine woman, and that is no
despicable praise from one who is accustomed to
the elegance of fashionable beauty.

Har. I would not compare her to any thing so trifling and insipid.

Sir Loft. She has one advantage which fashionable beauty seldom possesses.

Har. What do you mean ?

Sir Loft. A large fortune.

Har. (looking disappointed.) Poo, it is not the heiress I mean.

Sir Loft. Is it t'other girl you are raving about, she is showy at a distance, I admit, but as awkward as a dairy maid when near you ; and her tongue goes as fast as if she were repeating a pater noster.

Har. What, do you think I am silly enough to be caught with that magpie ?

Sir Loft. Who is it then, Harwood ? I see no body with Miss Withrington but Miss Eston, and the poor little creature her cousin.

Har. Good god ! what a contemptible perversion of taste do interest and fashion create! But it is all affectation. *(Looking contemptuously at him.)*

Sir Loft. (smiling contemptuously in return.) Ha, ha, ha! I see how it is with you, Harwood, and I beg pardon too. The lady is very charming, I dare say ; upon honour I never once looked in her face. She is a dependant relation of Miss Withrington's, I believe : now I never take notice of such girls, for if you do it once they expect you to do it again. I dont choose that every little creature should say she is acquainted with Sir Loftus Prettyman ; I am sparing of my attentions, that she on whom I really bestow them may have the more reason to boast.

Har. You are right, Prettyman, she who boasts of your attentions should receive them all herself, that nobody else may know how little worth they are.

Sir Loft. You are severe this morning, Mr. Harwood, but you do not altogether comprehend me, I believe. I know perhaps more of the polite world than a studious templar can be supposed to do, and I assure you, men of fashion, upon this principle, are sparing of their words too, that they may be listened to more attentively when they do speak.

Har. You are very right still, Sir Loftus, for if they spoke much, I'll be hang'd if they would get any body to listen to them at all.

Sir Loft. (haughtily.) There is another reason why men of fashion are not profuse of their words, inferior people are apt to forget themselves, and despise what is too familiar.

Har. Dont take so much pains to make me comprehend that the more fools speak the more people will despise them; I never had a clearer conviction of it in my life.

Sir Loft. (haughtily.) Good morning, sir, I see Lord Saunter in the other walk, and I must own I prefer the company of one who knows, at least, the common rules of politeness.　　　[Exit.

Har. (alone.) What a contemptible creature it is! He would prefer the most affected ideot, who

P

boasts a little fashion or consequence, as he calls it, to the most beautiful native character in the world.   Here comes another fool, who has been gazing too, but I will not once mention her before him.

Enter OPAL.

Op. Good morning, Harwood, I have been fortunate just now ! I have met some fine girls, 'faith !

Har. I am glad you have met with any thing so agreeable ; they are all equally charming to you, I suppose.

Op. Nay, Harwood, I know how to distinguish. There is a little animated creature amongst them, all life and spirit, on my soul I could almost be in love with her.

Har. Ha ! thou hast more discernment than I reckoned upon.   If that goose, Sir Loftus, did not spoil thee, Jack, thou would'st be a very good fellow after all.   Why I must tell you, my good Opal, that lady whom you admire, is the sweetest little gipsey in England.

Op. Is she indeed ? I wish I had taken a better look of her face then ; but she wears such a cursed plume of blue feathers nodding over her nose, there is scarcely one half of it to be seen.

Har. (staring at him with astonishment.) As I breathe ! he has fallen in love with the magpie !

Op. And what is so surprising in this pray ? Does not all the world allow Miss Withrington the heiress to be a fine woman ?

Har. That is not thc heiress, Jack, *(pointing off the stage)* the tall lady in the middle is she. But if your Dulcinea could coin her words into farthings, she would be one of the best matches in the kingdom.

Op. Pcst take it! she was pointcd out to me as Miss Withrington. Pest take my stupidity! the girl is well enough, but she is not altogether— *(Mumbling to himself.)*

Har. So you bestowcd all your attention on this bluc feathered lady, and let the other two pass by unnoticcd.

Op. No, not unnoticed ncither : Miss Withrington is too fine a figure to be overlooked any where, and for the other poor little creature, who hung upon her arm so familiarly, I could not help observing her too, because I wondered Miss Withrington allowed such a dowdy looking thing to walk with her in publick. Faith? Prettyman and I locked a vulgar looking dcvil up in the stable the othēr morning, who insisted upon going with us to the pump-room : men of fashion, you know, are always plagued with paltry fellows dangling after them.

Har. Hang your men of fashion! mere paltry fellows are too good company for them.

Op. Damn it, Harwood! speak more rcspectfully of that class of men to whom I havc the honour to belong.

Har. You mistake me, Opal, it was only the men of fashion I abused, I am too well bred to

speak uncivilly in your presence of the other class
you mentioned.

Op. I scorn your insinuation, sir ; but whatever
class of men I belong to, I praise heaven, I have
nothing of the sour plodding book-worm about me.

Har. You do well to praise heaven for the endowments it has bestowed upon you, Opal ; if all
men were as thankful as you for this blessed gift
of ignorance, we could not be said to live in an
ungrateful generation.

Op. Talk away, laugh at yuor own wit as much
as you please, I dont mind it. I dont trouble
my head to find out bons mots of a morning.

Har. You are very right, Jack, for it would be
to no purpose if you did.

Op. I speak whatever comes readiest to me : I
dont study speeches for company, Harwood.

Har. I hope so, Opal ; you would have a laborious life of it indeed, if you could not speak
nonsense extempore.

Op. *(Drawing himself up, and walking haughtily
to the other side of the stage.)* I had no business to
be so familiar with him. Sir Loftus is right ; a
reserved manner keeps impertinent people at a
distance. *(aside—Turns about, makes a very stiff
bow to* Harwood, *and* Exit.]

Har. *(alone.)* I am glad he is gone. What do I
see ! *(here* Mariane, Agnes, *and* Miss Eston *walk
over the bottom of the stage, attended by* Sir Loftus
and Opal, *and* Exeunt *by the opposite side.* Har.
looking after them.) Alas, now ! that such impudent

fellows should be so successful, whilst I stand gazing at a distance! how lightly she trips! does she not look about to me? by heaven I'll run to her! (*Runs to the bottom of the stage, and stops short.*) Oh no! I cannot do it! but see, her uncle comes this way. He look'd so kindly at her, I could not help loving him; he must be a good man, I'll make up to him, and he perhaps will join the ladies afterwards.

[EXIT.

ACT. II—SCENE I.

A Lodging-house. Enter ROYSTON *and* HUMPHRY, *followed by* JONATHAN, *carrying a portmanteau.*

Roy. What a world of business I have got upon my hands! I must set about it immediately. Come here Jonathan; I shall send you out in the first place,

Jon. Well, sir.

Roy. Take the black trunk, that is left in the hall, upon your shoulder, Jonathan, and be sure you dont run against any body with it, for that might bring us into trouble. And perhaps as you go along, you may chance to meet with some of the Duke of Bigwell's servants, or with some body who can tell you where his Grace lodges in this town, and you may enquire of them, without saying I desired you: you understand me, Jonathan?

Jon. O yes, your honour!

Roy. But first of all, however, if you see any de-

cent hair-dresser's shop in your way, desire them to
send some body here for my wig; and like enough
they may tell you, at the same time, where there is
an honest Town cryer to be had; I'll have Phebe's
black whelp cry'd directly; and hark ye, Jonathan,
you may say as though the dog were your own,
you understand, they will expect such a devil of a
reward else; and pri'thee man! step into the corn
market, if thou can'st find out the way, and
enquire the price of oats.

Jon. Yes, please your honour, but am I to go
trudging about to all these places with that great
heavy trunk upon my shoulder?

Roy. No! numskull! did I not bid you carry it
to the Inn, where the London stage puts up? by
the bye you had better take it to the waggon—
but first ask the coachman, what he charges for the
carriage: you can take it to the waggon afterwards,
I will suffer no man to impose upon me; you
will remember all this distinctly now, as I have
told it you Jonathan?

Jon. (counting to himself upon his fingers) O yes,
your honour! I'll manage it all I warrant! Exit.

Roy. What a world of business I have upon my
hands, Humphry, I am as busy as a minister of
state.

Re-enter JONATHAN, *scratching his head.*

Jon. La your honour! I have forgot all about
his Grace, and the black whelp.

Roy. Damn your muddle pate; did not I bid

1

you enquire where his Grace lives, and if you happen to see—

Jon. Ods bodickins! I remember it every word now! and the whelp is to be call'd by the Town cryer, just as one would call any thing that is lost.

Roy. Yes yes, go about it speedily *(Exit* JON.*)* Now in the first place, my good Humphry, I must see after the heiress I told you of, and it is a business, which requires a great deal of management too; for—

Re-enter JONATHAN, *scratching his head.*

Damn that dunder-headed fool! here he is again.

Jon. Your honour wont be angry now, but hang me, if I can tell whether I am to take that there trunk, to the coach, or the waggon.

Roy. Take it to the coach—no, no, to the waggon—yes, yes, I should have said—pest take it! carry it where thou wilt, fool, and plague me no more about it. *(Exit* JON.*)* one might as well give directions to a horse-block. Now, as I was saying, Humphry, this requires a great deal of management; for if the lady dont like me, she may happen to like my son: so I must feel my way a little, before I speak directly to the purpose.

Humph. Ay, your honour is always feeling your way.

Roy. And as for the Duke, I will ply him as close as I can with solicitations in the mean time, without altogether stating my request; for if I get the lady, George shall have the office, and if he gets the lady, I shall have the office. So we shall have two chances in our favour both ways, my good Humphry.

Humph. Belike, sir, if we were to take but one business in hand at a time, we might come better off at the long run.

Roy. O! thou hast no head for business, Humphry: thou hast no genius for business, my good Humphry. (*smiling conceitedly.*)

Humph. Why, for certain your honour has a marvellous deal of wit, but I dont know how it is, nothing that we take in hand ever comes to any good; and what provokes me, more than all the rest, is, that the more pains we take about it, the worse it always succeeds.

Roy. Humph, we can't guard against every cross accident.

Humph. To be sure sir, cross accidents will happen to every body, but certes! we have] more than our own share of them.

Roy. Well, dont trouble yourself about it: I have head enough to manage my own affairs, and more than my own too. Why, my lord Slumber can't even grant a new lease, nor imprison a vagabond for poaching, without my advice and direction: did I not manage all Mr. Harebrain's election for him; and, but for one of those cursed accidents or two, had brought him in for his Borough, as neatly as my glove; nay, if his Grace and I get into good understanding together, there is no knowing, but I may have affairs of the nation upon my hands; ha, ha, ha! poor Humphry, thou hast no comprehension of all this: thou think'st me a very wonderful man, dost thou not?

Humph. I must own I do sometimes marvel at your honour.

Enter Mr. WITHRINGTON,

Roy. Ha! how do you do, my dear cousin! I hope I have the happiness of seeing you in good health; I am heartily rejoiced to see you, my very good sir. *(Shaking him heartily by the hand.)*

With. I thank you, sir, you are welcome to Bath, I did not expect the pleasure of seeing you here.

Roy. Why, my dear worthy sir, I am a man of so much business, so toss'd about, so harass'd with a multiplicity of affairs, that I protest, I can't tell myself one day, what part of the world I shall be in the next.

With. You give yourself a great deal of trouble, Mr. Royston.

Roy. O! hang it! I never spare myself: I must work, to make others work, cousin Withrington; I have got a world of new alterations, going on at Royston-hall; if you would take a trip down to see them.

With. I am no great traveller, sir.

Roy. I have plough'd up the bowling-green, and cut down the elm-trees; I have built new

6

stables, and fill'd up the horse pond; I have dug up the orchard, and pull'd down the old fruit wall, where that odd little temple used to stand.

With. And is the little temple pull'd down too? pray, what has become of your Vicar's sister, Mrs. Mary? we drunk tea with her there, I remember, is she married yet? she was a very modest looking gentlewoman.

Roy. So you remember her too; well I have pull'd down every foot of it, and built a new cart-house with the bricks.—Good commodious stalls for thirty horses, cousin Withrington, they beat Sir John Houndly's all to nothing; it is as clever, a well constructed building as any in the country.

With. Has Sir John built a new house in the country.

Roy. No, no, the stables I say.

With. O you are talking of the stables again.

Roy. But when I get the new addition to the mansion-house finish'd, that will be the grand improvement; the best carpenters' work in the country, my dear sir, all well season'd timber from Norway.

Humph. It is part of a disputed wreck, sir, and if the law suit about the right to it turns out in my master's favour, as it should do, it will be the cheapest built house in the county; O! let his honour alone for making a bargain.

With. So you have got a law suit on your hands, Mr. Royston? I hope you are not much addicted to this kind of amusement, you will find it a very expensive one.

Roy. Bless you, my good sir, I am the most peaceable creature in the world, but I will suffer no man to impose upon me.

With. (*smiling.*) But you suffer the women sometimes to do so, do you not?

Humph. No, nor the women neither, sir; for it was but t'other day that he prosecuted widow Gibson, for letting her chickens feed amongst his corn, and it was given in his honour's favour, as in right it should have been.

With. (*archly.*) And who was adjudged to pay the expences of court, Mr. Humphry?

Humph. Ay, to be sure, his honour was obliged to pay that.

With. (*archly.*) But the widow paid swingingly for it, I suppose.

Humph. Nay 'faith, after all, they but fined her in a sixpence; yet that always shew'd, you know, that she was in the wrong.

With. To be sure, Mr. Humphry, and the sixpence would indemnify your master for the costs of suit.

Humph. Nay, as a body may say, he might as well have let her alone, for any great matter he made of it that way; but it was very wrong in her, you know, sir, to let her hens go amongst his honour's corn, when she knew very well, she was too poor to make up the loss to his honour.

With. Say no more about it, my good Hum-

phry, you have vindicated your master most ably,
and I have no doubts at all in regard to the pro-
priety of his conduct.

Humph. (*very well pleased.*) Ay, thank god, I do
sometimes make shift in my poor way to edge
in a word for his honour.

Roy. (*not so well pleased.*) Thou art strangely
given to prating this morning. (*to Humph.*) By the
bye, cousin Withrington, I must consult you about
my application to his Grace.

Humph. (*aside to* Withrington, *pulling him by
the sleeve.*) You forget to ask for the lady, sir.

With. (*turning round.*) What did you say of his
Grace?

Roy. No, no, I should—I meant—did I not say
the gracious young lady your niece; I hope she is
well?

With. (*smiling.*) She is very well; you shall go
home with me, and visit her.

Roy. I am infinitely obliged to you, my worthy
good sir, I shall attend you with the greatest pleasure; some ladies have no dislike to a good looking gentleman-like man, although he may be past
the bloom of his youth, cousin? however young
men do oftener carry the day, I believe, my son
George is a good likely fellow, I expect him in
Bath every hour, I shall have the honour of following you, my dear sir. Remember my orders
Humphry.

[EXEUNT.

Enter HARWOOD *hastily, looking round as if he sought some one, and was disappointed.*

Har. (*alone.*) He is gone, I have miss'd the good uncle of Agnes—what is the matter with me now, that the sound of an old man's voice should agitate me thus? did I not feel it was the sound of something which belong'd to her? in faith! I believe, if her kitten was to mew, I should hasten to hold some intercourse with it.—I can stay in this cursed house no longer, and when I do go out, there is but one way these legs of mine will carry me, the alley which leads to her dwelling—Well, well, I have been but six times there to-day already; I may have a chance of seeing her at last—I'll run after the old gentleman even now—what a delightful witch it is!   [EXIT *hastily.*

SCENE II.

WITHRINGTON'S *house.* AGNES *and* MARIANE, *discovered,* Mariane *reading a letter, and* Agnes *looking earnestly and gladly in her face.*

Ag. My friend Edward is well, I see; pray what does the traveller say for himself?

Mar. (*putting up the letter.*) You shall read it all by and by, every thing that is pleasant and kind.

Ag. Heaven prosper you both! you are happier than I am with all my fortune, Mariane, you have a right true lover.

Mar. And so have you, Agnes, my Harwood will

bear the trial: I have watch'd him closely, and I will venture my word upon him.

Ag. (*taking her in her arms.*) Now if thou art not deceiv'd, thou art the dearest sweet cousin on earth! (*Pausing and looking seriously.*) Ah no! it cannot be! I am but an ordinary looking girl, as my uncle says; (*with vivacity*;) I would it were so!

Enter SERVANT.

Ser. Sir Loftus Prettyman and Mr. Opal.

Mar. I am at home. (*Exit* SERVANT.) I can't entertain these fools till I have put up my letter: do you receive them, I will soon return. [EXIT.

Enter SIR LOFTUS *and* OPAL *dress'd pretty much alike.* SIR LOFTUS *makes a haughty distant bow to* AGNES, *and* OPAL *makes another very like it.*

Ag. Have the goodness to be seated, sir. *(to Sir Loftus)* Pray, sir, (*to Opal, making a courteous motion as if she wish'd them to sit down.*) Miss Withrington will be here immediately. (Sir Loftus *makes a slight bow without speaking*; Opal *does the same, and both saunter about with their hats in their hands.*)

Ag. I hope you had a pleasant walk after we left you, Sir Loftus?

Sir Loft. (*Looking affectedly, as if he did not understand her.*) I beg pardon——O! you were along with Miss Withrington. (*Mumbling something which is not heard.*)

Ag. to Op. You are fond of that walk, Mr. Opal, I think I have seen you there frequently.

Op. Ma'am you are very—(*mumbling something which is not heard, in the same manner with* Sir Loftus, *but still more absurd.*) I do sometimes walk—(*mumbling again.*)

Ag. to Sir Loft. The country is delightful round Bath.

Sir Loft. Ma'am!

Ag. Dont you think so, Mr. Opal?

Op. 'Pon honou *:* I never attended to it. (*A long pause,* Sir Loftus *and* Opal *strut about conceitedly. Enter* Mariane, *and both of them run up to her at once, with great alacrity and satisfaction.*)

Sir Loft. I hope I see Miss Withrington entirely recovered from the fatigues of the morning?

Mar. Pretty well, after the fatigue of dressing too, which is a great deal worse, Sir Loftus. (*carelessly.*)

Op. For the ball, I presume?

Sir Loft. I am delighted—

Mar. (*addressing herself to* Agnes, *without attending to him.*) Do you know what a provoking mistake my milliner has made?

Ag. I dont know.

Sir Loft. I hope madam—

Mar. to Ag. She has made up my whole suit of trimmings with the colour of all others I dislike.

Op. This is very provoking, indeed I would—

Mar. (*Still speaking to* Ag. *without attending to*

them.) And she has sent home my petticoat all patch'd over with scraps of gold foil, like a may-day dress for a chimney-sweeper.

Sir Loft. (*Thrusting in his face near* Mariane, *and endeavouring to be attended to.*) A very good comparison, ha, ha!

Op. (*Thrusting in his face at the other side of her.*) Very good indeed, ha, ha, ha!

Mar. (*Still speaking to* Agnes, *who winks at her without attending to them.*) I'll say nothing about it but never employ her again,

Sir Loft. (*going round to her other ear, and making another attempt.*) I am delighted, Miss Withrington.

Mar. (*carelessly.*) Are you, Sir Loftus? (*To* Agnes.) I have broken my fan, pray put it by with your own, my dear Agnes! (*Exit* Agnes *into the adjoining room, and* Sir Loftus *gives* Opal *a significant look, upon which he retires to the bottom of the stage, and, after sauntering a little there,* Exit.)

Sir Loft. (*seeming a little piqued.*) If you would have done me the honour to hear me, Ma'am, I should have said, I am delighted to see you dress'd, as I hope I may presume from it, you intend going to the ball to-night.

Mar. Indeed I am too capricious to know whether I do or not; do you think it will be pleasant?

Sir Loft. Very pleasant, if the devotions of a thousand admirers can make it so.

Mar. O! the devotions of a thousand admirers,

are like the good will of every body, one steady friendship is worth it all.

Sir Loft. From which may I infer that one faithful adorer, in your eyes, outvalues all the thousand? *(Affecting to be tender.)* Ah! so would I have Miss Withrington to believe! and if that can be any inducement, she will find such a one there, most happy to attend her.

Mar. Will she? I wonder who this may be: what kind of man is he pray?

Sir Loft. *(With a conceited simper, at the same time in a pompous manner.)* Perhaps it will not be boasting too much to say, he is a man of fashion, and of some little consequence in the world.

Mar. Handsome and accomplish'd too, Sir Loftus?

Sir Loft. I must not presume, ma'am, to boast of my accomplishments.

Mar. *(Affecting a look of disappointment.)* O! lud! so it is yourself after all! I have not so much penetration as I thought. *(Yawning twice very wide.)* Bless me! what makes me yawn so? I forgot to visit my old woman, who sells the cakes, this morning that must be it. *(Yawning again.)* Do you love gingerbread, Sir Loftus? (Sir Loftus *bites his lip, and struts proudly away to the other side of the stage, whilst* Agnes *peeps from the closet, and makes signs of encouragement to* Mariane.*)*

Mar. Well, after all, I believe, it will be pleasant enough to go to the ball, with such an accomplish'd attendant.

Q

Sir Loft. (*Taking encouragement, and smothering his pride.*) Are you so obliging, Miss Withrington? will you permit me to have the happiness of attending you?

Mar. If you'll promise to make it very agreeable to me; you are fond of dancing, I suppose?

Sir Loft. I'll do any thing you desire me, but why throw away time so precious in the rough familiar exercise of dancing? is there not something more distinguished, more refined, in enjoying the conversation of those we love?

Mar. In the middle of a crowd, Sir Loftus?

Sir Loft. What is that crowd to us? we have nothing to do but to despise it, whilst they stare upon us with vulgar admiration, we shall talk together, smile together, attend only to each other, like beings of a superiour order.

Mar. O! that will be delightful! but dont you think we may just peep slyly over our shoulder now and then, to see whether they are admiring us? (Sir Loftus *bites his lips again, and struts to the bottom of the stage, whilst* Agnes *peeps out again from the closet, and makes signs to* Mariane.)

Mar. (*Carelessly pulling a small case from her pocket.*) Are not these handsome brilliants, Sir Loftus?

Sir Loft. (*Very much struck with the sparkling of the diamonds, but pretending not to look at them.*) Upon my word, ma'am, I am no judge of trinkets.

Mar. They are clumsily set, I shall give them to my cousin.

Sir Loft. (*Forgetting himself.*) Why, ma'am, do you seriously mean—They are of a most incomparable water.

Mar. (*archly.*) I thought you had not attended to them.

Sir Loft. (*tenderly.*) It is impossible in the presence of Miss Withrington, to think of any thing but the cruelty with which she imposes silence on a heart which adores her.

Mar. Nay, you entirely mistake me, Sir Loftus, I am ready to hear you with the greatest good nature imaginable.

Sir Loft. It is a theme, perhaps, on which my tongue would too long dwell.

Mar. O! not at all, I have leisure, and a great deal of patience at present, I beg you would by no means hurry yourself.

Sir Loft. (*After a pause, looking foolish and embarrassed.*) Few words, perhaps, will better suit the energy of passion.

Mar. Just as you please, Sir Loftus, if you chuse to say it in few words I am very well satisfied. (*Another pause. Sir Loftus very much embarrassed.*)

Enter WITHRINGTON *and* HARWOOD, *and* Sir Loftus *seems very much relieved.*

Sir Loft. (*aside*) Heaven be praised! they are come.

Mar. to With. I thought you were to have brought Mr. Royston with you.

With. He left us at a shop by the way, to en-

quire the price of turnip seed; but he will be here
by-and-by, if a hundred other things do not prevent
him. *(Bows to* Sir Loftus; *then turns to* Harwood,
*and speaks as if he resumed a conversation which had
just been broken off, whilst* Sir Loftus *and* Mariane
retire to the bottom of the stage.) I perfectly agree
with you, Mr Harwood, that the study and prepa-
ration requisite for your profession is not altogether
a dry treasuring up of facts in the memory, as
many of your young students conceive : he who
pleads the cause of man before fellow-men, must
know what is in the heart of man as well as what
is in the book of records, and what study is there
in nature so noble, so interesting as this ?

Har. But the most pleasing part of our task,
my good sir, is not the least difficult. Where
application only is wanting I shall not be left behind, for I am not without ambition, though the
younger son of a family by no means affluent ;
and I have a widow mother whose hopes of seeing me respectable, must not be disappointed. I
assure you there is nothing—   *(Listening.)*

With. Go on, Mr. Harwood, I have great pleasure in hearing you.

Har. I thought I heard a door move.

With. It is Agnes in the next room, I dare say,
she is always making a noise.

Har. In the next room !

With. But you was going to assure me—Have
the goodness to proceed.

Har. I was going to say—I rather think I said—
I am sure—   *(Listening again.)*

With. Poo! there is no body there.

Har. Well, I said—I think I told you—In faith, my good sir, I will tell you honestly, I have forgot what I meant to say.

With. No matter, you will remember it again. Ha, ha, ha! it puts me in mind of a little accident which happened to myself when I was in Lincoln's Inn. Two or three of us met one evening, to be a little cheerful together, and—*(Whilst* Withrington *begins his story,* Agnes *enters softly from the adjoining closet unperceived; but* Harwood *on seeing her, runs eagerly up to her, leaving* Withrington *astonished, in the middle of his discourse.)*

Har. to Ag. Ha! after so many false alarms, you steal upon us at last like a little thief.

Ag. And I steal something very good from you too, if you lose my uncle's story by this interruption; for I know by his face he was telling one.

With. Raillery is not always well-timed, Miss Agnes Withrington.

Ag. Nay, do not be cross with us, sir. Mr. Harwood knew it was too good to be spent upon one pair of ears, so he calls in another to partake.

With. Get along, baggage.

Ag. So I will, uncle; for I know that only means with you that I should perk myself up by your elbow.

With. Well, two or three of us young fellows were met—did I not say—

Ag. At Lincoln's Inn. (Withrington *hesitates.)*

Har. She has named it, sir.

With. I know well enough it was there. And if I remember well, George Buckner was one of us. (Agnes *gives a gentle hem to suppress a cough.*)

Har. (eagerly.) You was going to speak, Miss Withrington?

Ag. No, indeed, I was not.

With. Well, George Buckner and two three more of us—We were in a very pleasant humour that night—(Agnes *making a slight motion of her hand to fasten some pin in her dress.*)

Har. (eagerly.) Do you not want something? (*To* Agnes.)

Ag. No, I thank you, I want nothing.

With. (Half amused, half peevish.) Nay, say what you please to one another, for my story is ended.

Har. My dear sir, we are perfectly attentive.

Ag. Now, pray, uncle!

With. to Ag. Now pray hold thy tongue. I forgot, I must consult the Court Calendar on Royston's account. (*Goes to a table and takes up a red book, which he turns over.*)

Ag. to Har. How could you do so to my uncle? I would not have interrupted him for the world.

Har. Ay, chide me well: I dearly love to be chidden.

Ag. Do not invite me to it. I am said to have a very good gift that way, and you would soon have too much of it, I believe.

Har. O no! I would come every hour to be chidden!

Ag. And take it meekly too ?

Har. Nay, I would have my revenge : I should call you scolding Agnes, and little Agnes, and my little Agnes.

Ag. You forget my dignity, Mr Harwood.

Har. Oh! you put all dignity out of countenance! The great Mogul himself would forget his own in your presence.

Ag. Am I, as the good folks say, such a very humbling sight ? But they are going to the garden : I am resolved to be one of the party. *(As she goes to join* Sir Loftus *and* Mariane, *who open a glass door leading to the garden,* Harwood *goes before, walking backwards, and his face turned to her.)* You will break your pate presently, if you walk with that retrograde step, like a dancing-master giving me a lesson. Do you think I shall follow you as if you had the fiddle in your hand ?

Har. Ah, Miss Withrington ! it is you who have got the fiddle, and I who must follow.

[EXEUNT *into the garden.*

Re-enter Sir LOFTUS *from the Garden, looking about for his hat.*

Sir Loft. O! here it is.

Enter OPAL.

Op. What, here alone ?

Sir Loft. She is in the garden, I shall join her immediately.

Op. All goes on well, I suppose ?

Sir Loft. Why, I dont know how it is—no-body hears us ? *(Looking round.)* I dont know how it is, but she does not seem to comprehend perfectly in what light I am regarded by the world ; that is to say, by that part of it which deserves to be called so.

Op. No! that is strange enough.

Sir Loft. Upon my honour, she treats me with as much careless familiarity as if I were some plain neighbour's son in the country.

Op. 'Pon honour, this is very strange.

Sir Loft. I am not without hopes of succeeding; but I will confess to you, I wish she would change her manner of behaving to me. On the word of a gentleman, it is shocking ! Suppose you were to give her a hint of the consequence I am honoured with in the fashionable circles, that she may just have an idea of the respect which is paid by every well-bred person—You understand me, Opal ?

Op. O ! perfectly. I shall give her to know that men like us, my dear friend, are accustomed to be looked upon as a class of superiour beings.

Sir Loft. (not quite satisfied.) I dont know— Suppose you were to leave out all mention of yourself—Your own merit could not fail to be inferred.

Op. Well, I shall do so.

Sir Loft. Let us go the garden.   [EXEUNT.

Enter Miss ESTON, *speaking as she enters.*
I have been all over the town, and here am I at

last quite tired to death. How do you ?—*(Look-ing round.)* O la! there is nobody here. Mr. Opal is gone too. I'll wait till their return. *(Takes up a book, then looks at herself in the glass, then takes up the book again. Yawning.)* 'Tis all about the imagination, and the understanding, and I dont know what—I dare say it is good enough to read of a Sunday. *(Yawns, and lays it down.)* O la! I wish they would come.

Enter ROYSTON, *and takes* Miss ESTON *for* Miss WITHRINGTON.

Roys. Madam, I have the honour to be your very humble servant. I hoped to have been here sooner, but I have been so overwhelmed with a multiplicity of affairs; and you know, madam, when that is the case—

Est. (Taking the word out of his mouth.) One is never master of one's time for a moment. I'm sure I have been all over the town this morning, looking after a hundred things; till my head has been put into such a confusion! La, ma'am! said my millener, do take some lavender drops, you look so pale. Why, says I, I dont much like to take them, Mrs. Trollop, they a'nt always good.

Roys. No more they are, ma'am, you are very right; and if a silly fellow, I know, had taken my advice last year, and bought up the lavender drops, he would have made—

Est. (Taking the word from him again.) A very good fortune, I dare say. But people never will take advice, which is very foolish in them, to be sure. Now I always take—

Roys. Be so good as to hear me, ma'am.

Est. Certainly, sir; For I always say if they give me advice it is for my good, and why should not I take it?

Roys. (Edging in his word as fast as he can.) And the damn'd foolish fellow too! I once saved him from being cheated in a horse; and—

Est. La! there are such cheats! a friend of mine bought a little lap-dog the other day—

Roys. But the horse, madam, was—

Est. Not worth a guinea, I dare say. Why they had the impudence to palm it on my friend.

Both speaking together.

Est. As a pretty little dog, which had been bred
Roys. It was a good mettled horse, and might
E. up for a lady of quality, and when she had
R. have passed as a good purchase at the money,
E. just made a cushion for it at the foot of her
R. but on looking his fore feet—*(Stops short, and lets her go on.)*
own bed, she found it was all over mangy. I'm sure I would rather have a plain wholesome cat, than the prettiest mangy dog in the kingdom.

Roys. Certainly, ma'am. And I assure you the horse—for says I to the groom—

Both speaking together.

Est. O! I dare say it was—and who would

Roys. What is the matter with this pastern,
E. have suspected that a dog bred up on pur-
R. Thomas? it looks as if it were rubbed—*(Stops short again, and looks at her with astonishment as she goes on talking.)*
E. pose for a lady of quality, should be all over so? nasty creature! It had spots upon its back as large as my watch. *(Taking up her watch.)* O la! I am half an hour after my time. My mantua-maker is waiting for me. Good morning, sir.

[EXIT, *hastily.*

Roys. (Looking after her.) Clack, clack, clack, clack! What a devil of a tongue she has got! 'Faith! George shall have her, and I'll e'en ask the place for myself. *(Looking out.)* But there is company in the garden! I'll go and join them.

[EXIT *to the garden.*

ACT III.—SCENE I.

Mr. WITRINGTON's *house. A loud laughing without. Enter* ROYSTON, *in a great rage.*

Roys. Ay, ay, laugh away, laugh away, madam, you'll weep by-and-by, mayhap. *(Pauses and listens, laughing still heard.)* What an infernal noise the jade makes. I wish she had a peck of chaff in her mouth, I am sure it is wide enough to hold it.

Enter HUMPHRY.

Humph. I have been seeking your honour every where—Lord, sir! I have something to tell you.

Roys. Confound your tales! dont trouble me with a parcel of nonsense.

Humph. (*Staring at him, and hearing the laughing without.*) For certain, your honour, there's somebody in this house merrier than you or I.

Roys. Damn you, sir! how do you know I am not merry? Go home, and do what I ordered you directly. If that fellow Jonathan is not in the way, I'll horse-whip him within an inch of his life. Begone, I say, why do you stand staring at me, like a madman?   [EXEUNT.

Enter MARIANE *and* AGNES, *by opposite sides.*

Mar. (*holding her sides.*) Oh how my poor sides ach! I shan't be able to laugh again for a month.

Ag. You have got rid of one lover who will scarcely attempt you a second time. I have met him hurrying through the hall, and muttering to himself like a madman. It is not your refusal of his son that has so roused him.

Mar. No, no, he began his courtship in a doubtful way, as if he would recommend a gay young husband to my choice, but a sly compliment to agreeable men of a middle age, brought him soon to speak plainly for himself.

Ag. But how did you provoke him so?

Mar. I will tell you another time. It is later than I thought. (*Looking at her watch.*)

Ag. Dont go yet. How stands it with you and a certain gentleman I recommended to your notice?

Mar. O! he does not know whether I am tall or short, brown or fair, foolish or sensible, after all the pains I have taken with him : he has eyes, ears, and understanding, for nobody but you, Agnes, and I will attempt him no more. He spoke to me once with animation in his countenance, and I turned round to listen to him eagerly, but it was only to repeat to me something you had just said, which, to deal plainly with you, had not much wit in it neither. I dont know how it is, he seemed to me at first a pleasanter man than he proves to be.

Ag. Oh! say not so, Mariane! he proves to be most admirable!

Mar. Well, be it so, he cannot prove better than I wish him to do, and I can make up my list without him. I have a love letter from an Irish baronet in my pocket, and Opal will declare himself presently.—I thought once he meant only to plead for his friend, but I would not let him off so, for I know he is a mercenary creature. I have flattered him a little at the expence of Sir Loftus, and I hope ere long to see him set up for a great man upon his own bottom.

Ag. So it was only to repeat to you something that I had been saying?

Mar. Ha! you are thinking of this still. I be-

lieve indeed he sets down every turn of your eye
in his memory, and acts it all over in secret.

Ag. Do you think so? give me your hand, my
dear Mariane, you are a very good cousin to me—
Marks every turn of mine eye! I am not quite
such an ordinary girl as my uncle says—My com-
plexion is as good as your own, Mariane, if it were
not a little sun-burnt. (Mariane *smiles.)* Yes,
smile at my vanity as you please, for what makes
me vain, makes me so good humoured too, that
I will forgive you. But here comes uncle. *(Skip-
ping as she goes to meet him.)* O! I am light as an
air-ball! *(Enter* Mr Withrington.) My dear sir, how
long you have been away from us this morning!
I am delighted to see you so pleased and so happy.

With. (*with a very sour face.)* You are mistaken, young lady, I am not so pleased as you
think.

Ag. O no, sir! you are very good humoured.
Is'nt he, Mariane?

With. But I say I am in very bad humour.
Get along with your foolery!

Ag. Is it really so? Let me look in your face,
uncle? To be sure your brows are a little knit,
and your eyes a little gloomy, but poo! that is
nothing to be called bad humour; if I could not
contrive to look crabbeder than all this comes to,
I would never pretend to be ill humoured in my
life. (Mariane *and* Agnes *take him by the hands
and begin to play with him.)*

With. No, no, young ladies, I am not in a

mood to be played with. I can't approve of every
farce you please to play off in my family, nor to
have my relations affronted, and driven from my
house for your entertainment.

Mar. Indeed, sir, I treated Royston better than
he deserved, for he would not let me have time to
give a civil denial, but ran on planning settle-
ments and jointures, and a hundred things besides;
I could just get in my word to stop his career with
a flat refusal, as he was about to provide for our
descendants of the third generation. O! if you
had seen his face then, uncle!

With. I know very well how you have treated
him.

Ag. Dont be angry, sir. What does a man
like Royston care for a refusal? he is only angry
that he can't take the law of her for laughing at
him.

With. Let this be as it may, I dont chuse to
have my house in a perpetual bustle from morning till night, with your plots and your pastimes.
There is no more order nor distinction kept up in
my house, than if it were a cabin in Kamschatka,
and common to a whole tribe. I can't set my nose
into a room of it but I find some visitor, or show-
man, or millener's apprentice, loitering about:
my best books are cast upon footstools and win-
dow-seats, and my library is littered over with
work-bags: dogs, cats, and kittens, take possession
of every chair, and refuse to be disturbed: kitchen
wenches flaunt up stairs with their new top-knots

2

on, to look at themselves in the pier glasses; and
the very beggar children go hopping about my hall,
with their half-eaten scraps in their hands, as
though it were the entry to a work-house.

Ag. (Clapping his shoulder gently.) Now dont
be impatient, my dear sir, and every thing shall
be put into such excellent order as shall delight
you to behold.   And as for the beggar children, if
any of them dare but to set their noses within the
door, I'll—What shall I do with them, sir? *(Pauses
and looks in his face, which begins to relent.)* I
believe we must e'en give them a little pudding
after all.   *(Both take his hands and coax him.)*

With. Come, come, off hands and let me sit
down.   I am tired of this.

Ag. Yes, uncle, and here is one seat, you see,
with no cat upon it. (Withrington *sits down, and*
Agnes *takes a little stool and sits down at his feet,
curling her nose as she looks up to him, and making
a good humoured face.*)

With. Well, it may be pleasant enough, girls,
but allow me to say all this playing, and laughing,
and hoidening about is not gentlewomanlike, nay,
I might say, is not maidenly.   A high bred elegant woman is a creature which man approaches
with awe and respect; but nobody would think of
accosting you with such impressions, any more
than if your were a couple of young female
tinkers.

Ag. Dont distress yourself about this, sir, we
shall get the men to bow to us, and tremble be-

fore us too, as well as e'er a hoop-petticoat or long ruffles of them all.

With. Tremble before you! ha, ha, ha! *(to Agnes)* Who would tremble before thee dost thou think?

Ag. No despicable man perhaps: What think you of your favourite, Harwood?

With. Poo, poo, poo! he is pleased with thee as an amusing and good natured creature, and thou thinkest he is in love with thee, forsooth.

Ag. A good natured creature! he shall think me a vixen and be pleased with me.

With. No, no, not quite so far gone, I believe.

Ag. I'll bet you two hundred pounds that it is so. If I win you shall pay it to Mariane for wedding trinkets, and if you win you may build a couple of alms-houses.

With. Well, be it so. We shall see, we shall see.

Mar. Indeed we shall see you lose your bet, uncle.

With. to Mar. Yes, baggage, I shall have your prayers against me I know.

Enter SERVANT, *and announces* Mr. Opal. *Enter* OPAL.

Op. to Mar. I hope I have the pleasure of seeing Miss Withrington well this morning. *(Bows distantly to* Withrington, *and still more so to* Agnes, *after the manner of* Sir Loftus.)

R

With. Your servant, sir.

Mar. to Op. How did you like the ball last night? There was a gay, genteel looking company.

Op. (With affected superiority.) Excepting Lord Saunter, and Lord Poorly, and Sir Loftus, and one or two more of us, I did not know a soul in the room.

With. There were some pretty girls there, Mr. Opal?

Op. I am very glad to hear it, 'pon honour. I did not—*(Mumbling.)*

With. (aside.) Affected puppy, I can't bear to look at him.   [EXIT.

Mar. (Assuming a gayer air as Withrington *goes out.)* You will soon have a new beau to enrich your circle, Mr. Opal, the handsome and accomplished Colonel Beaumont. He is just returned from abroad, and is now quite the fashion at court. *(To* Agnes.) Dont you think Mr. Opal resembles him?

Ag. O! very much indeed.

Op. (Bowing very graciously.) Does he not resemble Sir Loftus too? I mean in his air and his manner.

Mar. O! not at all! That haughty coldness of his is quite old fashioned now; so unlike the affable frankness so much admired in the Colonel: you have seen him I presume?

Op. I have never had that honour.

Mar. Then you will not be displeased at the likeness we have traced, when you do.

Op. (*Relaxing from his dignity, and highly pleased.*) The greatest pleasure of my life, ma'am, will be to resemble what pleases you. (Mariane *tips* Agnes *the wink, and she retires to the bottom of the stage.*)

Mar. You flatter me infinitely.

Op. Ah! call it not flattery, charming Miss Withrington! for now I will have the boldness to own to you frankly, I have been, since the first moment I beheld you, your most sincere, your most passionate admirer. Upon hon—(*correcting himself*) 'faith I have!

Mar. Nothing but my own want of merit can make me doubt of any thing Mr. Opal asserts upon his honour or his faith. (*Turning and walking towards the bottom of the stage, whilst* Opal *follows her stalking in dumb show ; then* Agnes *joins them, and they all come forward to the front.*)

Ag. to Mar. How much that turn of his head puts me mind of the Colonel.

Mar. So it does, my Agnes. (*To* Opal.) Pray have the goodness to hold it so for a moment! There now, it is just the very thing. (Opal *holds his head in a constrained ridiculous posture, and then makes a conceited bow.*) His very manner of bowing too! one would swear it was the Colonel!

Ag. Yes, only the Colonel is more familiar, more easy in his carriage.

Op. O! Ma'am! I assure you I have formerly—It is my natural manner to be remarkably easy—But I—*(pauses.)*

Mar. Have never condescended to assume any other than your natural manner, I hope.

Op. O! not at all, I detest affectation; there is nothing I detest so much—But upon my soul! I can't tell how it is, I have been graver of late. I am, indeed, sometimes thoughtful.

Mar. O fye upon it! dont be so any more. It is quite old fashioned and ridiculous now. *(To* Agnes, *winking at her.)* Did you see my gloves any where about the room, cousin?

Op. I'll find them. *(Goes to look for them with great briskness.—Servant announces* Miss Eston.)

Op. Pest take her! I stared at her once in a mistake, and she has ogled and followed me ever since.

Enter Miss Eston, *running up to* Mariane *and* Agnes, *and pretending not to see* Opal, *though she cannot help looking askance at him while she speaks.*

Est. O my dear creatures! you can't think how I have longed to see you. Mrs. Thomson kept me so long this morning, and you know she is an intolerable talker. *(Pretending to discover* Opal) O! how do you do, Mr. Opal? I declare I did not observe you!

Op. *(With a distant haughty bow.)* I am obliged to you, ma'am.

Est. I did see your figure, indeed, but I mistook it for Sir Loftus.

Op. (*Correcting himself, and assuming a cheerful frank manner.*) O ma'am! you are very obliging to observe me at all. I believe Prettyman and I may be nearly of the same height. (*Looking at his watch.*) I am beyond my appointment I see. Excuse me : I must hurry away.   [EXIT, *hastily.*

Est. (*Looking after him with marks of disappointment.*) I am very glad he is gone. He does so haunt me, and stare at me, I am quite tired of it. The first time I ever saw him, you remember how he looked me out of countenance. I was resolved before I came not to take notice of him.

Mar. So you knew you should find him here, then.

Est. O la! one dont know of a morning who one may meet ; as likely him as any body else, you know. I really wonder now what crotchet he has taken in his head about me. Do you know, last night, before twilight, I peeped past the blind, and saw him walking with slow pensive steps, under my window.

Mar. Well, what happened then ?

Est. I drew in my head, you may be sure; but a little while after, I peeped out again, and, do you know, I saw him come out of the perfumer's shop, just opposite to my dressing-room, where he had been all the while.

Mar. Very well, and what happened next ?

Est. La! nothing more. But was it not very

odd? What should he be doing all that time in that little paltry shop? The great shop near the Circus is the place where every body buys perfumery.

Ag. No, there is nothing very odd in Mr. Opal's buying perfumes at a very paltry shop, where he might see and be seen by a very pretty lady.

Est. (*With her face brightning up.*) Do you think so? O no! you dont?

Ag. To be sure I do. But I know what is very strange.

Est. O la! dear creature! What is it?

Ag. He bought his perfumes there before you came, when there was no such inducement. Is not that very odd? (Eston *pauses, and looks silly.*)

Enter Mr. WITHRINGTON, *but upon perceiving* Eston, *bows and retreats again.*

Est. (*Recovering herself.*) Ha! how do you do, Mr. Withrington? I have just seen your friend, Lady Fade. Poor dear soul! she says—

With. I am sorry, ma'am, it is not in my power at present—I am in a hurry, I have an appointment. Your servant, ma'am. [Exit.

Est. Well, now this is very odd! Wherever I go, I find all the men just going out to some appointment. O, I forgot to tell you, Mrs. Thomson has put a new border to her drawing room, just like the one up stairs. Has it not a dark blue ground? (*To Mariane.*)

Mar. I'm sure I cannot tell, let us go up stairs
and see.   [EXEUNT.

SCENE II.

Before Mr. WITHRINGTON'S *House.   Enter* HAR-
WOOD.

Well, here I am again, yet devil take me if I
can muster up resolution enough to take the
knocker in my hand! What a fool was I to call
twice this morning! for with what face can I now
visit her again? The old gentleman will look
strangely at me; the fine heiress her cousin will
stare at me; nay, the very servants begin already
to smile with impertinent significance, as I enquire
with conscious foolishness, if the ladies are at
home.   Then Agnes herself will look so drolly at
me—Ah! but she will look so pleasantly too!—
'Faith! I'll e'en go. *(Goes to the door, puts his
hand up to the knocker, stops short, and turns from it
again.   Pauses.)* What a fool am I, to stand thinking about it here! If I were but fairly in the room
with her, and the first salutation over, I should not
care if the devil himself made faces at me. Oh no!
every body is good humoured, every thing is happy
that is near her! the kitten who plays by her side
takes hold of her gown unchidden. How pleasant it is to love what is so blessed! I would hate
the fairest womsn on earth if she were not of a
sweet temper.   Come away, come away, every
thing favours me here, but my own foolish fancies.

(As he goes to the door again, it opens, and enters from the house, Betty, *crying, with a bundle in her hand.)*

Bet. O dear me! O dear me!

Har. What is the matter with you, my good girl?

Bet. I'm sure it was not my fault, and she has abused me worser than a heathen.

Har. That is hard indeed.

Bet. Indeed it is, sir; and all for a little nasty essence bottle, which was little better than a genteel kind of a stink at the best, and I am sure I did but take out the stopper to smell to it, when it came to pieces in my hand like an egg shell; if bottles will break, how can I help it; but la! sir, there is no speaking reason to my mistress, she is as furious and as ill tempered as a dragon.

Har. Dont distress yourself, Miss Agnes Withrington will make amends to you for the severity of your mistress.

Bet. She truly! she is my mistress herself, and she has abused me, O dear me—If it had been Miss Withrington, she would not have said a word to me, but Miss Agnes is so cross, and so ill natured, there is no living in the house with her.

Har. Girl, you are beside yourself.

Bet. No, sir, god be praised! but she is beside herself, I believe. Does she think I am going to live in her service to be call'd names so, and compared to a blackamoor too? if I had been waiting maid to the queen, she would not have compared me to a blackamoor, and will I take such usage from her? what do I care for her cast gowns.

Har. Well, but she is liberal to you?

Bet. She liberal! shc'll keep every thing that is worth keeping to herself, I warrant; and lord pity those who are bound to live with her! I'll seek out a new place for myself, and let the devil, if he will, wait upon her next, in the shape of blacka-moor; they will be fit company for one another, and if hc gets the better of her for scolding, he is a better devil than I take him for: and I am sure, sir, if you were to see her——

Har. Get along! get along! your are too pas-sionate yourself, to be credited.

Bet. I know what I know, I dont care what no body says, no more I do; I know who to com-plain to.   [EXIT, *grumbling.*

Har. (alone.) What a malicious toad it is! I dare say now, she has done something very pro-voking, I cannot bear these pert chamber-maids, the very sight of them is offensive to me.

Enter JONATHAN.

Jon. Good evening to your honour, can you tell me if Mr. Withrington be at home? for as how, my master has sent me with a message to him.

Har. (Impatiently.) Go to the house and enquire, I know nothing about it. *(Jonathan goes into the house.)*

Har. (Alone, after musing some time.) That girl has put me out of all heart though, with her

2

cursed stories,—No, no, it cannot be—it is impos₃ sible!

Re-enter JONATHAN *from the house, scratching his head, and looking behind.*

Jon. 'Faith there is hot work going on amongst them! thank heaven I am out again!

Har. What do you mean?

Jon. 'Faith! that little lady, in that there house, is the best hand at a scold, saving Mary Macmurrock, my wife's mother, that ever my too blessed eyes looked upon, lord sir! *(going nearer him)* her tongue goes ting, ting, ting, as shrill as the bell of any pieman, and then, sir, *(going nearer him)* her two eyes look out of her head, as though they were a couple of glow-worms, and then sir, he, he, he! *(laughing, and going close up to him)* she claps her little hands so, as if—

Har. Shut your fool's mouth and be damn'd to you! *(Kicks Jonathan off the stage in a violent passion; then leans his back to a tree, and seems thoughtful for some time, and very much troubled.)*

Enter AGNES *from the house, with a stormy look on her face.*

Ag. So you are still loitering here, Harwood? you have been very much amused I suppose, with the conversation of those good folks, you have talked with.

Har. No, not much amused, madam, though

somewhat astonished, I own; too much astonish'd indeed, to give it any credit.

Ag. O! it is true though, I have been very cross with the girl, and very cross with every-body, and if you dont clear up that dismal face of yours, I shall be cross with you too: what could possess you to stay so long under that chesnut-tree a little while ago, always appearing as if you were coming to the house, and always turning back again?

Har. (*eagerly.*) And is it possible, you were then looking at me, and observing my motions?

Ag. Indeed I was just going to open my window and beckon to you, when that creature broke my phial of sweet essence, and put me quite out of temper.

Har. Hang the stupid jade! I could—

Ag. So you are angry too? O! well done! we are fit company for one another, come along with me, come, come, (*impatiently. As she turns to go something catches hold of her gown.*) What is this? confounded thing! (*Pulls away her gown in a pas-sion, and tears it.*)

Har. (*aside.*) Witch that she is, she should be beaten for her humours. I will not go with her.

Ag. (*Looking behind.*) So you wont go in with me? good evening to you then: we did want a fourth person to make up a party with us, but since you dont like it we shall send to Sir Loftus or Opal, or Sir Ulock O'Grady, or some other good creature; I dare say Sir Loftus will come.

Har. (*Half aside.*) Cursed Coxcomb! If he sets his snout within the door, I'll pistol him.

Ag. (*Overhearing him.*) Ha! well said! you will make the best company in the world, come along, come along, (*he follows her half unwillingly,*) why dont you offer your arm here? dont you see how rough it is? (*He offers his arm.*) Poo, not that arm. (*Offers her the other.*) Poo, not so neither, on t'other side of me.

Har. What a humoursome creature you are! I have offer'd you two arms, and neither of them will do, do you think I have a third to offer you?

Ag. You are a simpleton, or you would have half a dozen at my service.

[EXEUNT *into the house.*

ACT IV.—SCENE I.

HARWOOD's *Lodgings. He is discovered walking about with an irregular disturbed step, his hair and dress all neglected and in disorder; he comes forward to the front of the stage.*

Har. I have neither had peace nor sleep since I beheld her; O! that I had never known her! or know her only such as my first fond fancy conceived her!—I would my friend were come, I will open my heart to him, he perhaps will speak comfort to me, for surely that temper must be violent indeed, which generous affection cannot subdue;

and she must be extravagant beyond all bounds of nature, who would ruin the fond husband who toils for her; no, no, nature makes not such, but when she sets her scowling mark upon them to warn us from our ruin. (*Pauses, walks up and down, then comes forward again.*) Insipid constitutions, good nature is a tiresome thing: passion subdued by reason is worth a score of it—and passion subdued by love?—O! that were better still!—yesterday, as I enter'd her door, I heard her name me to her cousin, with so much gentle softness in her voice, I blest her as she spoke.—Ah! if this were so, all might still be well; who would not struggle with the world, for such a creature as this— Ay, and I must struggle!—O! that this head of mine would give over thinking, but for one half hour! (*Rings the bell.*)

Enter THOMAS.

What brings you here, Thomas?

Thom. Your bell rung, sir.

Har. Well, well, I did want something but I have forgot it. Bring me a glass of water. (EXIT Thomas. Harwood *sits down by a small writing-table, and rests his head upon his hand. Re-enter* Thomas, *with the water.*) You have made good haste, Thomas.

Thom. I did make good haste, sir, lest you should be impatient with me.

Har. I am sometimes impatient with you, then? I fear indeed I have been too often so of late;

but you must not mind it, Thomas, I mean you no unkindness.

Thom. Lord love you, sir! I know that very well! a young gentleman who takes an old man into his service, because other gentlemen do not think him quick enough, nor smart enough for them, as your honour has taken me, can never mean to show him any unkindness, I know it well enough; I am only uneasy because I fear you are not so well of late.

Har. I thank you, Thomas, I am not very well— I am not ill neither, I shall be better. *(Pauses.)* I think I have heard you say, you were a soldier in your youth?

Thom. Yes, sir.

Har. And you had a wife too, a woman of fiery mettle, to bear about your napsack?

Thom. Yes, sir, my little stout spirity Jane; she had a devil of a temper, to be sure.

Har. Yet you loved her notwithstanding?

Thom. Yes, to be sure, I did, as it were, bear her some kindness.

Har. I'll be sworn you did!—and you would have been very sorry to have parted with her.

Thom. Why death parts the best of friends, sir: we lived but four years together.

Har. And so, your little spirity Jane was taken so soon away from you? Give me thy hand, my good Thomas. *(Takes his hand and presses it.)*

Thom. *(Perceiving tears in his eyes.)* Lord, sir! dont be so distress'd about it; she did die, to be sure, but truly, between you and I, although I did make a kind of whimpering at the first, I was not ill pleased afterwards to be rid of her ; for, truly, sir, a man who has got an ill tempered wife, has but a dog's life of it at the best.—Will you have your glass of water, sir ?

Har. (*Looking at him with dissatisfaction.*) No, no, take it away ; I have told you a hundred times not to bring me that chalky water from the court-yard. (*Turns away from him.*)

Enter Colonel HARDY. — HARWOOD *signs to* Thomas, *and he goes out.*

Har. My dear Colonel, this is kind; I am very glad to see you.

Col. It is so seldom that a young fellow has any inclination for the company of an old man, that I should feel myself vain of the summons you have sent me, were I not afraid, from this dishabille, my dear Harwood, that you are indisposed.

Har. You are very good ; I am not indisposed. I have indeed been anxious—I rested indifferently last night—I hope I see you well.

Col. Very well, as you may guess from the speed I have made in coming to you. These legs do not always carry me so fast; but you have something particular to say to me.

Har. I am very sensible of your friendship.— Pray, Colonel, be seated !—(*They sit down—a long pause.*—Colonel Hardy, *like one expecting to hear something* ; Harwood, *like one who knows not how to begin.)*—There are moments in a man's life, Colonel Hardy, when the advice of a friend is of the greatest value ; particularly one, who has also been his father's friend.

Col. My heart very warmly claims both those relations to you, Harwood ; and I shall be happy to advise you, as well as I am able.

Har. (After another pause.) I am about to commence a laborious profession.—The mind is naturally anxious.—*(Pauses.)*

Col. But you are too capable of exercising well that profession, to suffer much uneasiness.

Har. Many a man, with talents superiour to mine, has sunk beneath the burden.

Col. And many a man, with talents vastly inferiour to yours, has borne it up with credit.

Har. Ah ! What avails the head with an estranged heart !

Col. You are disgusted, then, with your profession, and have, perhaps, conceived more favourably of mine ? I am sorry for it : I hoped to see you make a figure at the bar; and your mother has long set her heart upon it.

Har. (With energy.) O, no ! she must not ! she shall not be disappointed!—Pardon me, my expressions have gone somewhat wide of my meaning.—I meant to have consulted you in regard to other difficulties.—

Col. And pardon me likewise, for interrupting you ; but it appears to me, that an unlearned soldier is not a person to be consulted in these matters.

Har. It was not, altogether, of these matters I meant to speak—But, perhaps, we had better put it off for the present.

Col. No, no!

Har. Perhaps, we had better walk out a little way ; we may talk with less restraint as we go.

Col. No, no, there are a thousand impertinent people about. Sit down again, and let me hear every thing you wish to say.

Har. (*Pausing, hesitating, and much embarrassed.*) There are certain attachments in which a man's heart may be so deeply interested—I would say so very—or rather I should say so strangely engaged, that—(*hesitates and pauses.*)

Col. O, here it is ! I understand it now. But pray dont be so foolish about it, Harwood ! You are in love ?

Har. (*Appearing relieved.*) I thank your quickness, my dear Colonel, I fear it is somewhat so with me.

Col. And whence your fear ? Not from the lady's cruelty ?

Har. No, there is another bar in my way, which does, perhaps, too much depress my hopes of happiness.

Col. You have not been prudent enough to fall in love with an heiress ?

Har. No, my dear sir, I have not.

Col. That is a great mistake, to be sure, Har-

s

wood; yet many a man has not advanced the less rapidly in his profession, for having a portionless wife to begin the world with. It is a spur to industry.

Har. (*Looking pleased at him.*) Such sentiments are what I expected from Colonel Hardy; and, were it not for female failings, there would be little risk in following them.—I dont know how to express it—I am perhaps too delicate in these matters—We ought not to expect a faultless woman.

Col. No, surely; and, if such a woman were to be found, she would be no fit companion for us.

Har. (*Getting up, and pressing the Colonel's hand between his.*) My dearest friend! your liberality and candour delight me!—I do, indeed, believe that many a man has lived very happily with a woman far from being faultless; and, after all, where is the great injury he sustains, if she should be a little violent and unreasonable?

Col. (*Starting up from his seat.*) Nay, heaven defend us from a violent woman; for that is the devil himself! — (*Seeing* Harwood's *countenance change*)—What is the matter with you, Harwood? She is not ill temper'd, I hope?

Har. (*Hesitating.*) Not—not absolutely so— She is of a very quick and lively disposition, and is apt to be too hasty and unguarded in her emotions.—I do not, perhaps, make myself completely understood.

Col. O! I understand you perfectly,—I have

known ladies of this lively disposition, very hasty and unguarded too in their demands upon a man's pocket as well as his patience; but she may be of a prudent and economical turn. Is it so, Harwood?

Har. (*Throwing himself into a chair very much distress'd.*) I do not say it is, Colonel.

Col. (*Putting his hand kindly upon his shoulder.*) I am sorry to distress you so much, my dear friend, yet it must be so. I see how it is with you : pardon the freedom of friendship, but indeed an expensive and violent temper'd woman is not to be thought of: he who marries such a one forfeits all peace and happiness. Pluck up some noble courage, and renounce this unfortunate connexion.

Har. (*Starting up.*) Renounce it, Colonel Hardy ! Is it from you I receive so hard, so unfeeling a request, who have suffered so much yourself from the remembrance of an early attachment ? I thought to have been pitied by you.

Col. I was early chagrined with the want of promotion, and disappointed in my schemes of ambition, which gave my countenance something of a melancholy cast, I believe, and the ladies have been kind enough to attribute it to the effects of hopeless love; but how could you be such a ninny, my dear Harwood ?

Har. I am sorry, sir, we have understood one another so imperfectly.

Col. Nay, nay, my young friend, do not carry

yourself so distantly with me. You have sought a love-worn companion, and you have found a plain spoken friend. I am sorry to give you pain ; deal more openly with me : when I know who this bewitching creature is, I shall, perhaps, judge more favourably of your passion.

Har. It is Miss Agnes Withrington.

Col. Cousin to Miss Withrington the heiress ?

Har. Yes it is she. What have I said to amaze you ?

Col. You amaze me, indeed!—That little—fogive me if I were almost to say,—plain looking girl ! Friendship would sympathize in your feelings ; but, pardon me, Harwood, you have lost your wits.

Har. I believe I have, Colonel, which must plead my pardon, likewise, for expecting this friendship from you.

Col. You distress me.

Har. I distress myself still more, by suffering so long the pain of this conversation.

Col. Let us end it, then, as soon as you please. When you are in a humour to listen to reason, I shall be happy to have the honour of seeing you.

Har. When I am in that humour, sir, I will not balk it so much as to intrude upon your time.

Col. Let me see you, then, when you are not in that humour, and I shall the more frequently have the pleasure of your company. *(Both bow coldly.* EXIT, Colonel Hardy.)

Har. (alone.) What a fool was I to send for this man !—A little plain looking girl ! What do the people mean ? They will drive me mad amongst them. Why does not the little witch wear high heels to her shoes, and stick a plume of feathers in her cap ? Oh ! they will drive me distracted !

SCENE II.

Mr. WITHRINGTON's *House.* AGNES *discovered embroidering at a small table,* HARWOOD *standing by her, and hanging fondly over her as she works.*

Har. How pretty it is ! Now you put a little purple on the side of the flower.

Ag. Yes, a very little shade.

Har. And now a little brown upon that.

Ag. Even so.

Har. And thus you work up and down, with that tiny needle of yours, till the whole flower is completed. (*Pauses, still looking at her working.*) Why, Agnes, you little witch ! you're doing that leaf wrong.

Ag. You may pick it out then, and do it better for me. I'm sure you have been idle enough all the morning, it is time you were employed about something.

Har. And so I will. (*Sitting down by her, and taking hold of the work.*)

Ag. (*Covering the flower with her hand*) O ! no, no !

Har. Take away that little perverse hand, and let me begin. *(Putting his hand upon hers.)*

Ag. What a good for nothing creature you are! you can do nothing yourself, and you will suffer no body else to do any thing. I should have had the whole pattern finished before now, if you had not loitered over my chair so long.

Har. So you can't work when I look over you? Then I have some influence upon you? O you sly girl! you are caught in your own words at last.

Ag. Indeed, Harwood, I wish you would go home again to your law-books and your precedent hunting; you have mispent a great deal of time here already.

Har. Is it not better to be with you in reality than only in imagination? Ah! Agnes! you little know what my home studies are.—Law, said you! how can I think of law, when your countenance looks upon me from every black lettered page that I turn? When your figure fills the empty seat by my side, and your voice speaks to me in the very mid-day stillness of my chamber? Ah! my sweet Agnes! you will not believe what a foolish fellow I have been, since I first saw you.

Ag. Nay, Harwood, I am not at all incredulous of the fact, it is only the cause of it which I doubt.

Har. Saucy girl! I must surely be revenged upon you for all this.

Ag. I am tired of this work. *(Getting up.)*

Har. O! do not give over.—Let me do something for you—Let me thread your needle for you—I can thread one most nobly.

Ag. There then. (*Gives him a needle and silk.*)

Har. (*Pretending to scratch her hand with it.*) So ought you to be punished. (*Threads it awkwardly.*)

Ag. Ay, nobly done, indeed! but I shall work no more to-day.

Har. You must work up my needleful.

Ag. I am to work a fool's cap in the corner by-and-by, I shall keep your needleful for that. I am going to walk in the garden.

Har. And so am I.

Ag. You are?

Har. Yes, I am. Go where you will, Agnes, to the garden or the field, the city or the desert, by sea or by land, I must e'en go too. I will never be where you are not, but when to be where you are is impossible.

Ag. O! there will be no getting rid of you at this rate, unless some witch will have pity upon me, and carry me up in the air upon her broomstick.

Har. There, I will not pretend to follow you, but as long as you remain upon the earth, Agnes, hang me! if I can find in my heart to budge an inch from your side.

Ag. You are a madman.

Har. You are a sorceress.

Ag. You are an idler.

Har. You are a little mouse.

Ag. Come, come, get your hat then, and let us go. (*Aside, while he goes to the bottom of the stage for his hat.*) Bless me! I have forgot to be ill-humour'd all this time.   [EXIT, *hastily.*

Har. (*Coming forward.*) Gone for her shawl, I suppose. How delightful she is! how pleasant every change of her countenance! How happy must his life be, spent even in cares and toil, where leisure hours are cheer'd with such a creature as this!

Ag. (*Without, in an angry voice.*) Dont tell me so: I know very well how it is, and you shall smart for it too, you lazy, careless, impudent fellow! And, besides all this, how dare you use my kitten so?

Har. (*Who listened with a rueful face.*) Well, now, but this is humanity: she will not have a creature ill used.—I wish she would speak more gently though.

Ag. (*Entering.*) Troublesome, provoking, careless fellow!

Har. It is very provoking in him to use the poor kitten ill.

Ag. So it is; but it is more provoking still to mislay my clogs, as he does.

Enter SERVANT, *with clogs.*

Ser. Here they are, madam.

Ag. Bring them here, I say, (*looks at them.*) These are Miss Withrington's clogs, you blockhead! (*Throws them to the other side of the stage in a passion.)* I must go without them, I find. (*To* Harwood.) What are you musing about? If you dont chuse to go with me, good morning.

Har. (*Sighing deeply.*) Ah, Agnes! you know too well that I cannot stay behind you. [EXEUNT.

SCENE III.

Miss WITHRINGTON's *Dressing-room. Enter* MA-
RIANE, *who turns back again towards the door,
and calls to* AGNES *without.*

Mar. Agnes, cousin Agnes, where are you going?

Ag. (*Without.*) I am returning to Miss Eston, whom I have left in the parlour, talking to the dog.

Mar. Well, let her talk to the dog a little longer, and let me talk to you.

Enter AGNES.

Ag. I have set Betty to watch at the higher windows to give notice of Sir Loftus's approach, that we may put ourselves in order to receive him; for I am resolved to have one bout more with him, and discharge him for good, I am quite tired of him now.

Ag. Do you expect him?

Mar. I am pretty sure he will come about this time, and I must be prepared for him. I have a good mind to tell him, at once, I despise him, and that will be a plain easy way of finishing the business.

Ag. No, no, my sweet Mariane! we must send him off with eclat. You have played your part very well hitherto; keep it up but for this last time, and let Eston and I go into the closet and enjoy it.

Mar. Well then, do so: I shall please you for this once.

Enter BETTY, *in haste.*

Bet. to Mar. Sir Loftus is just coming up the side path, madam, and he'll be at the door immediately.

Ag. I'll run and bring Eston directly.   [EXIT.

Mar. (*Looking at the door of the closet.*) Yes, it is very thin: they will hear well, and see through the key hole.

Re-enter AGNES *with* MISS ESTON, *in a great hurry.*

Est. La! I have torn my gown in my haste.

Ag. Come along, come along.

Est. It it is not so bad a tear though as Mrs. Thomson got the—

Ag. Come, come, we must not stay here. (*Pushes* Eston *into the closet, and follows.* Mariane *and* Betty *place a table with books, and a chair, near the front of the stage.*)

Est. (*Looking from the closet.*) La! Mariane, how I long to hear you and him begin.   I shall be so delighted!

Mar. For heaven sake shut the door! he will be here immediately. (*Shuts the door upon her, and continues to set the room in order.*)

Est. (*Looking out again.*) La! Mariane, do you know how many yards of print Lady Squat has got round her new—(Agnes *from behind, claps her hand on* Eston's *mouth, and draws her into the closet.—*Mariane *seats herself by the table, pretending to read.* EXIT Betty, *and enter* Sir LOFTUS, *a servant announcing him.*)

Sir Loft. You are very studious this morning, Miss Withrington.

Mar. (Carelessly.) Ha! how do you do?

Sir Loft. You have been well amus'd, I hope?

Mar. So, so. I must put in a mark here, and not lose my place. *(Looking on the table.)* There is no paper—O, there is some on the other table: pray do fetch it me! *(Pointing to a table at the bottom of the stage.)* I am very lazy. *(Sits down again indolently.)*

Sir Loft. (Fetching the paper, and presenting it with a condescending yet self-important air.) I have the honour to obey you, ma'am.

Mar. I thank you; you are a very serviceable creature, I am sure.

Sir Loft. (Drawing himself up proudly, but immediately correcting himself.) I am always happy to serve Miss Withrington.

Mar. O! I know very well the obliging turn of your disposition. *(Tosses her arm upon the table, and throws down a book.)* I am very stupid this morning. (Sir Loftus *picks up the book, and gives it to her rather sulkily; and she in receiving it drops an ivory ball under the table.)* Bless me! What is the matter with all these things? pray lift it for me, good Sir Loftus! I believe you must creep

2

under the table for it though. (*He stoops under the table with a very bad grace, and she slyly gives it a touch with her foot, which makes it run to the other side of the stage.*) Nay, you must go further off for it now. I am very troublesome.

Sir Loft. (*Goes after it rather unwillingly, and presenting it to her with still a worse grace.*) Madam, this is more honour than I—(*mumbling.*)

Mar. O, no! Sir Loftus, it is only you that are too good. (*Lolling carelessly in her chair.*) It is so comfortable to have such a good creature by one! your fine fashionable men are admired to be sure, but I dont know how, I feel always restrained in their company. With a good obliging creature like you now, I can be quite at my ease: I can just desire you to do any thing.

Sir Loft. Upon my honour, madam, you flatter me very much indeed. Upon my honour, I must say, I am rather at a loss to conceive how I have merited these commendations.

Mar. O! Sir Loftus, you are too humble, too diffident of yourself. I know very well the obliging turn of your disposition to every body.

Sir Loft. (*aside.*) Damn it! is she an ideot? (*aloud.*) Your good opinion, madam, does me a great deal of honour, but I assure you, ma'am, it is more than I deserve. I have great pleasure in serving Miss Withrington;—to be at the service of every body is an extent of benevolence I by no means pretend to.

Mar. Now why are you so diffident, Sir Loftus?

Did not old Mrs. Mumblecake tell me the other day, how you ran nine times to the apothecary's to fetch green salve to rub her monkey's tail.

Sir Loft. She told you a damn'd lie then! (*Biting his lip, and walking up and down with hasty strides.*) Damn it! this is beyond all bearing! I run nine times to the apothecary's to fetch green salve for her monkey's tail! If the cursed hag says so again I'll bury her alive!

Mar. Nay, dont be angry about it. I'm sure I thought it very good in you, and I said so to every body.

Sir Loft. You have been so obliging as tell all the world too?

Mar. And why should not I have the pleasure of praising you?

Sir Loft. Hell and the devil! (*Turning on his heel, and striding up and down, and muttering as he goes, whilst she sits carelessly with her arms crossed.*)

Mar. My good Sir Loftus, you will tire yourself. Had you not better be seated?

Sir Loft. (*Endeavouring to compose himself.*) The influence you have over me, ma'am, gets the better of every thing. I would not have you mistake my character, however; if love engages me in your service you ought to receive it so. I have been less profuse of these attentions to women of the very first rank and fashion; I might therefore have hoped that you would lend a more favourable ear to my passion.

Mar. Indeed you wrong me. You dont know

how favourable my ear may be disposed : sit down here and tell me all about it. (*Sir Loftus revolts again at her familiarity, but stifles his pride and sits down by her.*)

Sir Loft. Permit me to say, madam, that it is time we should come to an explanation of each other's sentiments.

Mar. Whenever you please, sir.

Sir Loft. (*Bowing.*) I hope then, I may be allowed to presume, that my particular attentions to you, pardon me, ma'am, have not been altogether disagreeable to you.

Mar. O! not at all, Sir Loftus.

Sir Loft. (*Bowing again.*) I will presume then, still farther, ma'am, and declare to you, that from the very day which gave birth to my passion, I have not ceased to think of you with the most ardent tenderness.

Mar. La! Sir Loftus, was it not of a Wednesday ?

Sir Loft. (*Fretted.*) Upon my word I am not so very accurate: it might be Wednesday, or Friday, or any day.

Mar. Of a Friday, do you think? it runs strangely in my head that we saw one another first of a Wednesday.

Sir Loft. (*Very much fretted.*) I say, ma'am, the day which gave birth to my love—

Mar. O! very true! You might see me first of a Wednesday, and yet not fall in love with me till the Friday. (*Sir Loftus starts up in a passion, and strides up and down.*—Mariane *rising from her seat carelessly.*) I wonder where William has put the nuts I bought for Miss Eston's squirrel. I think I hear a mouse in the cupboard. (*Goes to the bottom of the room, and opens a small cupboard in the wall, whilst* Sir Loftus *comes forward to the front.*)

Sir Loft. (*aside.*) Damn her freaks! I wish the devil had the wooing of her. (*Pauses.*) I must not lose her for a trifle though; but when she is once secured, I'll be revenged! I'll vex her! I'll drive the spirit out of her. (*Aloud, as she comes forward from the cupboard.*) My passion for you, Miss Withrington, is too generous and disinterested to merit this indifference.

Mar. I'm glad they have not eat the nuts though.

Sir Loft. (*aside.*) Curse her and her nuts! I'll tame her! (*aloud.*) My sentiments for you, ma'am, are of so delicate and tender a nature, they do indeed deserve your indulgence. Tell me then, can the most disinterested, the most fervent love, make any impression on your heart? I can no longer exist in this state of anxiety! at your feet let me implore you— (*Seems about to kneel, but rather unwilling, as if he wished to be prevented.*)

Mar. Pray, Sir Loftus, dont kneel there! my maid has spilt oil on the floor.

Sir Loft. Since you will not permit me to have the pleasure of kneeling at—

Mar. Nay, I will not deprive you of the pleasure—There is no oil spilt here. (*Pointing to a part of the floor very near the closet door.*)

Sir Loft. I see it would be disagreeable to you.

Mar. I see very well you are not inclined to condescend so far.

Sir Loft. (*Kneeling directly.*) Believe me, madam, the pride, the pleasure of my life, is to be devoted to the most adorable—(Mariane *gives a significant cough, and* Agnes *and* Eston *burst from the closet, the door opening on the outside, comes against* Sir Loftus *as he kneels, and lays him sprawling on the floor.*)

Ag. Est. and Mar. (*Speaking together.*) O Sir Loftus! poor Sir Loftus! (*All coming about him, pretending to assist him to get up, but in reality hindering him.*)

Sir Loft. Damn their bawling! they will bring the whole family here!

Enter Mr. WITHRINGTON *and* OPAL, *and* Sir Loftus, *mad with rage, makes a desperate effort, and gets upon his legs.* Opal *stands laughing at him without any ceremony, whilst he bites his lips, and draws himself up haughtily.*

Mar. to Sir Loft. I'm afraid you have hurt yourself?

Sir Loft. (*Shortly.*) No, ma'am.

Ag. Hav'nt you rubbed the skin of your shins, Sir Loftus?

Sir Loft. No, ma'am.

6

Est. Nor off your toes, Sir Loftus?

Sir Loft. No, ma'am.

Ag. I'm sure he has hurt his poor dear nose, but he is ashamed to own it.

Sir Loft. Neither toes nor nose! Devil take it!

With. Get along, girls, and dont torment this poor man any longer. I am afraid, Sir Loftus, the young gipsies have been making a fool of you.

Sir Loft. Sir, it is neither in your power nor their's to make a fool of me.

Op. Ha, ha, ha, ha! 'Faith Prettyman you must forgive me! ha, ha, ha, ha! I never thought in my life to have caught you at such low prostrations. But dont be so angry, man! though you do make a confounded silly figure, it must be confess'd. Ha, ha, ha, ha!

Sir Loft. to Op. Sir, your impertinence and yourself are equally contemptible: and I desire you would no longer take the trouble of intruding yourself into my company, nor of affronting me, as you have hitherto done, with your awkward imitation of my figure and address.

Op. What the devil do you mean? I imitate your figure and address! I scorn to—I will not deny that I may have insensibly acquired a little of them both for—for—*(Hesitating.)*

Ag. For he has observed people laughing at him of late.

Sir Loft. (Turning on his heel.) He is beneath my resentment.

Mar. Be not so angry, good Sir Loftus! let us

T

end this business for the present, and when I am at leisure to hear the remainder of your declara-tions, which has been so unfortunately interrupted, I'll send and let you know.

Sir Loft. No, 'faith, madam! you have heard the last words I shall ever say to you upon the subject. A large fortune may make amends for an ordinary person, madam, but not for vulgarity and imperti-nence. Good morning. *(As he is going out enter* Servant.)

Ser. Lord Saunter, and Colonel Gorget are coming up stairs, to see how Sir Loftus Prettyman does after his fall.

Sir Loft. Hell and damnation! I'll go out by the other door.

Mar. That door is locked ; you can't go that way.

Sir Loft. I'll burst it open then. *(Runs to the door : they all get about him to prevent him.)*

Sir Loft. (Struggling.) What, is there no get-ting out from this den of devils? *(Breaks from them, and* Exit, *leaving them laughing provokingly behind him.)*

With. (Shaking his head.) This is too bad, this is too bad, young ladies! I am ashamed to have all this rioting and absurdity going on in my house.

Ag. Come away, uncle, and see him go down the back walk, from the parlour windows. I'll warrant you he'll stride it away most nobly. (Withring-ton *follows, shrugging up his shoulders.)*

[Exeunt.

ACT V.—SCENE I.

Mr. WITHRINGTON's *Library*.   Mr. WITHRING-
TON *discovered seated by a table.*

With. Who waits there ? *(Enter* SERVANT.) Tell
Miss Agnes Withrington I wish to see her. [EXIT
servant.) What an absurd fellow this Harwood is,
to be so completely bewitched with such a girl as
Agnes ! If she were like the women I remember,
there would indeed be some—(Agnes *entering
softly behind him, gives him a tap on the shoulder.)*

Ag. Well, uncle, what are you grumbling
about ? Have you lost your wager ? Harwood has
just left you, I hear.

With. I believe you may buy those trinkum,
trankum ornaments for Mariane whenever you
please.

Ag. Pray look not so ungraciously upon the
matter ! But you can't forgive him, I suppose, for
being such a ninny as to fall in love with a little
ordinary girl, eh ?

With. And so he is a ninny, and a fool, and a
very silly fellow.

Ag. Do tell me what he has been saying to
you.

With. Why, he confesses thou art ill-tempered,
that thou art freakish, that thou art extravagant ;
and that of all the friends he has spoken with upon
the subject, there is not one who will allow thee
beauty enough to make a good looking pot-girl.

Ag. Did he say so?

With. Why, something nearly equivalent to it, Agnes. Yet, notwithstanding all this, there is something about thee so unaccountably delightful to him, that, poor as thou art, he will give up the fair hopes of opulence, and the pleasures of freedom, to watch for thee, drudge for thee, pinch himself for thee, if thou wilt have the condescension, in return, to plague and torment him for life.

Ag. Foolish enough indeed, yet heaven bless him for it! What a fortunate woman am I! I sought a disinterested lover, and I have found a most wonderful one.

With. I dare say you think yourself very fortunate.

Ag. And dont you, likewise, my good sir? but you seem displeased at it.

With. You guess rightly enough: I must speak without disguise, Agnes, I am not pleased.

Ag. Ah! his want of fortune—

With. Poo! you know very well I despise all mercenary balancing of property. It is not that which disturbs me. To be the disinterested choice of a worthy man is what every woman, who means to marry at all, would be ambitious of; and a point in regard to her marriage, which a woman of fortune would be unwilling to leave doubtful. But there are men whose passions are of such a violent over-bearing nature, that love in them, may be considered as a disease of the mind; and the object of it claims no more perfection or pre-eminence amongst women, than chalk, lime, or oatmeal may do amongst dainties, because some diseased stomachs do prefer them to all things. Such men as these, we sometimes see attach themselves even to ugliness and infamy, in defiance of honour and decency. With such men as these, women of sense and refinement can never be happy; nay, to be willingly the object of their love is disrespect-able. *(Pauses.)* But you dont care for all this, I suppose? It does well enough for an old uncle to perplex himself with these niceties: it is you yourself the dear man happens to love, and none of those naughty women I have been talking of. So all is very right. *(Pauses, and she seems thoughtful.)*

Ag. *(Assuming a grave and more dignified air.)* No, sir, you injure me: prove that his love for me is stronger than his love of virtue, and I will—

With. What will you do, Agnes?

Ag. I will give him up for ever.

With. Ay, there spoke a brave girl! you deserve the best husband in Christendom for this.

Ag. Nay, my husband-hunting will end here. If Harwood endures not the test, I will indeed re-nounce him, but no other man shall ever fill his place.

With. Well, well, we shall see, we shall see. *(Walks up and down. She is thoughtful.)* You are very thoughtful, Agnes; I fear I have distres-sed you.

Ag. You have distressed me, yet I thank you for it. I have been too presumptuous, I have ventured farther than I ought. Since it is so, I will not shrink from the trial. *(Pauses.)* Dont you think he will go through it honourably ?

With. (Shaking his head.) Indeed I know not— I hope he will.

Ag. You hope? I thank you for that word, my dear sir ! I hope he will too. *(She remains thoughtful: he takes a turn or two cross the stage.)*

With. (Clapping her shoulder affectionately.) What are you thinking of, niece?

Ag. How to set about this business.

With. And how will you do it ?

Ag. I will write a letter to Lady Fade, asking pardon for having told some malicious falsehoods of her, to a relation of whom she is dependant upon, and begging she will make up the matter, and forgive me ; promising at the same time, most humbly, if she will not expose me for this time, never to offend so any more. Next time he comes I will make him direct the letter himself, that when it falls into his hands again, he may have no doubt of its authenticity. Will this do ?

With. Yes, very well. If he loves you after this, his love is not worth the having.

Ag. Ah, uncle ! you are very hard hearted ! But you are very right : I know you are very right. Pray does not Royston lodge in the same house with Harwood ?

With. He does.

Ag. I wish, by his means, we could conceal ourselves somewhere in his apartments, where we might see Harwood have the letter put into his hands, and observe his behaviour. I dont know any body else who can do this for us : do you think you could put him into good humour again?

With. I rather think I can, for he hath still a favour to ask of me.

Ag. We must give him a part to act ; do you think he can do it?

With. He is a very blundering fellow, but he will be so flattered with being let into the secret, that I know he will do his best.

Enter MARIANE.

Mar. What have you been about so long together ?

With. Hatching a new plot, girl ! and we set about it directly too.

Mar. I am very sure the plot is of your own hatching, then, for I never saw Agnes with any thing of this kind in her head, wear such a grave spiritless face upon it before.

With. You are mistaken, ma'am, it is of her own contrivance, but you shall know nothing about it. And I give you warning that this shall be the last of them, if you have got any more poor devils on your hands to torment, do it quickly ; for I will have an end put to all this foolery. I will have my family put in order again, and well dressed people to drink tea with me, as I used to have, instead of all this up and down irregular kind of living, which I abhor.

Mar. Very well, uncle, I have just been following your advice. I have discarded Sir Ullock O'Grady, and I have only now poor Opal to reward for his services. I have got a promise of marriage from him, in which he forfeits ten thousand pounds if he draws back, I shall torment him with this a little. It was an extraordinary thing to be sure for an heiress to demand, but I told him it was the fashion ; and now that he has bound himself so securely, he is quite at heart's ease, and thinks every thing snug and well settled.

Enter ROYSTON, *a Servant announcing him.*

With. Your servant, Mr. Royston, I am very glad to see you. Dont start at seeing the ladies with me, I know my niece, Mariane, and you have had a little misunderstanding, but when I have explained the matter to you, you will be friends with her again, and laugh at it yourself.

Roy. (coldly.) I have the honour to wish the ladies good morning.

With. Nay, cousin, you dont understand how it is ; these girls have been playing tricks upon every man they have met with since they came here ; and when that wild creature, *(pointing to* Mariane,) was only laughing at the cheat she had passed upon them all, which I shall explain to you presently, you thought she was laughing at you;

shake hands, and be friends with her, cousin; nobody minds what a foolish girl does.

Roy. (With his face brightening up.) O! for that matter, I mind these things as little as any body, cousin Withrington. I have too many affairs of importance in my hands, to attend to such little matters as these. I am glad the young lady had a hearty laugh with all my soul; and I shall be happy to see her as merry again whenever she has a mind to it. I mind it! no, no, no!

Mar. I thank you, sir, and I hope we shall be merry again, when you shall have your own share of the joke.

Roy. Yes, yes, we shall be very merry. By the bye, Withrington, I came here to tell you, that I have got my business with the duke put into so good a train, that it can hardly misgive.

With. I am happy to hear it.

Roy. You must know I have set very artfully about it, cousin; but I dare say you would guess as much, he, he, he! You know me of old, eh? I have got Mr. Cullyfool to ask it for me on his own account; I have bribed an old-house-keeper, who is to interest a great lady in my favour; I have called eleven times on his grace's half cousin, till she has fairly promised to write to my lady dutchess upon the business; I have written to the steward, and promised his son all my interest at next election, if he has any mind to stand for our borough, you know, and I have applied by a friend—No, no, he has applied through the medium of another friend, or rather, I believe, by that friend's wife, or aunt, or some way or other, I dont exactly remember, but it is a very good channel, I know.

With. O! I make no doubt of it.

Roy. Nay, my landlady, has engaged her apothecary's wife to speak to his grace's physician about it; and a medical man, you know, sometimes asks a favour with great advantage, when a patient believes that his life is in his hands. The duke has got a most furious fit of gout, and it has been in his stomach too, ha, ha, ha, ha!— If we can't succeed without it, I have a friend who will offer a round sum for me, at last, but I hope this will not be necessary. Pray, do you know of any other good channel to solicit by?

With. 'Faith, Royston! you have found out too many roads to one place already, I fear you'll lose your way amongst them all.

Roy. Nay, nay, cousin, I won't be put off so. I have been told this morning you are acquainted with Mr. Sucksop, the duke's greatest friend and adviser. Come, come! you must use your interest for me.

With. Well, then, come into the other room, and we shall speak about it. I have a favour to ask of you too.

Roy. My dear sir, any favour in my power you may absolutely command at all times. I'll follow you, cousin. (*Goes to the door with* Withrington *with great alacrity, but, recollecting that he has for-*

l

gotten to pay his compliments to the ladies, hurries back again, and, after making several very profound bows to them, follows Withrington *into another room.)*

Mar. (Imitating him.) Ha, ha, ha, ha !

Ag. Softly, Mariane ; let us leave this room, if you must laugh, for he will overhear you.

[EXEUNT.

SCENE II.

ROYSTON's *Lodgings : enter* ROYSTON, *conducting in* AGNES, MARIANE, *and* WITHRINGTON.

Roy. Now, pray compose yourselves, young ladies, and sit down a little. I'll manage every thing : dont give yourselves any trouble; I'll set the whole plot a going.

With. We depend entirely upon you, Royston.

Roy. I know you do, many a one depends upon me, cousin Withrington. I'll shew you how I'll manage it. Jonathan, come here, Jonathan ! *(Enter* Jonathan.) Bring me that screen from the other room. *(Exit* Jonathan.) We'll place it here, if you please, cousin, and then you and the ladies can stand as snugly behind it, as kings and queens in a puppet-show, till your time comes to appear. *(Enter* Jonathan *with screen.)* Come hither with it, Jonathan: place it here. *(Pointing.)* No, no, jolter-head, nearer the wall with it. *(Going behind it, and coming out again.)* It will do better a little more to this side, for then it will be farther from the window.

Ag. O ! it will do very well, sir, you take too much trouble.

Roy. Trouble, my dear ma'am ! if it were a hundred times more trouble, I should be happy to serve you. I dont mind trouble, if I can get the thing done cleverly and completely. That's my way of doing things. No, it dont stand to please me yet, it is too near the door now, and the ladies may catch cold, perhaps.

Ag. (*Very uneasy.*) Indeed, it stands very well! Harwood will be here before we are ready.

Roy. to Jon. Blockhead, that thou art ! can'st thou not set it up even ? Now that will do. (*Getting behind it.*) This will do. (*Coming out again.*) Yes, this will do to a nicety.

Mar. (*Aside.*) Heaven be praised this grand matter is settled at last !

Roy. Now, he'll think it odd, perhaps, that I have a screen in my room; but I have a trick for that, ladies; I'll tell him I mean to purchase lands in Canada, and have been looking over the map of America. (Agnes *looks to* Withrington *very uneasy.*)

With. Dont do that, Royston, for then he will examine the screen.

Roy. Or, I may say, there is a chink in the wall, and I placed it to keep out the air.

Ag. No, no, that wont do. For heaven's sake, sir!

Roy. Then I shall just say, I love to have a screen in my room, for I am used to it at home.

Mar. Bless me, Mr. Royston! can't you just leave it alone, and he'll take no notice of it.

Roy. O! if he takes no notice of it, that is a different thing, Miss Withrington; but dont be uneasy, I'll manage it all : I'll conduct the whole business.

Ag. (*Aside to* Withrington.) O! my good sir! this fool will ruin every thing.

With. Be quiet, Agnes, we are in for it now.

Roy. Let me remember my lesson too. Here is the letter for him, with the seal as naturally broken, as if the lady had done it herself. Harwood will wonder, now, how I came to know about all this. 'Faith! I believe, he thinks me a strange diving, penetrating, kind of a genius, already, and he is not far wrong, perhaps. You know me, cousin Withrington : ha, ha, ha, ha! You know me.

Ag. O! I wish it were over, and we were out of this house again!

Roy. Dont be uneasy, ma'am, I'll manage every thing. Jonathan, *(Enter* Jonathan,) dont you go and tell Mr. Harwood that I have got company here.

Jon. No, no, your honour, I knows better than that ; for the ladies are to be behind the screen, sir, and he must know nothing of the matter, to be sure. I'ficken! it will be rare sport!

Ag. (*Starting.*) I hear a knock at the door.

Roy. It is him, I dare say, run Jonathan.
[EXIT, *Jonathan.*

Ag. Come, come, let us hide ourselves. *(All get behind the screen but* Royston.)

Roy. Ay, ay, it will do very well. *(Looking at the screen.)*

Ag. (Behind.) Mariane, dont breathe so loud.

Mar. (*Behind.*) I dont breathe loud.

Ag. (Behind.) Do uncle draw in the edge of your coat.

With. (*Behind.*) Poo, silly girl! they can't see a bit of it.

Enter Colonel HARDY *and* HARWOOD.

Roy. Ha! your servant, my dear Colonel. How goes it, Harwood? I bid my man tell you I was alone, and very much disposed for your good company; but I am doubly fortunate. *(Bowing to the* Colonel.)

Col. Indeed, Royston, I have been pretty much with him these two days past, and I dont believe he gives me great thanks for my company. I am like an old horse running after a colt, the young devil never fails to turn now and then, and give him a kick for his pains.

Har. Nay, my good friend, I must be an ass's colt, then. I am sure, I mean it not, but I am not happy, and I fear I have been peevish with you.

Roy. (*Attempting to look arch.*) Peevish, and all that, perhaps, the young man is in love, Colonel.

Col. No more, if you please, Royston : we are to speak of this no more.

Enter JONATHAN.

Jon. Did your honour call ?

Roy. No, sirrah. (Jonathan *goes, as if he were looking for something, and takes a sly peep behind the screen, to see if they are all there.*) What are you peeping there for ? get along, you hound ! Does he want to make people believe I keep rary shews behind the wainscot ? (EXIT, Jonathan.) But as I was a saying, Colonel, perhaps the young man is in love. He, he, he !

Col. No, no, let us have no more of it.

Roy. But 'faith, I know that he is so ! and I know the lady too. She is a cousin of my own, and I am as well acquainted with her, as I am with my own dog.—But you dont ask me what kind of a girl she is. (*To the* Colonel.)

Col. Give over now, Royston : she is a very good girl, I dare say.

Roy. Well, you may think so, but—(*Making significant faces*) But—I should not say all I know of my own cousin, to be sure, but—

Har. What are all those cursed grimaces for ? Her faults are plain and open as her perfections : these she disdains to conceal, and the others it is impossible.

Roy. Softly, Harwood, dont be in a passion, unless you would imitate your mistress ; for she has not the gentlest temper in the world.

Har. Well, well, I love her the better for it.
I can't bear your insipid passionless women : I
would as soon live upon sweet curd all my life,
as attach myself to one of them.

Roy. She is very extravagant.

Har. Heaven bless the good folks ! would they
have a man to give up the woman of his heart,
because she likes a bit of lace upon her petticoat.

Roy. Well, but she is——

Col. Devil take you, Royston ! can't you hold
your tongue about her ? you see he can't bear it.

Roy. (*Making signs to the Colonel.*) Let me
alone ; I know when to speak, and when to hold
my tongue, as well as another. Indeed, Harwood, I am your friend ; and though the lady is
my relation, I must say, I wish you had made a
better choice. I have discovered something in
regard to her this morning, which shews her to
be a very improper one. I cannot say, however,
that I have discovered any thing which surprised
me, I know her too well.

Har. (*Vehemently.*) You are imposed upon by
some damn'd falsehood.

Roy. But I have proof of what I say ; the lady
who is injured by her, gave me this letter to shew
to Mr. Withrington. (*Taking out the letter.*)

Har. It is some fiend who wants to undermine
her, and has forged that scrawl to serve her
spiteful purpose.

Roys. I would be glad it were so, my dear

friend ; but Lady Fade is a woman, whose veracity has never been suspected.

Har. Is it from Lady Fade? Give it me. *(Snatching the letter.)*

Roy. It is Agnes's hand, is it not?

Har. It is, at least, a good imitation of it.

Roy. Read the contents, pray!

Har. Madam, what I have said to the prejudice of your ladyship's character to your relation, Mr. Worthy, I am heartily sorry for ; and I am ready to beg pardon on my knees if you desire it; to acknowledge before Mr. Worthy himself, that it is a falsehood, or make any other reparation, in a private way, that you may desire. Let me, then, conjure your ladyship not to expose me, and I shall ever remain your most penitent and grateful A. Withrington.

Roy. The lady would not be so easily pacified, though ; for she blackened her character, in order to make her best friend upon earth quarrel with her; so she gave me the letter to shew to her uncle. Is it forged, think you?

Har. It is possible !—I will venture to say— Nay, I am sure it is.

Roy. If it is, there is one circumstance which may help to discover the author, it is directed by a different hand on the back. Look at it.

Har. (In great perturbation.) Is it? *(Turns hastily the folds of the letter, but his hand trembles so much, he can't find the back.)*

Col. My dear Harwood! this is the back of

U

the letter ; and methinks the writing is somewhat
like your own. (Harwood *looks at it*; *then stag-
gering back, throws himself into a chair, which
happens to be behind him, and covers his upper face
with his hand.*)

Col. My dear Harwood !

Roy. See how his lips; quiver, and his bosom
heaves ! Let us unbutton him : I fear he is going
into a fit. (Agnes *comes from behind the screen in
a fright, and* Withrington *pulls her in again.*)

Col. (With great tenderness.) My dear Harwood !

Har. *(With a broken voice.)* I'll go to mine own
chamber. *(Gets up hastily from his chair, and then
falls back again in a faint.)*

Col. He's gone off.

Roys. Help, help, here ! *(Running about.)* Who
has got hartshorn, or lavender, or water! help
here. *(They all come from behind the screen. Agnes runs to* Harwood, *and sprinkles him over with
lavender, rubbing his temples, &c. whilst* Colonel
Hardy *stares at them all in amazement.)*

Ag. Alas! we have carried this too far? Harwood ! my dear Harwood !

Col. to Roys. What is all this ?

Roys. I thought we should amaze you. I knew
I should manage it.

Col. You have managed finely indeed, to put
Harwood into such a state, with your mummery.

Ag. Will he not come to himself again ! get
some water, Mariane—See how pale he is. *(He*

recovers.) O! he recovers! Harwood! do you know me, Harwood?

Har. (*Looking upon* Agnes, *and shrinking back from her.*) Ha! what has brought you here? leave me! leave me! I am wretched enough already.

Ag. I come to bring you relief, my dear Harwood.

Har. No, madam, it is misery you bring. We must part for ever.

Ag. O! uncle! do you hear that? He says we must part for ever.

With. (*Taking hold of* Agnes.) Dont be in such a hurry about it.

Har. (*Rising up.*) How came you here? (*to* Withrington,) and these ladies?

Roys. O! it was all my contrivance.

With. Pray now, Royston, be quiet a little— Mr. Harwood, I will speak to you seriously. I see you are attached to my niece, and I confess she has many faults; but you are a man of sense, and with you she will make a more respectable figure in the world than with any other. I am anxious for her welfare, and if you will marry her I will give her such a fortune as will make it no longer an imprudent step to follow your inclinations.

Har. No, sir, you shall keep your fortune and your too bewitching niece together. For her sake I would have renounced all ambition, I would have shared with her poverty and neglect, I would have borne with all her faults and weaknesses of nature, I would have toiled, I would have bled for her, but I can never yoke myself with unworthiness.

Ag. (Wiping her eyes, and giving two skips upon the floor.) O! admirable! admirable! speak to him, uncle! tell him all, my dear uncle! for I can't say a word.

Col. (Aside to Royston.) Isn't she a little wrong in the head, Royston?

With. Give me your hand, Harwood: you are a noble fellow, and you shall marry this little girl of mine after all. This story of the letter and Lady Fade, was only a concerted one amongst us, to prove what mettle you are made of. Agnes, to try your love, affected to be shrewish and extravagant; and afterwards, at my suggestion, to try your principles, contrived this little plot, which has just now been unravelled: but I do assure you, on the word of an honest man, there is not a better girl in the kingdom. I must own, however, she is a fanciful little toad. (Harwood *runs to* Agnes, *catches her in his arms, and runs two or three times round with her, then takes her hand and kisses it, and then puts his knee to the ground.)*

Har. My charming, my delightful Agnes! Oh! what a fool have I been! how could I suppose it.

Ag. We took some pains upon you, and it would have been hard if we could not have deceived you amongst us all.

Har. And so thou art a good girl, a very **good** girl. I know thou art. I'll be hang'd if thou hast one fault in the world.

With. No, no, Harwood, not quite so perfect. I can prove her still to be an arrant cheat; for she pretended to be careless of you when she thought of you all the day long, and she pretended to be poor with an hundred thousand pounds, independant of any one, in her possession. She is Miss Withrington the heiress, and this lady, *(pointing to* Mariane,) has only been her representative, for a time, for reasons which I shall explain to you by-and-by. (Harwood *lets go* Agnes's *hand, and steps back some paces with a certain gravity and distance in his air.)*

With. What is the matter now, Hrwood, does this cast a damp upon you?

Roys. It is a weighty distress, truly. Ha, ha, ha, ha!

Col. By heaven! this is good.

Ag. (Going up to Harwood, *and holding out her hand.)* Do not look so distantly upon me, Harwood. You was willing to marry me as a poor woman; if there is any thing in my fortune which offends you, I scatter it to the winds.

Har. My admirable girl, it is astonishment, it is something I cannot express, which overcomes, I had almost said distresses me at present. *(Presenting her to the Colonel.)* Colonel Hardy, this is the woman I have raved about, this is the woman I have boasted of, this is my Agnes. And this, Miss Withrington, is Colonel Hardy, my own, and my father's friend.

Ag. (Holding out her hand to the Colonel.) He shall be mine too. Every friend of your's shall be my friend, Harwood; but the friend of your father my most respected one.

Har. Do you hear that, Colonel?

Col. I hear it, my heart hears it, and I bless you both.

Har. to With. My dear sir, what shall I say to you for all this goodness?

Ag. Tell him he is the dearest good uncle on earth, and we will love him all our lives for it. Yes, indeed, we will, uncle, (*clapping his shoulder,*) very, very dearly.

Roys. Now, good folks, have not I managed it cleverly?

Mar. Pray let me come from the back ground a little: and since I must quit all the splendour of heiresship, I desire, at least, that I may have some respect paid me for having filled the situation so well, as the old Mayor receives the thanks of the corporation, when the new Mayor—Bless me! here comes Opal! I have not just done with it yet.

With. Your servant, Mr. Opal.

Mar. to Op. Are not you surprised to find us all here?

Op. Harwood I know is a very lucky fellow, but I knew you were here. It is impossible, you see, to escape me. But (*half aside to* Marianc) I wanted to tell you Colonel Beaumont is come to Bath. Now I should like to be introduced to him on his arrival. He will be very much the fashion I dare say, and I should like to have a friendship for him. You understand me ? You can procure this for me, I know.

With. Come, Mr. Opal, you must join in our good humour here, for we have just been making up a match. My niece, Agnes, with a large fortune bestows herself on a worthy man, who would have married her without one ; and, Mariane, who for certain reasons has assumed her character of heiress since we came to Bath, leaves all her borrowed state, in hopes that the man who would have married with a fortune, will not now forsake her.

Op. (*Stammering.*) Wh—Wh—What is all this?

Roy. (*Half aside to* Opal.) You seem disturbed, Mr. Opal, you have not been paying your addresses to her, I hope.

Op. (*Aside to* Royston.) No, not paying my addresses ; that is to say, not absolutely. I have paid her some attention to be sure.

Roy. (*Nodding significantly.*) It is well for you it is no worse.

Mar. (*Turning to* Opal, *who looks very much frightened.*) What is it you say? Dont you think I overheard it ? Not paid your addresses to me ! O ! you false man ! can you deny the declarations you have made ? the oaths you have sworn ? O ! you false man !

Op. Upon honour, madam, we men of fashion dont expect to be called to an account for every foolish thing we say.

Mar. What you have written then shall witness

against you.   Will you deny this promise of marriage in your own hand-writing ? (*Taking out a
paper.*)

Roy. (*Aside to* Opal.) What, a promise of marriage, Mr. Opal ? The devil himself could not
have put it into your head to do a worse thing
than this.

Op. (*Very frightened, but making a great exertion.*)
Dont think, ma'am, to bully me into the match.
I can prove that promise to be given to you under
the false character of an heiress, therefore your
deceit loosens the obligation.

With. Take care what you say, sir, (*to* Opal,) I
will not see my niece wronged.   The law shall do
her justice, whatever expence it may cost me.

Mar. Being an heiress or not has nothing to do
in the matter, Mr. Opal ; for you expressly say in
this promise, that my beauty and perfections alone
have induced you to engage yourself, and I will
take all the men in court to witness, whether I
am not as handsome to-day as I was yesterday.

Op. I protest there is not such a word in the
paper.

Mar. (*Holding out the paper.*) O base man ! will
you deny your own writing ?   (Opal *snatches the
paper from her, tears it to pieces.*)

Mar. (*Gathering up the scattered pieces.*) O ! I
can put them together again.   (Opal, *snatching up
one of the pieces, crams it into his mouth and chews
it.*)

Roy. Chew fast, Opal, she will snatch it out

of your mouth else. There is another bit for you. (*Offering him another piece.*)

Mar. (*Bursting into a loud laugh, in which all the company join.*) Is it very nice, Mr. Opal? You munch it up as expeditiously as a bit of plumb-cake.

Op. What the deuce does all this mean?

With. This naughty girl, Mr. Opal, has only been amusing herself with your promise, which she never meant to make any other use of; she is already engaged to a very worthy young man, who will receive with her a fortune by no means contemptible.

Op. Well, well, much good may it do him: what do I care about—(*mumbling to himself.*)

Roy. (*Clapping Opal's shoulder.*) Ha, ha, ha! dont look so foolish, man; you did not know a word of all this, now. Ha, ha, ha! how some people do get themselves into scrapes! They have no more notion of managing their affairs than if they were so many sheep. Ha, ha, ha, ha!

Enter HUMPHRY.

Humph. to Roy. I would speak a word with your honour. (*Whispers to* Royston.)

Roy. (*In a rage.*) What! given away the place! It is impossible! It is some wicked machination! it is some damn'd trick!

With. Be moderate, Royston: what has good Mr. Humphry been telling you?

Roy. O! the devil of a bite! his grace has

given away the place to a poor simpleton, who had never a soul to speak for him.

With. Who told you this, Mr. Humphry?

Humph. Truly, sir, I called upon his Grace's gentleman, just to make up a kind of acquaintance with him, as his honour desired me, and he told me it was given away this morning.

Roy. What cursed luck!

Humph. Why, says I, I thought my master was to have had it, Mr. Smoothly; and so he would, says he, but one person came to the Duke after another, teazing him about Mr. Royston, till he grew quite impatient; for there was but one of all those friends, says he, winking with his eye so, who did speak at last to the purpose, but then upon Mr. Sucksop's taking up your master's interest, he shrunk back from his word, which offended his grace very much.

Roy. Blundering blockhead!

Humph. But after all, says he, it might have come round again, if the gout had not stung him so wickedly, when in came the doctor, who has promised to cure him these three weeks, and only made it so much the worse, and upon his likewise presuming to teaze him about Mr. Royston, he fell into a violent passion, and gave away the place directly to poor Mr. Drudgewell, who had no recommendation at all, but fifteen years hard service in the office.

Roy. Well, now! well, now! you see how the world goes: simpletons and ideots carry every thing before them.

With. Nay, Royston, blame yourself too. Did not I tell you, you had found out too many roads to one place, and would lose your way amongst them?

Roy. No, no, it is all that cursed perverse fate of mine! By the Lord, half the trouble I have taken for this paltry office, would have procured some people an archbishoprick. There is Harwood, now, fortune presses herself upon him, and makes him, at one stroke, an idle gentleman for life.

Har. No, sir, an idle gentleman I will never be: my Agnes shall never be the wife of any thing so contemptible.

Ag. I thank you, Harwood; I do, indeed, look for an honourable distinction in being your wife; you shall still exert your powers in the profession you have chosen: you shall be the weak ones stay, the poor man's advocate; you shall gain fair fame in recompense, and that will be our nobility.

With. Well said, my children! you have more sense than I thought you had amongst all these whimsies. Now, let us take our leave of plots and story-telling, if you please, and all go to my house to supper. Royston shall drown his disappointment in a can of warm negus, and Mr. Opal shall have something more palatable than his last spare morsel.   [EXEUNT.

THE END OF THE TRYAL.

DE MONFORT:

A TRAGEDY.

PERSONS OF THE DRAMA.

MEN.

DE MONFORT.

REZENVELT.

COUNT FREBERG, *Friend to* De Monfort *and* Rezenvelt.

MANUEL, *Servant to* De Monfort.

JEROME, De Monfort's *old Landlord.*

GRIMBALD, *an artful knave.*

BERNARD, *a Monk.*

Monks, Gentlemen, Officers, Page, &c. &c.

WOMEN.

JANE DE MONFORT, *sister to* De Monfort.

COUNNESS FREBERG, *Wife to* Freberg.

THERESA, *Servant to the* Countess.

Abbess, Nuns, *and a* Lay Sister, Ladies, &c.

Scene, a Town in Germany.

DE MONFORT.

ACT I.—SCENE I.

JEROME's *House.* *A large old fashioned Chamber.*

Jer. (*speaking without.*) This way good masters.

Enter JEROME, *bearing a light, and followed by* Manuel, *and* Servants *carrying luggage.*

                        Rest your burdens here.
This spacious room will please the Marquis best.
He takes me unawares; but ill prepar'd:
If he had sent, e'en tho' a hasty notice,
I had been glad.
    Man.   Be not disturb'd, good Jerome;
Thy house is in most admirable order;
And they who travel o'cold winter nights
Think homeliest quarters good.
    Jer. He is not far behind?
    Man.   A little way.
(*To the servants.*) Go you and wait below till he
    arrives.
    Jer. (*Shaking* Manuel *by the hand.*) Indeed, my
    friend, I'm glad to see you here,

                2

Yet marvel wherefore.

Man. I marvel wherefore too, my honest Jerome:
But here we are, pri'thee be kind to us.

Jer. Most heartily I will. I love your master:
He is a quiet and a lib'ral man:
A better inmate never cross'd my door.

Man. Ah! but he is not now the man he was.
Lib'ral he will, God grant he may be quiet

Jer. What has befallen him ?

Man.   I cannot tell thee ;
But faith, there is no living with him now.

Jer. And yet, methinks, if I remember well,
You were about to quit his service, Manuel,
When last he left this house. You grumbled
      then.

Man. I've been upon the eve of leaving him
These ten long years ; for many times is he
So difficult, capricious, and distrustful,
He galls my nature—yet, I know not how,
A secret kindness binds me to him still.

Jer. Some, who offend from a suspicious nature,
Will afterwards such fair confession make
As turns e'en the offence into a favour.

Man. Yes, some indeed do so : so will not he ;
He'd rather die than such confession make.

Jer. Ay, thou art right, for now I call to mind
That once he wrong'd me with unjust suspicion,
When first he came to lodge beneath my roof ;
And when it so fell out that I was proved
Most guiltless of the fault, I truly thought
He would have made profession of regret :

But silent, haughty, and ungraciously
He bore himself as one offended still.
Yet shortly after, when unwittingly
I did him some slight service, o'the sudden
He overpower'd me with his grateful thanks ;
And would not be restrain'd from pressing on me
A noble recompense. I understood
His o'erstrain'd gratitude and bounty well.
And took it as he meant.

  Man.   'Tis often thus.
I would have left him many years ago,
But that with all his faults there sometimes come
Such bursts of natural goodness from his heart,
As might engage a harder churl than I
To serve him still.—And then his sister too,
A noble dame, who should have been a queen :
The meanest of her hinds, at her command,
Had fought like lions for her, and the poor,
E'en o'er their bread of poverty had bless'd her—·
She would have griev'd if I had left my Lord.

  Jer. Comes she along with him ?

  Man. No, he departed all unknown to her,
Meaning to keep conceal'd his secret route ;
But well I knew it would afflict her much,
And therefore left a little nameless billet,
Which after our departure, as I guess,
Would fall into her hands, and tell her all.
What could I do ? O 'tis a noble lady!

  Jer. All this is strange—something disturbs his
    mind—
Belike he is in love.

Man.   No, Jerome, no.
Once on a time I serv'd a noble master,
Whose youth was blasted with untoward love,
And he with hope and fear and jealousy
For ever toss'd, led an unquiet life :
Yet, when unruffled by the passing fit,
His pale wan face such gentle sadness wore
As mov'd a kindly heart to pity him ;
But Monfort, even in his calmest hour,
Still bears that gloomy sternness in his eye
Which sullenly repells all sympathy.
O no! good Jerome, no, it is not love.
    Jer. Hear I not horses trampling at the gate?
                        (Listening.)
He is arriv'd—stay thou—I had forgot—
A plague upon't! my head is so confus'd—
I will return i'the instant to receive him.
                        (EXIT *hastily.*)
    (A great bustle without. EXIT Manuel *with
    lights, and returns again lighting in* DE
    MONFORT, *as if just alighted from his
    journey.)*
    Man. Your ancient host, my lord, receives you
        gladly,
And your apartment will be soon prepar'd.
    De Mon. 'Tis well.
    Man. Where shall I place the chest you gave
        in charge ?
So please you, say my lord.
    De Mon. (Throwing himself into a chair.) Where-
        e'er thou wilt.

Man. I would not move that luggage till you
    came.   (*Pointing to certain things.*)
De Mon. Move what thou wilt, and trouble me
    no more.

    (Manuel, *with the assistance of other Servants,*
    sets about putting the things in order, and
    De Monfort *remains sitting in a thoughtful*
    posture.)

Enter JEROME, *bearing wine, &c. on a salver. As*
he approaches De Monfort, Manuel *pulls him by*
the sleeve.

Man. (*Aside to* Jerome.) No, do not now; he
    will not be disturb'd.
Jer. What not to bid him welcome to my
    house,
And offer some refreshment?
Man.   No, good Jerome.
Softly, a little while: I pri'thee do.

    (Jerome *walks softly on tip-toes, till he gets*
    near De Montford, *behind backs, then peep-*
    ing on one side to see his face.)

Jer. (*Aside to* Manuel.) Ah, Manuel, what
    an alter'd man is here!
His eyes are hollow, and his cheeks are pale—
He left this house a comely gentleman.
De Mon. Who whispers there?
Man.   'Tis your old landlord, sir:
Jer. I joy to see you here—I crave your pardon—
I fear I do intrude.—

De Mon. No, my kind host, I am oblig'd to
   thee.

Jer. How fares it with your honour?

De Mon.   Well enough.

Jer. Here is a little of the fav'rite wine

That you were wont to praise.   Pray honour me.

                              (*Fills a glass.*)

De Mon. (*After drinking.*) I thank you, Jerome,
   'tis delicious.

Jer. Ay, my dear wife did ever make it so.

De Mon. And how does she?

Jer.   Alas, my lord! she's dead.

De Mon. Well, then she is at rest.

Jer.   How well, my lord?

De Mon. Is she not with the dead, the quiet
   dead,

Where all is peace.   Not e'en the impious wretch,

Who tears the coffin from its earthy vault,

And strews the mould'ring ashes to the wind

Can break their rest.

Jer. Woe's me! I thought you would have
   griev'd for her.

She was a kindly soul!   Before she died,

When pining sickness bent her cheerless head,

She set my house in order—

And but the morning ere she breath'd her last,

Bade me preserve some flaskets of this wine,

That should the Lord De.Monfort come again

His cup might sparkle still.   (De Monfort *walks*

               across the stage, and wipes his eyes.)

Indeed I fear I have distress'd you, sir:

I surely thought you would be griev'd for her.

De Mon. (*Taking* Jerome's *hand.*) I am, my
    friend.   How long has she been dead?

Jer. Two sad long years.

De Mon.   Would she were living still!
I was too troublesome, too heedless of her.

Jer. O no! she lov'd to serve you.

                    (*Loud knocking without.*)

De Mon. What fool comes here, at such un-
    timely hours,
To make this cursed noise. (*To* Manuel.)   Go to
    the gate.   [EXIT Manuel.
All sober citizens are gone to bed;
It is some drunkards on their nightly rounds,
Who mean it but in sport.

Jer. I hear unusual voices—here they come.

Re-enter MANUEL, *shewing in Count* FREBERG *and*
his LADY.

Freb. (*Running to embrace* De Monfort.)   My
    dearest Monfort! most unlook'd-for pleasure.
Do I indeed embrace thee here again?
I saw thy servant standing by the gate,
His face recall'd, and learnt the joyful tidings.
Welcome, thrice welcome here!

De Mon. I thank thee, Freberg, for this friendly
    visit,
And this fair Lady too.   (*Bowing to the Lady.*)

Lady.   I fear, my Lord,
We do intrude at an untimely hour:

But now returning from a midnight mask,
My husband did insist that we should enter.

   Freb. No, say not so ; no hour untimely call,
Which doth together bring long absent friends.
Dear Monfort, wherefore hast thou play'd so sly,
To come upon us thus all suddenly ?

   De Mon. O ! many varied thoughts do cross
       our brain,
Which touch the will, but leave the memory
       trackless ;
And yet a strange compounded motive make
Wherefore a man should bend his evening walk
To th' east or west, the forest or the field.
Is it not often so ?

   Freb. I ask no more, happy to see you here
From any motive.   There is one behind,
Whose presence would have been a double bliss :
Ah ! how is she ? The noble Jane de Monfort.

   De Mon. (*Confused.*)   She is—I have—I have
      left my sister well.

   Lady. (*To* Freberg.)   My Freberg, you are
      heedless of respect :
You surely meant to say the Lady Jane.

   Freb. Respect ! No, Madam ; Princess, Em-
      press, Queen,
Could not denote a creature so exalted
As this plain native appellation doth,
The noble Jane de Monfort.

   Lady. (*Turning from him displeased to* Monfort.)
You are fatigued, my Lord ; you want repose ;

Say, should we not retire?

Freb.   Ha! is it so?

My friend, your face is pale, have you been ill?

De Mon. No, Freberg, no; I think I have
  been well.

Freb. (*Shaking his head.*) I fear thou hast not,
  Monfort—Let it pass.

We'll re-establish thee : we'll banish pain.

I will collect some rare, some cheerful friends,

And we shall spend together glorious hours,

That gods might envy.   Little time so spent

Doth far outvalue all our life beside.

This is indeed our life, our waking life,

The rest dull breathing sleep.

De Mon. Thus, it is true, from the sad years of
  life

We sometimes do short hours, yea minutes strike,

Keen, blissful, bright, never to be forgotten ;

Which thro' the dreary gloom of time o'erpast

Shine like fair sunny spots on a wild waste.

But few they are, as few the heaven-fir'd souls

Whose magick power creates them.   Bless'd art
  thou,

If in the ample circle of thy friends

Thou canst but boast a few.

Freb. Judge for thyself: in truth I do not boast.

There is amongst my friends, my later friends,

A most accomplish'd stranger.   New to Amberg,

But just arriv'd ; and will ere long depart.

I met him in Franconia two years since.

He is so full of pleasant anecdote,

So rich, so gay, so poignant is his wit,
Time vanishes before him as he speaks,
And ruddy morning thro' the lattice peeps
Ere night seems well begun.

De Mon.   How is he call'd ?

Freb. I will surprise thee with a welcome face :
I will not tell thee now.

Lady to Mon. I have, my Lord, a small request
     to make,
And must not be denied.   I too may boast
Of some good friends, and beauteous country-
     women :
To-morrow night I open wide my doors
To all the fair and gay ; beneath my roof
Musick, and dance, and revelry shall reign.
I pray you come and grace it with your presence.

De Mon. You honour me too much to be denied.

Lady. I thank you, Sir ; and in return for this,
We shall withdraw, and leave you to repose.

Freb. Must it be so ? Good night—sweet sleep
     to thee. (*To* De Monfort.)

De Mon. to Freb. Good night. (*To Lady.*)
     Good-night, fair Lady.

Lady.   Farewel !

     [EXEUNT Freberg *and* Lady.]

De Mon. to Jer. I thought Count Freberg had
     been now in France.

Jer. He meant to go, as I have been inform'd.

De Mon. Well, well, prepare my bed ; I will to
     rest.   [EXIT Jerome.

De Mon. (*alone.*) I know not how it is, my
  heart stands back,
And meets not this man's love.—Friends ! rarest
  friends !
Rather than share his undiscerning praise
With every table wit, and book-form'd sage,
And paltry poet puling to the moon,
I'd court from him proscription ; yea abuse,
And think it proud distinction.   [Exit.

SCENE II.

A Small Apartment in Jerome's *House : a table and
breakfast set out.   Enter* De Monfort, *followed
by* Manuel, *and sets himself down by the table,
with a cheerful face.*

De Mon. Manuel, this morning's sun shines
  pleasantly :
These old apartments too are light and cheerful.
Our landlord's kindness has reviv'd me much ;
He serves as though he lov'd me. This pure air
Braces the listless nerves, and warms the blood :
I feel in freedom here.
        (*Filling a cup of coffee, and drinking.*)
Man.   Ah ! sure, my Lord,
No air is purer than the air at home.
De Mon. Here can I wander with assured steps,
Nor dread, at every winding of the path,
Lest an abhorred serpent cross my way,
And move—(*Stopping short.*)
Man.   What says your honour ?

There are no serpents in our pleasant fields.

De Mon. Think'st thou there are no serpents in
    the world
But those who slide along the grassy sod,
And sting the luckless foot that presses them?
There are who in the path of social life
Do bask their spotted skins in Fortune's sun,
And sting the soul—Ay, till its healthful frame
Is chang'd to secret, fest'ring, sore disease,
So deadly is the wound.

Man. Heaven guard your honour from such
    horrid skathe:
They are but rare, I hope?

De Mon. (*Shaking his head.*) We mark the hol-
    low eye, the wasted frame,
The gait disturb'd of wealthy honour'd men,
But do not know the cause.

Man. 'Tis very true.   God keep you well, my
    Lord!

De Mon. I thank thee, Manuel, I am very well.
I shall be gay too, by the setting sun.
I go to revel it with sprightly dames,
And drive the night away.
        (*Filling another cup, and drinking.*)

Man. I should be glad to see your honour gay.

De Mon. And thou too shalt be gay.   There,
    honest Manuel,
Put these broad pieces in thy leathern purse,
And take at night a cheerful jovial glass.
Here is one too, for Bremer; he loves wine;
And one for Jaques: be joyful all together.

Enter Servant.

Ser. My Lord, I met e'en now, a short way off,
Your countryman the Marquis Rezenvelt.

De Mon. (*Starting from his seat, and letting the
cup fall from his hand.*) Who, say'st thou?

Ser.   Marquis Rezenvelt, an' please you.

De Mon. Thou ly'st—it is not so—it is impossible.

Ser. I saw him with these eyes, plain as yourself.

De Mon. Fool! 'tis some passing stranger thou
hast seen,
And with a hideous likeness been deceiv'd.

Ser. No other stranger could deceive my sight.

De Mon. (*Dashing his clenched hand violently
upon the table, and overturning every thing.*)
Heaven blast thy sight! it lights on
nothing good.

Ser. I surely thought no harm to look upon
him.

De Mon. What, dost thou still insist? Him
must it be?
Does it so please thee well? (*Servant endeavours
to speak*) hold thy damn'd tongue.
By heaven I'll kill thee. (*Going furiously up to him.*)

Man. (*In a soothing voice.*) Nay harm him not,
my Lord; he speaks the truth;
I've met his groom, who told me certainly
His Lord is here. I should have told you so,
But thought, perhaps, it might displease your
honour.

De Mon. (*Becoming all at once calm, and turning*
    sternly to Manuel.) And how dar'st thou
    to think it would displease me?
What is't to me who leaves or enters Amberg?
But it displeases me, yea ev'n to frenzy,
That every idle fool must hither come
To break my leisure with the paltry tidings
Of all the cursed things he stares upon.
      (Servant *attempts to speak*—De Monfort
      stamps with his foot.)
Take thine ill-favour'd visage from my sight,
And speak of it no more.   [EXIT Servant.
  De Mon. And go thou too; I choose to be
    alone.   [EXIT Manuel.
    (De Monfort *goes to the door by which they*
    went out; opens it, and looks.)
But is he gone indeed? Yes, he is gone.
    (*Goes to the opposite door, opens it, and looks:*
    then gives loose to all the fury of gesture, and
    walks up and down in great agitation.)
It is too much: by heaven it is too much!
He haunts me—stings me—like a devil haunts—
He'll make a raving maniack of me—Villain!
The air wherein thou draw'st thy fulsome breath
Is poison to me—Oceans shall divide! (*Pauses.*)
But no; thou think'st I fear thee, cursed reptile!
And hast a pleasure in the damned thought.
Though my heart's blood should curdle at thy sight,
I'll stay and face thee still.
      (*Knocking at the chamber door.*)
  2   Ha! Who knocks there?

Freberg. (*Without.*) It is thy friend, De Monfort.
De Mon. (*Opening the door.*) Enter, then.

Enter FREBERG.

Freb. (*Taking his hand kindly.*) How art thou
    now ? How hast thou past the night ?
Has kindly sleep refresh'd thee ?
De Mon. Yes, I have lost an hour or two in
    sleep,
And so should be refresh'd.
Freb.   And art thou not ?
Thy looks speak not of rest.   Thou art disturb'd.
De Mon. No, somewhat ruffled from a foolish
    cause,
Which soon will pass away.
Freb. (*Shaking his head.*) Ah no, De Monfort!
    something in thy face
Tells me another tale.   Then wrong me not:
If any secret grief distracts thy soul,
Here am I all devoted to thy love ;
Open thy heart to me.   What troubles thee ?
De Mon. I have no grief: distress me not, my
    friend.
Freb. Nay, do not call me so.   Wert thou my
    friend,
Would'st thou not open all thine inmost soul,
And bid me share its every consciousness ?
De Mon. Freberg, thou know'st not man ; not
    nature's man,
But only him who, in smooth studied works

Of polish'd sages, shines deceitfully
In all the splendid foppery of virtue.
That man was never born whose secret soul
With all its motley treasure of dark thoughts,
Foul fantasies, vain musings, and wild dreams.
Was ever open'd to another's scan.
Away, away! it is delusion all.

 Freb. Well, be reserved then: perhaps I'm
  wrong.

 De Mon. How goes the hour?

 Freb. 'Tis early: a long day is still before us,
Let us enjoy it.   Come along with me;
I'll introduce you to my pleasant friend.

 De Mon. Your pleasant friend?

 Freb.   Yes, he of whom I spake.
      (*Taking his hand.*)
There is no good I would not share with thee,
And this man's company, to minds like thine,
Is the best banquet-feast I could bestow.
But I will speak in mystery no more,
It is thy townsman, noble Rezenvelt.

 De Mon. (*Pulls his hand hastily from* Freberg,
  and shrinks back.)   Ha! What is this?
  Art thou pain-stricken, Monfort?
Nay, on my life, thou rather seem'st offended:
Does it displease thee that I call him friend?

 De Mon. No, all men are thy friends.

 Freb. No, say not all men.   But thou art
  offended.
I see it well.   I thought to do thee pleasure.

But if his presence is not welcome here,
He shall not join our company to-day.

 De Mon. What dost thou mean to say ? What
   is't to me
Whether I meet with such a thing as Rezenvelt
To-day, to-morrow, every day, or never.

 Freb. In truth, I thought you had been well
   with him.
He prais'd you much.

 De Mon. I thank him for his praise—Come, let
   us move :
This chamber is confin'd and airless grown.

          (*Starting.*)

I hear a stranger's voice !

 Freb.   'Tis Rezenvelt.
Let him be told that we are gone abroad.

 De Mon. (*Proudly.*) No ; let him enter. Who
   waits there ? Ho ! Manuel !

     Enter MANUEL.

What stranger speaks below ?

 Man.   The Marquis Rezenvelt.
I have not told him that you are within.

 De Mon. (*Angrily.*) And wherefore dids't thou
   not ? Let him ascend.

  (*A long pause.* De Monfort *walking up and
  down with a quick pace.*)

 Enter REZENVELT, *and runs freely up to* De
     Monfort.

 Rez. to De Mon. My noble Marquis, welcome.

De Mon.   Sir, I thank you.

Rez. to Freb. My gentle friend, well met.
  Abroad so early ?

Freb. It is indeed an early hour for me.
How sits thy last night's revel on thy spirits ?

Rez. O, light as ever. On my way to you
E'en now I learnt De Monfort was arriv'd,
And turn'd my steps aside ; so here I am.

(*Bowing gaily to* De Monfort.)

De Mon. I thank you, Sir ; you do me too
  much honour.   (*Proudly.*)

Rez. Nay, say not so ; not too much honour,
  Marquis,
Unless, indeed, 'tis more than pleases you.

De Mon. (*Confused.*) Having no previous notice
  of your coming,
I look'd not for it.

Rez. Ay, true indeed ; when I approach you
  next,
I'll send a herald to proclaim my coming,
And make my bow to you by sound of trumpet.

De Mon. to Freb. (*Turning haughtily from* Rezenvelt *with affected indifference.*) How does
    your cheerful friend, that good old man ?

Freb. My cheerful friend ? I know not whom
  you mean.

De Mon. Count Waterlan.

Freb.   I know not one so named.

De Mon. (*Very confused.*) O pardon me—it was
  at Bâle I knew him.

Freb. You have not yet enquired for honest
     Reisdale.
I met him as I came, and mention'd you.
He seem'd amaz'd ; and fain he would have learnt
What cause procur'd us so much happiness.
He question'd hard, and hardly would believe
I could not satisfy his strong desire.
    Rez. And know you not what brings De Mon-
     fort here ?
    Freb. Truly, I do not.
    Rez.   O ! 'tis love of me.
I have but two short days in Amberg been,
And here with postman's speed he follows me,
Finding his home so dull and tiresome grown.
    Freb. to De Mon. Is Rezenvelt so sadly miss'd
     with you ?
Your town so chang'd ?
    De Mon.   Not altogether so :
Some witlings and jest-mongers still remain
For fools to laugh at.
    Rez. But he laughs not, and therefore he is
     wise.
He ever frowns on them with sullen brow
Contemptuous ; therefore he is very wise.
Nay, daily frets his most refined soul
With their poor folly, to its inmost core ;
Therefore he is most eminently wise.
    Freb. Fy, Rezenvelt ! You are too early gay ;
Such spirits rise but with the ev'ning glass.
They suit not placid morn.

(*To* De Monfort, *who after walking impatiently up and down, comes close to his ear, and lays hold of his arm.*)
                    What would you, Monfort?

De Mon. Nothing—Yet, what is't o'clock?
No, no—I had forgot—'tis early still.
                            (*Turns away again.*)

Freb. to Rez. Waltser informs me that you have
     agreed
To read his verses o'er, and tell the truth.
It is a dangerous task.

Rez.   Yet I'll be honest:
I can but lose his favour and a feast.

(*Whilst they speak,* De Monfort *walks up and down impatiently and irresolute; at last, pulls the bell violently.*)

Enter SERVANT.

De Mon. to Ser. What dost thou want?—

Ser.   I thought your honour rung.

De Mon. I have forgot—Stay; are my horses
     saddled?

Ser. I thought, my Lord, you would not ride
     to-day,
After so long a journey.

De Mon. (*Impatiently.*)   Well—'tis good.
Begone!—I want thee not.   [EXIT Servant.

Rez. (*Smiling significantly.*) I humbly crave your
     pardon, gentle Marquis.
It grieves me that I cannot stay with you,

And make my visit of a friendly length.
I trust your goodness will excuse me now ;
Another time I shall be less unkind.
(*To* Freberg.) Will you not go with me ?
   Freb. Excuse me, Monfort, I'll return again.
               [EXEUNT Rezenvelt *and* Freberg.
   De Mon. (*Alone, tossing his arms distractedly.*)
Hell hath no greater torment for th' accurs'd
Than this man's presence gives—
Abhorred fiend ! he hath a pleasure too,
A damned pleasure in the pain he gives !
Oh ! the side glance of that detested eye !
That conscious smile ! that full insulting lip !
It touches every nerve : it makes me mad.
What, does it please thee ? Dost thou woo my
       hate ?
Hate shalt thou have ! determin'd, deadly hate,
Which shall awake no smile. Malignant villain !
The venom of thy mind is rank and devilish,
And thin the film that hides it.
Thy hateful visage ever spoke thy worth :
I loath'd thee when a boy.
That —— should be besotted with him thus !
And Freberg likewise so bewitched is,
That like a hireling flatt'rer, at his heels
He meanly paces, off'ring brutish praise.
O ! I could curse him too.   [EXIT.

ACT II.—SCENE I.

A very splendid apartment in Count FREBERG'S
*house, fancifully decorated. A wide folding door
opened, shews another magnificent room lighted
up to receive company. Enter through the folding
doors the Count and Countess, richly dressed.*

Freb. (*Looking round.*) In truth, I like those de-
    corations well :
They suit those lofty walls.   And here, my love,
The gay profusion of a woman's fancy
Is well display'd.   Noble simplicity
Becomes us less on such a night as this
Than gaudy show.
Lady. Is it not noble, then ? (*He shakes his
    head.*) I thought it so,
And as I know you love simplicity,
I did intend it should be simple too.
Freb. Be satisfy'd, I pray ; we want to-night
A cheerful banquet-house, and not a temple.
How runs the hour ?
Lady. It is not late, but soon we shall be rous'd
With the loud entry of our frolick guests.

Enter a PAGE, *richly dressed.*

Page. Madam, there is a Lady in your hall,
Who begs to be admitted to your presence.
Lady. Is it not one of our invited friends ?
Page. No, far unlike to them ; it is a stranger.

Lady. How looks her countenance?

Page. So queenly, so commanding, and so noble,
I shrunk at first in awe; but when she smil'd,
For so she did to see me thus abash'd,
Methought I could have compass'd sea and land
To do her bidding.

Lady.　　　　Is she young or old?

Page. Neither, if right I guess, but she is fair;
For time hath laid his hand so gently on her,
As he too had been aw'd.

Lady.　　　　The foolish stripling !
She has bewitch'd thee. Is she large in stature?

Page. So stately and so graceful is her form,
I thought at first her stature was gigantick,
But on a near approach I found, in truth,
She scarcely does surpass the middle size.

Lady. What is her garb?

Page. I cannot well describe the fashion of it.
She is not deck'd in any gallant trim,
But seems to me clad in the usual weeds
Of high habitual state; for as she moves
Wide flows her robe in many a waving fold,
As I have seen unfurled banners play
With the soft breese.

Lady.　　　　Thine eyes deceive thee, boy,
It is an apparition thou hast seen.

Freb. (*Starting from his seat, where he has been*
sitting during the conversation between the Lady
and the Page.) It is an apparition he has seen.
Or it is Jane De Monfort.　　　[Exit, *hastily.*

1

Lady. (Displeased.) No; such description surely
    suits not her.
Did she enquire for me?
    Page. She ask'd to see the lady of Count Fre-
    berg.
    Lady. Perhaps it is not she—I fear it is—
Ha! here they come. He has but guess'd too
    well.

Enter FREBERG, *leading in* JANE DE MONFORT.

    Freb. (Presenting her to Lady.) Here, madam,
    welcome a most worthy guest.
    Lady. Madam, a thousand welcomes. Pardon
    me ;
I could not guess who honour'd me so far ;
I should not else have waited coldly here.
    Jane. I thank you for this welcome, gentle
    Countess,
But take those kind excuses back again ;
I am a bold intruder on this hour,
And am entitled to no ceremony.
I came in quest of a dear truant friend,
But Freberg has inform'd me—
(To Freberg.) And he is well you say ?
    Freb.   Yes, well, but joyless.
    Jane. It is the usual temper of his mind :
It opens not, but with the thrilling touch
Of some strong heart-string o'the sudden press'd.
    Freb. It may be so, I've known him otherwise.
He is suspicious grown.

Jane. Not so, Count Freberg, Monfort is too
        noble.
Say rather, that he is a man in grief,
Wearing at times a strange and scowling eye;
And thou, less generous than beseems a friend,
Hast thought too hardly of him.
      Freb. (Bowing with great respect.) So will I say
I'll own nor word, nor will, that can offend you.
      Lady. De Monfort is engag'd to grace our
        feast,
Ere long you'll see him here.
      Jane. I thank you truly, but this homely dress
Suits not the splendour of such scenes as these.
      Freb. (Pointing to her dress.) Such artless and
        majestick elegance,
So exquisitely just, so nobly simple,
Will make the gorgeous blush.
      Jane. (Smiling.) Nay, nay, be more consistent,
        courteous knight,
And do not praise a plain and simple guise
With such profusion of unsimple words.
I cannot join your company to-night.
      Lady. Not stay to see your brother?
      Jane. Therefore it is I would not, gentle hos-
        tess.
Here he will find all that can woo the heart
To joy and sweet forgetfulness of pain;
The sight of me would wake his feeling mind
To other thoughts.   I am no doting mistress,
No fond distracted wife, who must forthwith
Rush to his arms and weep.   I am his sister:

The eldest daughter of his father's house :
Calm and unwearied is my love for him ;
And having found him, patiently I'll wait,
Nor greet him in the hour of social joy,
To dash his mirth with tears.—
The night wears on; permit me to withdraw.

    Freb. Nay, do not, do not injure us so far !
Disguise thyself, and join our friendly train.

    Jane. You wear not masks to-night ?

    Lady. We wear not masks, but you may be con-
    ceal'd
Behind the double foldings of a veil.

    Jane. (*After pausing to consider.*) In truth, I feel
    a little so inclin'd.
Methinks unknown, I e'en might speak to him,
And gently prove the temper of his mind:
But for the means I must become your debtor.
                        (*To* Lady.)

    Lady. Who waits ? (*Enter her* Woman.) Attend
    this lady to my wardrobe,
And do what she commands you.
            [EXEUNT Jane *and* Waiting-woman.

    Freb. (*Looking after* Jane, *as she goes out, with
    admiration.*) Oh! what a soul she bears!
    see how she steps !
Nought but the native dignity of worth
E'er taught the moving form such noble grace.

    Lady. Such lofty mien, and high assumed gait
I've seen ere now, and men have call'd it pride.

    Freb. No, 'faith ! thou never did'st, but oft in-
    deed

The paltry imitation thou hast seen.
(*Looking at her.*) How hang those trappings on
      thy motly gown?
They seem like garlands on a May-day queen,
Which hinds have dress'd in sport.
    Lady. I'll doff it, then, since it displeases you.
    Freb. (*Softening.*) No, no, thou art lovely still
      in every garb.
But see the guests assemble.

*Enter groups of well dressed people, who pay their
    compliments to* Freberg *and his* Lady; *and fol-
    lowed by her pass into the inner apartment, where
    more company appear assembling, as if by another
    entry.*

    Freb. (*Who remains on the front of the stage,
      with a friend or two.*) How loud the hum
      of this gay meeting croud!
'Tis like a bee-swarm in the noonday sun.
Musick will quell the sound. Who waits without?
Musick strike up.
    (*A grand piece of musick is playing, and when
      it ceases, enter from the inner apartment
      *REZENVELT, *with several gentlemen, all
      richly dressed.*)
    Freb. (*To those just entered.*) What lively gal-
      lants quit the field so soon?
Are there no beauties in that moving crowd
To fix your fancy?
    Rez. Ay, marry, are there! men of ev'ry mind
May in that moving croud some fair one find,

To suit their taste, tho' whimsical and strange,
As ever fancy own'd.
Beauty of every cast and shade is there,
From the perfection of a faultless form,
Down to the common, brown, unnoted-maid,
Who looks but pretty in her Sunday gown.

 1st Gent. There is, indeed, a gay variety.

 Rez. And if the liberality of nature
Suffices not, there's store of grafted charms
Blending in one the sweets of many plants
So obstinately, strangely opposite,
As would have well defy'd all other art
But female cultivation, Aged youth,
With borrow'd locks in rosy chaplets bound,
Cloaths her dim eye, parch'd lip, and skinny cheek
In most unlovely softness.
And youthful age, with fat round trackless face,
The down-cast look of contemplation deep,
Most pensively assumes.
Is it not even so? The native prude,
With forced laugh, and merriment uncouth,
Plays off the wild coquet's successful charms
With most unskilful pains; and the coquet,
In temporary crust of cold reserve,
Fixes her studied looks upon the ground
Forbiddingly demure.

 Freb. Fy! thou art too severe.

 Rez.   Say, rather, gentle.
I' faith! the very dwarfs attempt to charm
With lofty airs of puny majesty,
Whilst potent damsels, of a portly make,

Totter like nurselings, and demand the aid
Of gentle sympathy.
From all those diverse modes of dire assault,
He owns a heart of hardest adamant,
Who shall escape to-night.

    Freb. (*To* De Monfort, *who has entered during
        Rezenvelt's speech, and heard the greatest
        part of it.)*   Ha, ha, ha, ha!
How pleasantly he gives his wit the rein,
Yet guides its wild career !

                    (De Monfort *is silent.*)

    Rez. (*Smiling archly.*) What, think you, Fre-
        berg, the same powerful spell
Of transformation reigns o'er all to-night?
Or that De Monfort is a woman turn'd,
So widely from his native self to swerve,
As grace my gai'ty with a smile of his ?

    De Mon. Nay, think not, Rezenvelt, there is no
        smile
I can bestow on thee.   There is a smile,
A smile of nature too, which I can spare,
And yet, perhaps, thou wilt not thank me for it.

                (*Smiles contemptuously.*)

    Rez. Not thank thee! It were surely most un-
        grateful
No thanks to pay for nobly giving me
What, well we see, has cost thee so much pain.
For nature hath her smiles, of birth more painful
Than bitt'rest execrations.

    Freb. These idle words will lead us to disquiet: •
Forbear, forbear, my friends.   Go, Rezenvelt,

             6

Accept the challange of those lovely dames,
Who thro' the portal comes with bolder steps
To claim your notice.

> (*Enter a group of* Ladies *from the other apart-*
> *ment.*   Rezenvelt *shrugs up his shoulders, as*
> *if unwilling to go.*)

1*st Gent. to Rez.* Behold in sable veil a lady
comes,
Whose noble air doth challange fancy's skill
To suit it with a countenance as goodly.

> (*Pointing to* Jane De Monfort, *who now enters*
> *in a thick black veil.*)

Rez. Yes, this way lies attraction.   (*To* Freberg.) With permission,

> (*Going up to* Jane.)

Fair lady, tho' within that envious shroud
Your beauty deigns not to enlighten us,
We bid you welcome, and our beauties here
Will welcome you the more for such conceal-
ment.
With the permission of our noble host—

> (*Taking her hand, and leading her to the front*
> *of the stage.*)

Jane to Freb. Pardon me this presumption,
courteous sir:
I thus appear, (*pointing to her veil,*) not careless
of respect
Unto the gen'rous lady of the feast.
Beneath this veil no beauty shrouded is,
That, now, or pain, or pleasure can bestow.
Within the friendly cover of its shade

I only wish unknown, again to see
One who, alas! is heedless of my pain.

De Mon. Yes, it is ever thus.   Undo that veil,
And give thy count'nance to the cheerful light.
Men now all soft, and female beauty scorn,
And mock the gentle cares which aim to please.
It is most damnable! undo thy veil,
And think of him no more.

Jane. I know it well, even to a proverb grown,
Is lovers' faith, and I had borne such slight:
But he who has, alas! forsaken me
Was the companion of my early days,
My cradle's mate, mine infant play-fellow.
Within our op'ning minds with riper years
The love of praise and gen'rous virtue sprung:
Thro' varied life our pride, our joys, were one;
At the same tale we wept: he is my brother.

De Mon. And he forsook thee?—No, I dare not
          curse him:
My heart upbraids me with a crime like his.

Jane. Ah! do not thus distress a feeling heart.
All sisters are not to the soul entwin'd
With equal bands; thine has not watch'd for
          thee,
Weep'd for thee, cheer'd thee, shar'd thy weal
          and woe,
As I have done for him.

De Mon. (Eagerly.)   Ha! has she not?
By heaven! the sum of all thy kindly deeds
Were but as chaff pois'd against the massy gold,
Compar'd to that which I do owe her love.

Oh pardon me ! I mean not to offend—
I am too warm—But she of whom I speak
Is the dear sister of my earliest love ;
In noble virtuous worth to none a second :
And tho' behind those sable folds were hid
As fair a face as ever woman own'd,
Still would I say she is as fair as thee.
How oft amidst the beauty-blazing throng,
I've proudly to th' inquiring stranger told
Her name and lineage ! yet within her house,
The virgin mother of an orphan race
Her dying parents left, this noble woman
Did, like a Roman matron, proudly sit,
Despising all the blandishments of love ;
Whilst many a youth his hopeless love conceal'd,
Or, humbly distant, woo'd her like a queen.
Forgive, I pray you ! O forgive this boasting !
In faith ! I mean you no discourtesy.

    Jane. (*Off her guard, in a soft natural tone of
       voice.)* Oh no! nor do me any.

    De Mon. What voice speaks now ? Withdraw,
       withdraw this shade !

For if thy face bear semblance to thy voice,
I'll fall and worship thee. Pray! pray undo!

    (*Puts forth his hand eagerly to snatch away the
      veil, whilst she shrinks back, and* Rezenvelt
      steps between to prevent him.)

    Rez. Stand off: no hand shall lift this sacred
      veil.

    De Mon. What, dost thou think De Monfort
      fall'n so low,

That there may live a man beneath heav'n's roof
Who dares to say he shall not?

Rez. He lives who dares to say—

*Jane. (Throwing back her veil, very much alarm-
ed, and rushing between them.)* Forbear,
forbear!

(Rezenvelt, *very much struck, steps back respectfully, and makes her a very low bow.
De Monfort stands for a while motionless,
gazing upon her, till she, looking expressively
to him, extends her arms, and he, rushing
into them, bursts into tears.* Freberg *seems
very much pleased. The company then gather
about them, and the Scene closes.)*

SCENE II.

De Monfort's *apartments. Enter* DE MONFORT,
*with a disordered air, and his hand pressed upon
his forehead, followed by* JANE.

De Mon. No more, my sister, urge me not
again:
My secret troubles cannot be revealed.
From all participation of its thoughts
My heart recoils: I pray thee be contented.

Jane. What, must I, like a distant humble
friend,
Observe thy restless eye, and gait disturb'd,
In timid silence, whilst with yearning heart
I turn aside to weep? O no! De Monfort!
A nobler task thy noble mind will give;

Thy true intrusted friend I still shall be.

 De Mon. Ah, Jane, forbear! I cannot e'en to
  thee.

 Jane. Then fy upon it! fy upon it, Monfort!
There was a time when e'en with murder stain'd,
Had it been possible that such dire deed
Could e'er have been the crime of one so piteous,
Thou would'st have told it me.

 De Mon. So would I now—but ask of this no
  more.
All other trouble but the one I feel
I had disclos'd to thee.   I pray thee spare me.
It is the secret weakness of my nature.

 Jane. Then secret let it be; I urge no farther.
The eldest of our valiant father's hopes,
So sadly orphan'd, side by side we stood,
Like two young trees, whose boughs, in early
  strength,
Screen the weak saplings of the rising grove,
And brave the storm together—
I have so long, as if by nature's right,
Thy bosom's inmate and adviser been,
I thought thro' life I should have so remain'd,
Nor ever known a change.   Forgive me, Monfort,
A humbler station will I take by thee:
The close attendant of thy wand'ring steps;
The cheerer of this home, by strangers sought;
The soother of those griefs I must not know,
This is mine office now: I ask no more,

 De Mon. Oh Jane! thou dost constrain me with
  thy love!

Would I could tell it thee!

   Jane. Thou shalt not tell me. Nay, I'll stop mine ears,

Nor from the yearnings of affection wring

What shrinks from utt'rance. Let it pass, my brother.

I'll stay by thee; I'll cheer thee, comfort thee:

Pursue with thee the study of some art,

Or nobler science, that compels the mind

To steady thought progressive, driving forth

All floating, wild, unhappy fantasies;

Till thou, with brow unclouded, smil'st again,

Like one who from dark visions of the night,

When th' active soul within its lifeless cell

Holds its own world, with dreadful fancy press'd

Of some dire, terrible, or murd'rous deed,

Wakes to the dawning morn, and blesses heaven.

   De Mon. It will not pass away: 'twill haunt me still.

   Jane. Ah! say not so, for I will haunt thee too;

And be to it so close an adversary,

That, tho' I wrestle darkling with the fiend,

I shall o'ercome it.

   De Mon.   Thou most gen'rous woman!

Why do I treat thee thus? It should not be—

And yet I cannot—O that cursed villain!

He will not let me be the man I would.

   Jane. What say'st thou, Monfort? Oh! what words are these?

They have awak'd my soul to dreadful thoughts.

I do beseech thee speak!

      (*He shakes his head and turns from her; she following him.*)

    z

By the affection thou didst ever bear me,
By the dear mem'ry of our infant days ;
By kindred living ties, ay, and by those
Who sleep i'the tomb, and cannot call to thee,
I do conjure thee speak.

> *(He waves her off with his hand, and covers his face with the other, still turning from her.)*

         Ha ! wilt thou not ?
(Assuming dignity.) Then, if affection, most un-
  wearied love,
Tried early, long, and never wanting found,
O'er gen'rous man hath more authority,
More rightful power than crown and sceptre give,
I do command thee.

> *(He throws himself into a chair greatly agitated.)*

De Monfort, do not thus resist my love.
Here I entreat thee on my bended knees.

            (Kneeling.)

Alas! my brother!

> (De Monfort *starts up, and, catching her in his arms, raises her up, then placing her in the chair, kneels at her feet.)*

 De Mon. Thus let him kneel who should the
  abased be,
And at thine honour'd feet confession make.
I'll tell thee all—but oh! thou wilt despise me.
For in my breast a raging passion burns,
To which thy soul no sympathy will own.
A passion which hath made my nightly couch
A place of torment; and the light of day,

With the gay intercourse of social man,
Feel like th' oppressive airless pestilence.
O Jane! thou wilt despise me.

 Jane.   Say not so:
I never can despise thee, gentle brother.
A lover's jealousy and hopeless pangs
No kindly heart contemns.

 De Mon.   A lover, say'st thou?
No, it is hate! black, lasting, deadly hate;
Which thus hath driv'n me forth from kindred
  peace,
From social pleasure, from my native home,
To be a sullen wand'rer on the earth,
Avoiding all men, cursing and accurs'd.

 Jane. De Monfort, this is fiend-like, frightful,
  terrible!
What being, by th' Almighty Father form'd,
Of flesh and blood, created even as thou,
Could in thy breast such horrid tempest wake,
Who art thyself his fellow?
Unknit thy brows, and spread those wrath-clench'd
  hands:
Some sprite accurst within thy bosom mates
To work thy ruin. Strive with it, my brother!
Strive bravely with it; drive it from thy breast:
'Tis the degrader of a noble heart;
Curse it, and bid it part.

 De Mon. It will not part. *(His hand on his*
  breast.)
       I've lodged it here too long;
With my first cares I felt its rankling touch,

       z 2

I loath'd him when a boy.

    Jane. Who did'st thou say ?

    De Mon.   Oh ! that detested Rezenvelt !
E'en in our early sports, like two young whelps
Of hostile breed, instinctively reverse,
Each 'gainst the other pitch'd his ready pledge,
And frown'd defiance.   As we onward pass'd
From youth to man's estate, his narrow art,
And envious gibing malice, poorly veil'd
In the affected carelessness of mirth,
Still more detestable and odious grew.
There is no living being on this earth
Who can conceive the malice of his soul,
With all his gay and damned merriment,
To those, by fortune or by merit plac'd
Above his paltry self.   When, low in fortune,
He look'd upon the state of prosp'rous men,
As nightly birds, rous'd from their murky holes,
Do scowl and chatter at the light of day,
I could endure it ; even as we bear
Th' impotent bite of some half-trodden worm,
I could endure it.   But when honours came,
And wealth and new-got titles fed his pride;
Whilst flatt'ring knaves did trumpet forth his
        praise,
And grov'ling idiots grinn'd applauses on him ;
Oh ! then I could no longer suffer it !
It drove me frantick.——What ! what would I
        give !
What would I give to crush the bloated toad,
So rankly do I loathe him !

June. And would thy hatred crush the very man
Who gave to thee that life he might have ta'en?
That life which thou so rashly did'st expose
To aim at his! Oh! this is horrible!

   De Mon. Ha! thou hast heard it, then? From
      all the world,
But most of all from thee, I thought it hid.

   Jane. I heard a secret whisper, and resolv'd
Upon the instant to return to thee.
Did'st thou receive my letter?

   De Mon. I did! I did! 'twas that which drove
      me hither.
I could not bear to meet thine eye again.

   Jane. Alas! that, tempted by a sister's tears,
I ever left thy house! these few past months,
These absent months, have brought us all this woe.
Had I remain'd with thee it had not been.
And yet, methinks, it should not move you thus.
You dar'd him to the field; both bravely fought;
He more adroit disarm'd you; courteously
Return'd the forfeit sword, which, so return'd,
You did refuse to use against him more;
And then, as says report, you parted friends.

   De Mon. When he disarm'd this curs'd, this
      worthless hand
Of its most worthless weapon, he but spar'd
From dev'lish pride, which now derives a bliss
In seeing me thus fetter'd, sham'd, subjected
With the vile favour of his poor forbearance;
Whilst he securely sits with gibing brow
And basely bates me, like a muzzled cur

Who cannot turn again.———
Until that day, till that accursed day,
I knew not half the torment of this hell,
Which burns within my breast.   Heaven's light-
          ning blast him !

Jane. O this is horrible ! Forbear, forbear !
Lest heaven's vengeance light upon thy head,
For this most impious wish.

          De Mon.   Then let it light.
Torments more fell than I have felt already
It cannot send.   To be annihilated ;
What all men shrink from ; to be dust, be no-
          thing,
Were bliss to me, compar'd to what I am.

          Jane. Oh ! would'st thou kill me with these
                    dreadful words ?

          De Mon. (*Raising his arms to heaven.*)   Let me
                    but once upon his ruin look,
Then close mine eyes for ever !

          (Jane, *in great distress, staggers back, and
                    supports herself upon the side scene.* De
                    Monfort, *alarm'd, runs up to her with a
                    soften'd voice.*)
Ha ! how is this ? thou'rt ill ; thou'rt very pale.
What have I done to thee ? Alas, alas !
I meant not to distress thee.—O my sister !

          Jane. (Shaking her head.)   I cannot speak to
                    thee.

          De Mon.   I have kill'd thee.
Turn, turn thee not away ! look on me still !

Oh ! droop not thus, my life, my pride, my
    sister !
Look on me yet again.
    Jane.   Thou too, De Monfort,
In better days, wert wont to be my pride.
    De Mon. I am a wretch, most wretched in
    myself,
And still more wretched in the pain I give.
O curse that villain ! that detested villain !
He hath spread mis'ry o'er my fated life :
He will undo us all.
    Jane. I've held my warfare through a troubled
    world,
And borne with steady mind my share of ill ;
For then the helpmate of my toil wert thou.
But now the wane of life comes darkly on,
And hideous passion tears thee from my heart,
Blasting thy worth.—I cannot strive with this.
    De Mon. (*Affectionately.*) What shall I do ?
    Jane.   Call up thy noble spirit,
Rouse all the gen'rous energy of virtue ;
And with the strength of heaven-endued man,
Repel the hideous foe. Be great ; be valiant.
O, if thou could'st ! E'en shrouded as thou art
In all the sad infirmities of nature,
What a most noble creature would'st thou be !
    De Mon. Ay, if I could: alas! alas ! I cannot.
    Jane. Thou can'st, thou may'st, thou wilt.
We shall not part till I have turn'd thy soul.

Enter MANUEL.

De Mon. Ha! some one enters. Wherefore
    com'st thou here ?

Man. Count Freberg waits your leisure.

De Mon. (*Angrily.*) Be gone, be gone.—I
    cannot see him now.   [EXIT, Manuel.

Jane. Come to my closet ; free from all in-
    trusion,

I'll school thee there ; and thou again shalt be
My willing pupil, and my gen'rous friend ;
The noble Monfort I have lov'd so long,
And must not, will not lose.

    De Mon. Do as thou wilt ; I will not grieve
      thee more.   [EXEUNT.

SCENE III.

Count FREBERG'S *House.* *Enter the* COUNTESS,
followed by the PAGE, *and speaking as she enters.*

    Lady. Take this and this. (*Giving two packets.*)
      And tell my gentle friend,

I hope to see her ere the day be done.

    Page. Is there no message for the Lady Jane?

    Lady. No, foolish boy, that would too far ex-
      tend

Your morning's route, and keep you absent long.

    Page. O no, dear Madam! I'll the swifter run.

The summer's light'ning moves not as I'll move,
If you will send me to the Lady Jane.

    Lady. No, not so slow, I ween. The summer's
      light'ning!

Thou art a lad of taste and letters grown:
Would'st poetry admire, and ape thy master.
Go, go ; my little spaniels are unkempt ;
My cards unwritten, and my china broke :
Thou art too learned for a lady's page.
Did I not bid thee call Theresa here ?

Page. Madam, she comes.

Enter THERESA, *carrying a robe over her arm.*

Lady to Ther. What has employ'd you all this
    dreary while ?
I've waited long.

Ther.   Madam, the robe is finish'd.

Lady. Well, let me see it.
           (Theresa *spreads out the robe.*)
(*Impatiently to the Page.*) Boy, hast thou ne'er
    a hand to lift that fold ?
See where it hangs.
    (Page *takes the other side of the robe, and
       spreads it out to its full extent before her,
       whilst she sits down and looks at it with
       much dissatisfaction.*)

Ther. Does not my lady like this easy form ?

Lady. That sleeve is all awry.

Ther.   Your pardon, madam;
'Tis but the empty fold that shades it thus.
I took the pattern from a graceful shape ;
The Lady Jane De Monfort wears it so.

Lady. Yes, yes, I see 'tis thus with all of you.
Whate'er she wears is elegance and grace,

2

Whilst ev'ry ornament of mine, forsooth,
Must hang like trappings on a May-day queen.
   (*Angrily to the* Page, *who is smiling to himself.*)
Youngster be gone.   Why do you loiter here?

[Exit Page.

Ther. What would you, madam, chuse to wear
   to-night?
One of your newest robes?

Lady.   I hate them all.

Ther. Surely, that purple scarf became you well,
With all those wreaths of richly hanging flowers.
Did I not overhear them say, last night,
As from the crouded ball-room ladies past,
How gay and handsome, in her costly dress,
The Countess Freberg look'd.

Lady.   Did'st thou o'erhear it?

Ther. I did, and more than this.

Lady. Well, all are not so greatly prejudic'd;
All do not think me like a May-day queen,
Which peasants deck in sport.

Ther.   And who said this?

Lady. (*Putting her handkerchief to her eyes.*) E'en
   my good lord, Theresa.

Ther. He said it but in jest.   He loves you well.

Lady. I know as well as thee he loves me well;
But what of that? he takes no pride in me.
Elsewhere his praise and admiration go,
And Jane De Monfort is not mortal woman.

Ther. The wond'rous character this lady bears
For worth and excellence; from early youth
The friend and mother of her younger sisters

Now greatly married, as I have been told,
From her most prudent care, may well excuse
The admiration of so good a man
As my good master is.   And then, dear madam,
I must confess, when I myself did hear
How she was come thro' the rough winter's storm,
To seek and comfort an unhappy brother,
My heart beat kindly to her.
    Lady. Ay, ay, there is a charm in this I find :
But wherefore may she not have come as well.
Through wintry storms to seek a lover too?
        Ther. No, madam, no, I could not think of this.
        Lady. That would reduce her in your eyes,
            mayhap,
To woman's level.—Now I see my vengeance!
I'll tell it round that she is hither come,
Under pretence of finding out De Monfort,
To meet with Rezenvelt.   When Freberg hears it
'Twill help, I ween, to break this magick charm.
        Ther. And say what is not, madam ?
        Lady. How can'st thou know that I shall say
            what is not ?
'Tis like enough I shall but speak the truth.
        Ther. Ah no! there is—
        Lady.   Well, hold thy foolish tongue.
Carry that robe into my chamber, do :
I'll try it there myself.   [EXEUNT.

ACT III.—SCENE I.

DE MONFORT *discovered sitting by a table reading. After a little time he lays down his book, and continues in a thoughtful posture. Enter to him* JANE DE MONFORT.

Jane. Thanks, gentle brother.—

(Pointing to the book.)

Thy willing mind has been right well employ'd.
Did not thy heart warm at the fair display
Of peace and concord and forgiving love ?
   De Mon. I know resentment may to love be
       turn'd ;
Tho' keen and lasting, into love as strong:
And fiercest rivals in th' ensanguin'd field
Have cast their brandish'd weapons to the ground,
Joining their mailed breasts in close embrace,
With gen'rous impulse fir'd.   I know right well
The darkest, fellest wrongs have been forgiven
Seventy times o'er from blessed heavenly love :
I've heard of things like these; I've heard and
       wept.
But what is this to me ?
   Jane.   All, all, my brother!
It bids thee too that noble precept learn,
To love thine enemy.
   De Mon. Th' uplifted stroke that would a wretch
       destroy
Gorg'd with my richest spoil, stain'd with my blood,

I would arrest and cry, hold! hold! have mercy:
But when the man most adverse to my nature;
Who e'en from childhood hath, with rude male-
   volence,
Withheld the fair respect all paid beside,
Turning my very praise into derision;
Who galls and presses me where'er I go,
Would claim the gen'rous feelings of my heart,
Nature herself doth lift her voice aloud,
And cries, it is impossible.
  Jane. (Shaking her head.)—Ah Monfort, Mon-
   fort!
  De Mon. I can forgive th' envenom'd reptile's
   sting,
But hate his loathsome self.
  Jane. And canst thou do no more for love of
   heaven?
  De Mon. Alas! I cannot now so school my
   mind
As holy men have taught, nor search it truly:
But this, my Jane, I'll do for love of thee;
And more it is than crowns could win me to,
Or any power but thine. I'll see the man.
Th' indignant risings of abhorrent nature;
The stern contraction of my scowling brows,
That, like the plant, whose closing leaves do shrink
At hostile touch, still knit at his approach;
The crooked curving lip, by instinct taught,
In imitation of disgustful things,
To pout and swell, I strictly will repress;
And meet him with a tamed countenance,

E'en as a townsman, who would live at peace,
And pay him the respect his station claims.
I'll crave his pardon too for all offence
My dark and wayward temper may have done ;
Nay more, I will confess myself his debtor
For the forbearance I have curs'd so oft.
Life spar'd by him, more horrid than the grave
With all its dark corruption!   This I'll do.
Will it suffice thee ?   More than this I cannot.

    Jane. No more than this do I require of thee
In outward act, tho' in thy heart, my friend,
I hop'd a better change, and still will hope.
I told thee Freberg had propos'd a meeting.

    De Mon. I know it well.

    Jane.   And Rezenvelt consents.
He meets you here ; so far he shews respect.

    De Mon. Well, let it be ; the sooner past the
        better.

    Jane. I'm glad to hear you say so, for, in truth,
He has propos'd it for an early hour.
'Tis almost near his time ; I came to tell you.

    De Mon. What, comes he here so soon ? shame
        on his speed!
It is not decent thus to rush upon me.
He loves the secret pleasure he will feel
To see me thus subdued.

    Jane. O say not so! he comes with heart sincere.

    De Mon. Could we not meet elsewhere ? from
        home—i' the fields,
Where other men—must I alone receive him ?
Where is your agent, Freberg, and his friends,

1

That I must meet him here?
        (*Walks up and down very much disturbed.*)
Now did'st thou say?—how goes the hour?—e'en
        now!
I would some other friend were first arriv'd.
    Jane. See, to thy wish comes Freberg and his
        dame.
    De Mon. His lady too! why comes he not
        alone?
Must all the world stare upon our meeting?

Enter COUNT FREBERG *and his* COUNTESS.

    Freb. A happy morrow to my noble marquis
And his most noble sister.
    Jane.   Gen'rous Freberg,
Your face, methinks, forbodes a happy morn
Open and cheerful.   What of Rezenvelt?
    Freb. I left him at his home, prepar'd to follow:
He'll soon appear.   (*To* De Monfort.) And now,
        my worthy friend,
Give me your hand; this happy change delights
        me.
        (De Monfort *gives him his hand coldly, and
        they walk to the bottom of the stage together,
        in earnest discourse, whilst* Jane *and the*
        Countess *remain in the front.*)
    Lady. My dearest madam, will you pardon me?
I know Count Freberg's bus'ness with De Monfort,
And had a strong desire to visit you,
So much I wish the honour of your friendship.
For he retains no secret from mine ear.

Jane, archly. Knowing your prudence.—You are
    welcome, madam,
So shall Count Freberg's lady ever be.

    (De Monfort *and* Freberg *returning towards
    the front of the stage, still engaged in
    discourse.*)

Freb. He is indeed a man, within whose breast,
Firm rectitude and honour hold their seat,
Tho' unadorned with that dignity
Which were their fittest garb. Now, on my life!
I know no truer heart than Rezenvelt.

    De Mon. Well, Freberg, well, there needs not
    all this pains
To garnish out his worth ; let it suffice.
I am resolv'd I will respect the man,
As his fair station and repute demand.
Methinks I see not at your jolly feasts
The youthful knight, who sung so pleasantly,

    Freb. A pleasant circumstance detains him
    hence ;
Pleasant to those who love high gen'rous deeds
Above the middle pitch of common minds ;
And, tho' I have been sworn to secrecy,
Yet must I tell it thee.
This knight is near a kin to Rezenvelt
To whom an old relation, short while dead,
Bequeath'd a good estate, some leagues distant.
But Rezenvelt, now rich in fortune's store,
Disdain'd the sordid love of further gain,
And gen'rously the rich bequest resign'd
To this young man, blood of the same degree

To the deceas'd, and low in fortune's gifts,
Who is from hence to take possession of it.
Was it not nobly done?

De Mon. 'Twas right, and honourable.
This morning is oppressive, warm, and heavy :
There hangs a foggy closeness in the air ;
Dost thou not feel it ?

Freb. O no! to think upon a gen'rous deed
Expands my soul, and makes me lightly breath.

De Mon. Who gives the feast to night ? His
name escapes me.
You say I am invited.

Freb. Old Count Waterlan.
In honour of your townsman's gen'rous gift
He spreads the board.

De Mon. He is too old to revel with the gay.

Freb. But not too old is he to honour virtue.
I shall partake of it with open soul ;
For, on my honest faith, of living men
I know not one, for talents, honour, worth,
That I should rank superiour to Rezenvelt.

De Mon. How virtuous he hath been in three
short days!

Freb. Nay, longer, Marquis, but my friendship
rests
Upon the good report of other men ;
And that has told me much.

(De Monfort *aside, going some steps hastily
from* Freberg, *and rending his cloak with
agitation as he goes.*)
Would he were come ! by heaven I would he were!

A A

This fool besets me so.

> (*Suddenly correcting himself, and joining the*
> Ladies, *who have retired to the bottom of the*
> *stage, he speaks to* Countess Freberg *with*
> *affected cheerfulness.*)

The sprightly dames of Amberg rise by times
Untarnish'd with the vigils of the night.

Lady. Praise us not rashly, 'tis not always so.

De Mon. He does not rashly praise who praises
 you ;
For he were dull indeed—

> (*Stopping short, as if he heard something.*)

Lady.   How dull indeed ?

De Mon. I should have said—It has escap'd me
 now

> (*Listening again, as if he heard something.*)

Jane to De Mon. What, hear you ought ?

De Mon. (hastily.)   'Tis nothing.

Lady to De Mon. Nay, do not let me lose it so,
 my lord.
Some fair one has bewitch'd your memory,
And robs me of the half-form'd compliment.

Jane. Half-utter'd praise is to the curious mind,
As to the eye half-veiled beauty is,
More precious than the whole.   Pray pardon him.
Some one approaches.   (*Listening.*)

Freb. No, no, it is a servant who ascends ;
He will not come so soon.

Mon. (Off his guard.) 'Tis Rezenvelt : I heard
 his well-known foot !
From the first stair-case, mounting step by step.

Freb. How quick an ear thou hast for distant
    sound!
I heard him not.
    (De Monfort *looks embarrassed, and is silent.*)

Enter REZENVELT.

(De Monfort, *recovering himself, goes up to
receive* Rezenvelt, *who meets him with a
cheerful countenance.*)
De Mon. to Rez. I am, my lord, beholden to you
    greatly.
This ready visit makes me much your debtor.
    Rez. Then may such debts between us, noble
    marquis,
Be oft incurr'd, and often paid again.
    To Jane. Madam, I am devoted to your service,
And ev'ry wish of yours commands my will.
    To Countess. Lady, good morning. (*To Freb.*)
    Well, my gentle friend,
You see I have not linger'd long behind.
    Freb. No, thou art sooner than I look'd for
    thee.
    Rez. A willing heart adds feather to the heel,
And makes the clown a winged mercury.
    De Mon. Then let me say, that with a grateful
    mind
I do receive these tokens of good will;
And must regret that, in my wayward moods,
I have too oft forgot the due regard
Your rank and talents claim.
    Rez.   No, no, De Monfort,

You have but rightly curb'd a wanton spirit,
Which makes me too, neglectful of respect.
Let us be friends, and think of this no more.

Freb. Ay, let it rest with the departed shades
Of things which are no more ; whilst lovely concord,
Follow'd by friendship sweet, and firm esteem,
Your future days enrich. O heavenly friendship!
Thou dost exalt the sluggish souls of men,
By thee conjoin'd, to great and glorious deeds ;
As two dark clouds, when mix'd in middle air,
The vivid lightning's flash, and roar sublime.
Talk not of what is past, but future love.

De Mon. (With dignity.) No, Freberg, no, it
    must not. *(To* Rezenvelt.*)* No, my lord.
I will not offer you an hand of concord
And poorly hide the motives which constrain me.
I would that, not alone these present friends,
But ev'ry soul in Amberg were assembled,
That I, before them all, might here declare
I owe my spared life to your forbearance.
(Holding out his hand.) Take this from one who
    boasts no feeling warmth,
But never will deceive.

    (Jane *smiles upon* De Monfort *with great*
    approbation, and Rezenvelt *runs up to him*
    with open arms.)

Rez. Away with hands ! I'll have thee to my
    breast.
Thou art, upon my faith, a noble spirit !

De Mon. (Shrinking back from him.) Nay, if you
    please, I am not so prepar'd—

My nature is of temp'rature too cold—
I pray you pardon me. (*Jane's countenance changes.*)
But take this hand, the token of respect ;
The token of a will inclin'd to concord ;
The token of a mind that bears within
A sense impressive of the debt it owes you ;
And cursed be its power, unnerv'd its strength,
If e'er again it shall be lifted up
To do you any harm.

   Rez. Well, be it so, De Monfort, I'm contented ;
I'll take thy hand since I can have no more.
(*Carelessly.*) I take of worthy men whate'er they
     give.
Their heart I gladly take ; if not, their hand :
If that too is withheld, a courteous word,
Or the civility of placed looks ;
And, if e'en these are too great favours deem'd,
'Faith, I can set me down contentedly
With plain and homely greeting, or, God save ye !
    (De Monfort *aside, starting away from him*
    some paces.)
By the good light, he makes a jest of it !
    (Jane *seems greatly distressed, and* Freberg
    endeavours to cheer her.)
   Freb. to Jane. Cheer up, my noble friend ; all
    will go well ;
For friendship is no plant of hasty growth.
Tho' planted in esteem's deep-fixed soil,
The gradual culture of kind intercourse
Must bring it to perfection.

(To the Countess.) My love, the morning, now, is
        far advanced ;
Our friends elsewhere expect us ; take your leave.

 Lady to Jane. Farewell ! dear madam, till the
        ev'ning hour.

 Freb. to De Mon. Good day, De Monfort. *(To
        Jane.)* Most devoutly yours.

 Rez. to Freb. Go not too fast, for I will follow
        you.

     [EXEUNT Freberg *and his* Lady.

(To Jane.) The Lady Jane is yet a stranger here:
She might, perhaps, in the purlieus of Amberg
Find somewhat worth her notice.

 Jane. I thank you, Marquis, I am much engaged;
I go not out to-day.

 Rez. Then fare ye well! I see I cannot now
Be the proud man who shall escort you forth,
And shew to all the world my proudest boast,
The notice and respect of Jane De Monfort.

 De Mon. (Aside, impatiently.) He says farewell,
        and goes not!

 Jane to Rez.   You do me honour.

 Rez. Madam, adieu! *(To* Jane.) Good morn-
        ing, noble marquis.   [EXIT.

 (Jane *and* De Monfort *look expressively to one
        another, without speaking, and then* EXEUNT,
        severally.)

SCENE II.

A splendid Banquetting Room. DE MONFORT, RE-
ZENVELT, FREBERG, MASTER OF THE HOUSE,
and GUESTS, *are discovered sitting at table,
with wine, &c. before them.*

SONG.—A GLEE.

Pleasant is the mantling bowl,
And the song of merry soul;
And the red lamps cheery light,
And the goblet glancing bright;
Whilst many a cheerful face, around,
Listens to the jovial sound.
Social spirits, join with me;
Bless the God of jollity.

Freb. to De Mon. (*Who rises to go away.*) Thou
wilt not leave us, Monfort? wherefore so?
De Mon. (*Aside to* Freberg.) I pray thee take
no notice of me now.
Mine ears are stunned with these noisy fools;
Let me escape. [EXIT, *hastily.*
Master of the House. What, is De Monfort
gone?
Freb. Time presses him.
Rez. It seem'd to sit right heavily upon him,
We must confess.
Master to Freb. How is your friend? he wears
a noble mien,
But most averse, methinks, from social pleasure.
Is this his nature?

Freb.   No, I've seen him cheerful,
And at the board, with soul-enliven'd face,
Push the gay goblet round.—But it wears late.
We shall seem topers more than social friends,
If the returning sun surprise us here.
(To Mast.) Good rest, my gen'rous host; we will
    retire.
You wrestle with your age most manfully,
But brave it not too far.   Retire to sleep.
Mast. I will, my friend, but do you still remain,
With noble Rezenvelt, and all my guests.
Ye have not fourscore years upon your head;
Do not depart so soon.   God save you all!
      [Exit Master, *leaning upon a* Servant.
Freb. to the Guests. Shall we resume?
Guests.   The night is too far spent.
Freb. Well then, good rest to you.
Rez. to Guests.   Good rest, my friends.
      [Exeunt *all but* Freberg *and* Rezenvelt.
Freb. Alas! my Rezenvelt!
I vainly hop'd the hand of gentle peace,
From this day's reconciliation sprung,
These rude unseemly jarrings had subdu'd:
But I have mark'd, e'en at the social board,
Such looks, such words, such tones, such untold
    things,
Too plainly told, 'twixt you and Monfort pass,
That I must now despair.
Yet who could think, two minds so much refin'd,
So near in excellence, should be remov'd,
So far remov'd, in gen'rous sympathy.

Rez. Ay, far remov'd indeed.

Freb. And yet, methought, he made a noble effort,

And with a manly plainness bravely told

The galling debt he owes to your forbearance.

Rez. 'Faith! so he did, and so did I receive it;

When, with spread arms, and heart e'en mov'd to tears,

I frankly proffer'd him a friend's embrace:

And, I declare, had he as such receiv'd it,

I from that very moment had forborne

All opposition, pride-provoking jest,

Contemning carelessness, and all offence;

And had caress'd him as a worthy heart,

From native weakness such indulgence claiming:

But since he proudly thinks that cold respect,

The formal tokens of his lordly favour,

So precious are, that I would sue for them

As fair distinction in the world's eye,

Forgetting former wrongs, I spurn it all;

And but that I do bear the noble woman,

His worthy, his incomparable sister,

Such fix'd profound regard, I would expose him;

And as a mighty bull, in senseless rage,

Rous'd at the baiter's will, with wretched rags

Of ire-provoking scarlet, chaffs and bellows,

I'd make him at small cost of paltry wit,

With all his deep and manly faculties,

The scorn and laugh of fools.

    Freb. For heaven's sake, my friend! restrain your wrath;

For what has Monfort done of wrong to you,
Or you to him, bating one foolish quarrel,
Which you confess from slight occasion rose,
That in your breasts such dark resentment dwells,
So fix'd, so hopeless ?

Rez. O! from our youth he has distinguish'd
    me
With ev'ry mark of hatred and disgust.
For e'en in boyish sports I still oppos'd
His proud pretensions to pre-eminence ;
Nor would I to his ripen'd greatness give
That fulsome adulation of applause
A senseless croud bestow'd. Tho' poor in fortune,
I still would smile at vain-assuming wealth :
But when unlook'd-for fate on me bestow'd
Riches and splendour equal to his own,
Tho' I, in truth, despise such poor distinction,
Feeling inclin'd to be at peace with him,
And with all men beside, I curb'd my spirit,
And sought to soothe him. Then, with spiteful
    rage,
From small offence he rear'd a quarrel with me,
And dar'd me to the field. The rest you know.
In short, I still have been th' opposing rock,
O'er which the stream of his o'erflowing pride
Hath foam'd and bellow'd. See'st thou how it is ?

Freb. Too well I see, and warn thee to beware.
Such streams have oft, by swelling floods sur-
    charg'd,
Borne down with sudden and impetuous force
The yet unshaken stone of opposition,

Which had for ages stopp'd their flowing course.
I pray thee, friend, beware.

 Rez. Thou canst not mean—he will not murder me?

 Freb. What a proud heart, with such dark passion toss'd,

May, in the anguish of its thoughts, conceive,
I will not dare to say.

 Rez.   Ha, ha! thou know'st him not.

Full often have I mark'd it in his youth,
And could have almost lov'd him for the weakness;
He's form'd with such antipathy, by nature,
To all infliction of corporeal pain,
To wounding life, e'en to the sight of blood,
He cannot if he would.

 Freb.   Then fy upon thee!

It is not gen'rous to provoke him thus.
But let us part; we'll talk of this again.
Something approaches.—We are here too long.

 Rez. Well, then, to-morrow I'll attend your call.

Here lies my way.   Good night.   [EXIT.

Enter GRIMBALD.

 Grim. Forgive, I pray, my lord, a stranger's boldness.

I have presum'd to wait your leisure here,
Though at so late an hour.

 Freb.   But who art thou?

 Grim. My name is Grimbald, sir,

A humble suitor to your honour's goodness,
Who is the more embolden'd to presume,
In that the noble Marquis of De Monfort
Is so much fam'd for good and gen'rous deeds.
 Freb. You are mistaken, I am not the man.
 Grim. Then, pardon me ; I thought I could
  not err.
That mien so dignified, that piercing eye
Assur'd me it was he.
 Freb. My name is not De Monfort, courteous
  stranger ;
But, if you have a favour to request,
I may, perhaps, with him befriend your suit.
 Grim. I thank your honour, but I have a friend
Who will commend me to De Monfort's favour :
The Marquis Rezenvelt has known me long,
Who, says report, will soon become his brother.
 Freb. If thou would'st seek thy ruin from De
  Monfort,
The name of Rezenvelt employ, and prosper ;
But, if ought good, use any name but his.
 Grim. How may this be?
 Freb.   I cannot now explain.
Early to-morrow call upon Count Freberg ;
So am I call'd, each burgher knows my house,
And there instruct me how to do you service.
Good-night.   [EXIT.
 Grim. (*Alone.*) Well, this mistake may be of
  service to me ;
And yet my bus'ness I will not unfold
To this mild, ready, promise-making courtier ;

I've been by such too oft deceiv'd already :
But if such violent enmity exists
Between De Monfort and this Rezenvelt,
He'll prove my advocate by opposition.
For, if De Monfort would reject my suit,
Being the man whom Rezenvelt esteems,
Being the man he hates, a cord as strong,
Will he not favour me ?   I'll think of this.

[EXIT.

SCENE III.

A lower Apartment in JEROME'S *House, with a
wide folding glass door, looking into a garden,
where the trees and shrubs are brown and leafless.
Enter* DE MONFORT *with his arms crossed,
with a thoughtful frowning aspect, and paces
slowly across the stage,* Jerome *following behind
him with a timid step.* De Monfort *hearing
him, turns suddenly about.*

De Mon. (*Angrily.*)   Who follows me to this
   sequester'd room ?
Jer. I have presum'd, my lord. 'Tis some-
   what late :
I am inform'd you eat at home to-night ;
Here is a list of all the dainty fare
My busy search has found ; please to peruse it.
   De Mon. Leave me : begone ! Put hemlock in
      thy soup,
Or deadly night-shade, or rank hellebore,
And I will mess upon it.

Jer.   Heaven forbid !
Your honour's life is all too precious, sure—
  De Mon. (Sternly.) . Did I not say begone ?
  Jer. Pardon, my lord, I'm old, and oft forget.
                                       [Exit.
  De Mon. (Looking after him, as if his heart
    smote him.)   Why will they thus mistime
    their foolish zeal,
That I must be so stern ?
O ! that I were upon some desert coast !
Where howling tempests and the lashing tide
Would stun me into deep and senseless quiet ;
As the storm-beaten trav'ller droops his head,
In heavy, dull, lethargick weariness,
And, midst the roar of jarring elements,
Sleeps to awake no more.
What am I grown ? All things are hateful to me.

                  Enter MANUEL.

  (Stamping with his foot.)   Who bids thee break
    upon my privacy ?
  Man. Nay, good, my lord! I heard you speak
    aloud,
And dreamt not, surely, that you were alone.
  De Mon. What, dost thou watch, and pin
    thine ear to holes,
To catch those exclamations of the soul,
Which heaven alone should hear ? Who hir'd
    thee, pray ?
Who basely hir'd thee for a task like this?
  Man. My lord, I cannot hold. For fifteen years,

Long-troubled years, I have your servant been,
Nor hath the proudest lord in all the realm,
With firmer, with more honourable faith
His sov'reign serv'd, than I have served you ;
But, if my honesty is doubted now,
Let him who is more faithful take my place,
And serve you better.

    De Mon. Well, be it as thou wilt. Away with
        thee.
Thy loud-mouth'd boasting is no rule for me
To judge thy merit by.

Enter JEROME *hastily, and pulls* MANUEL *away.*

    Jer. Come, Manuel, come away ; thou art not
        wise.
The stranger must depart and come again,
For now his honour will not be disturb'd.

                    [EXIT Manuel *sulkily.*
    De Mon. A stranger said'st thou.
               (*Drops his handkerchief.*)
    Jer. I did, good sir, but he shall go away ;
You shall not be disturb'd.
            (*Stooping to lift the handkerchief.*)
          You have dropp'd somewhat.
    De Mon. (*Preventing him.*)   Nay, do not stoop,
        my friend! I pray thee not !
Thou art too old to stoop.—
I am much indebted to thee.—Take this ring—
I love thee better than I seem to do.
I pray thee do it—thank me not.—What stranger?
    Jer. A man who does most earnestly entreat
To see your honour, but I know him not.

De Mon. Then let him enter.   [EXIT Jerome.

A pause.   Enter GRIMBALD.

De Mon. You are the stranger who would
    speak with me ?
Grim. I am so far unfortunate, my lord,
That, though my fortune on your favour hangs,
I am to you a stranger.
    De Mon. How may this be ? What can I do
        for you ?
    Grim. Since thus your lordship does so frankly
        ask,
The tiresome preface of apology
I will forbear, and tell my tale at once.—
In plodding drudgery I've spent my youth,
A careful penman in another's office ;
And now, my master and employer dead,
They seek to set a stripling o'er my head,
And leave me on to drudge, e'en to old age,
Because I have no 'friend to take my part.
It is an office in your native town,
For I am come from thence, and I am told
You can procure it for me.   Thus, my lord,
From the repute of goodness which you bear,
I have presum'd to beg.
    De Mon. They have befool'd thee with a false
        report.
    Grim. Alas ! I see it is in vain to plead.
Your mind is pre-possess'd against a wretch,
Who has, unfortunately for his weal,
Offended the revengeful Rezenvelt.
                        3

De Mon. What dost thou say ?

Grim. What I, perhaps, had better leave unsaid.
Who will believe my wrongs if I complain ?
I am a stranger, Rezenvelt my foe,
Who will believe my wrongs ?

De Mon. (Eagerly catching him by the coat.)
         I will believe them !
Though they were base as basest, vilest deeds,
In ancient record told, I would believe them.
Let not the smallest atom of unworthiness
That he has put upon thee be conceal'd.
Speak boldly, tell it all ; for, by the light !
I'll be thy friend, I'll be thy warmest friend,
If he has done thee wrong.

  Grim. Nay, pardon me, it were not well
    advis'd,
If I should speak so freely of the man,
Who will so soon your nearest kinsman be.

  De Mon. What canst thou mean by this ?

  Grim.   That Marquis Rezenvelt
Has pledg'd his faith unto your noble sister,
And soon will be the husband of her choice.
So, I am told, and so the world believes.

  De Mon. 'Tis false ! 'tis basely false!
What wretch could drop from his envenom'd
    tongue
A tale so damn'd ?—It chokes my breath—
(Stamping with his foot.) What wretch did tell
    it thee ?

  Grim. Nay, every one with whom I have con-
    vers'd

Has held the same discourse.   I judge it not.
But you, my lord, who with the lady dwell,
You best can tell what her deportment speaks ;
Whether her conduct and unguarded words
Belie such rumour.

>   (De Monfort *pauses, staggers backwards,*
>   *and sinks into a chair ; then starting up*
>   *hastily.*)

De Mon. Where am I now ? 'midst all the
   cursed thoughts
That on my soul like stinging scorpions prey'd,
This never came before——Oh, if it be !
The thought will drive me mad.—Was it for this
She urged her warm request on bended knee ?
Alas ! I wept, and thought of sister's love,
No damned love like this.
Fell devil ! 'tis hell itself has lent thee aid
To work such sorcery! (*Pauses.*) I'll not believe it.
I must have proof clear as the noon-day sun
For such foul charge as this ! Who waits without !

>   (*Paces up and down furiously agitated.*)

Grim. (*Aside.*)   What have I done ? I've carried this too far.
I've rous'd a fierce ungovernable madman.

Enter JEROME.

De Mon. (*In a loud angry voice.*) Where did
   she go, at such an early hour,
And with such slight attendance ?
   Jer. Of whom inquires your honour?

2

De Mon. Why, of your lady.   Said I not my
  sister ?

Jer. The Lady Jane, your sister ?

De Mon. (*In a faultering voice.*)   Yes, I did
  call her so.

Jer. In truth, I cannot tell you where she went.
E'en now, from the short-beechen walk hard-by,
I saw her through the garden-gate return.
The Marquis Rezenvelt, and Freberg's Countess
Are in her company.   This way they come,
As being nearer to the back apartments ;
But I shall stop them, if it be your will,
And bid them enter here.

De Mon. No, stop them not.   I will remain unseen,
And mark them as they pass.   Draw back a little.
  (Grimbald *seems alarm'd, and steals off un-*
   noticed.   De Monfort *grasps* Jerome
   tightly by the hand, and drawing back with
   him two or three steps, not to be seen from
   the garden, waits in silence with his eyes
   fixed on the glass-door.)

De Mon. I hear their footsteps on the grating
  sand.
How like the croaking of a carrion bird,
That hateful voice sounds to the distant ear !
And now she speaks—her voice sounds cheerly
  too—
O curse their mirth !—
Now, now, they come, keep closer still ! keep
  steady !
   (*Taking hold of* Jerome *with both hands.*)

Jer. My lord, you tremble much.

De Mon.   What, do I shake?

Jer. You do, in truth, and your teeth chatter
   too.

De Mon. See! see they come! he strutting
   by her side.

   (Jane, Rezenvelt, *and* Countess Freberg *appear through the glass-door, pursuing their
   way up a short walk leading to the other
   wing of the house.*)

See how he turns his odious face to her's!

Utt'ring with confidence some nauseous jest.

And she endures it too—Oh! this looks vilely!

Ha! mark that courteous motion of his arm—

What does he mean?—He dares not take her
   hand!

   (Pauses and looks eagerly.) By heaven and
   hell he does!

   (*Letting go his hold of* Jerome, *he throws out
   his hands vehemently, and thereby pushes him
   against the scene.*)

Jer. Oh! I am stunn'd! my head is crack'd in
   twain:

Your honour does forget how old I am.

De Mon.   Well, well, the wall is harder than
   I wist.

Begone! and whine within.

   [Exit Jerome, *with a sad rueful countenance.*
   (De Monfort *comes forward to the front of
   the stage, and makes a long pause, expressive
   of great agony of mind.*)

It must be so ; each passing circumstance;
Her hasty journey here ; her keen distress
Whene'er my soul's abhorrence I express'd ;
Ay, and that damned reconciliation,
With tears extorted from me : Oh, too well !
All, all too well bespeak the shameful tale.
I should have thought of heav'n and hell conjoin'd,
The morning star mix'd with infernal fire,
Ere I had thought of this—
Hell's blackest magick, in the midnight hour,
With horrid spells and incantation dire,
Such combination opposite, unseemly,
Of fair and loathsome, excellent and base,
Did ne'er produce.—But every thing is possible,
So as it may my misery enhance!
Oh ! I did love her with such pride of soul !
When other men, in gayest pursuit of love,
Each beauty follow'd, by her side I stay'd ;
Far prouder of a brother's station there,
Than all the favours favour'd lovers boast.
We quarrel'd once, and when I could no more
The alter'd coldness of her eye endure,
I slipp'd o' tip-toe to her chamber door ;
And when she ask'd who gently knock'd—Oh! oh!
Who could have thought of this ?

> (*Throws himself into a chair, covers his face
> with his hand, and bursts into tears. After
> some time he starts up from his seat furiously.*)

Hell's direst torment seize th' infernal villain !
Detested of my soul! I will have vengeance!

I'll crush thy swelling pride—I'll still thy vaunt-
      ing—
I'll do a deed of blood—Why shrink I thus ?
If, by some spell or magick sympathy,
Piercing the lifeless figure on that wall
Could pierce his bosom too, would I not cast it ?
            (*Throwing a dagger against the wall.*)
Shall groans and blood affright me ? No, I'll do it.
Tho' gasping life beneath my pressure heav'd,
And my soul shudder'd at the horrid brink,
I would not flinch.—Fy, this recoiling nature!
O that his sever'd limbs were strew'd in air,
So as I saw him not !
      (*Enter* Rezenvelt *behind, from the glass door.*
      De Monfort *turns round, and on seeing him
      starts back, then drawing his sword, rushes
      furiously upon him.*)
Detested robber; now all forms are over :
Now open villany, now open hate !
Defend thy life.
      Rez.   De Monfort, thou art mad.
      De Mon. Speak not, but draw. Now for thy
      hated life !
      (*They fight :* Rezenvelt *parries his thrusts
      with great skill, and at last disarms him.*)
Then take my life, black fiend, for hell assists thee.
      Rez. No, Monfort, but I'll take away your
      sword.
Not as a mark of disrespect to you,
But for your safety. By to-morrow's eve

I'll call on you myself and give it back ;
And then, if I am charg'd with any wrong,
I'll justify myself. Farewell, strange man !

[EXIT.

(De Monfort *stands for some time quite motionless, like one stupified. Enter to him a*
SERVANT : *he starts.*)

De Mon. Ha! who art thou?

Ser. 'Tis I, an' please your honour.

De Mon. (*Staring wildly at him.*) Who art thou?

Ser. Your servant Jacques.

De Mon. Indeed I know thee not.
Leave me, and when Rezenvelt is gone,
Return and let me know.

Ser. He's gone already, sir.

De Mon. How, gone so soon ?

Ser. Yes, as his servant told me,
He was in haste to go, for night comes on,
And at the ev'ning hour he must take horse,
To visit some old friend whose lonely mansion
Stands a short mile beyond the farther wood;
And, as he loves to wander thro' those wilds.
Whilst yet the early moon may light his way,
He sends his horses round the usual road,
And crosses it alone.
I would not walk thro' those wild dens alone
For all his wealth. For there, as I have heard,
Foul murders have been done, and ravens scream;
And things unearthly, stalking thro' the night,
Have scar'd the lonely trav'ller from his wits.

(De Monfort *stands fixed in thought.*)

I've ta'en your mare, an please you, from her field,
And wait your farther orders.

(De Monfort *heeds him not.*)

Her hoofs are sound, and where the saddle gall'd
Begins to mend.   What further must be done?

(De Monfort *still heeds him not.*)

His honour heeds me not.   Why should I stay?

De Mon. (Eagerly, as he is going.) He goes alone
saidst thou?

Ser. His servant told me so.

De Mon.   And at what hour?

Ser. He 'parts from Amberg by the fall of eve.

Save you, my lord? how chang'd your count'-
nance is!

Are you not well?

De Mon.   Yes, I am well: begone!
And wait my orders by the city wall:
I'll that way bend, and speak to thee again.

[EXIT, Servant.

(De Monfort *walks rapidly two or three times
across the stage ; then siezes his dagger from
the wall; looks steadfastly at its point, and*
EXIT, *hastily.*)

ACT IV.—SCENE I.

*Moon-light. A wild path in a wood, shaded with
trees. Enter* De Monfort, *with a strong expression of disquiet, mixed with fear, upon his face,
looking behind him, and bending his ear to the
ground, as if he listened to something.*)

   De Mon. How hollow groans the carth beneath
      my tread !
Is there an echo here ? Methinks it sounds
As tho' some heavy footstep follow'd me.
I will advance no farther.
Deep settled shadows rest across the path,
And thickly-tangled boughs o'er-hang this spot.
O that a tenfold gloom did cover it !
That 'midst the murky darkness I might strike ;
As in the wild confusion of a dream,
Things horrid, bloody, terrible, do pass,
As tho' they pass'd not; nor impress the mind
With the fix'd clearness of reality.
         (*An owl is heard screaming near him.*)
(*Starting.*) What sound is that?
           (*Listens, and the owl cries again,*)
            It is the screech-owl's cry.
Foul bird of night ! what spirit guides thee here?
Art thou instinctive drawn to scenes of horrour ?
I've heard of this.   (*Pauses and listens.*)
How those fall'n leaves so rustle on the path,
With whisp'ring noise, as tho' the earth around me

Did utter secret things!
The distant river, too, bears to mine ear
A dismal wailing. O mysterious night!
Thou art not silent; many tongues hast thou.
A distant gath'ring blast sounds thro' the wood,
And dark clouds fleetly hasten o'er the sky:
O! that a storm would rise, a raging storm;
Amidst the roar of warring elements
I'd lift my hand and strike: but this pale light,
The calm distinctness of each stilly thing,
Is terrible. (*Starting.*) Footsteps are near—
He comes, he comes! I'll watch him farther on—
I cannot do it here.   [EXIT.

Enter REZENVELT, *and continues his way slowly
     across the stage, but just as he is going off the
     owl screams, he stops and listens, and the owl
     screams again.*

> *Rez.* Ha! does the night-bird greet me on my
>   way?
How much his hooting is in harmony
With such a scene as this! I like it well.
Oft when a boy, at the still twilight hour,
I've leant my back against some knotted oak,
And loudly mimick'd him, till to my call
He answer would return, and thro' the gloom
We friendly converse held.
Between me and the star-bespangl'd sky
Those aged oaks their crossing branches wave,
And thro' them looks the pale and placid moon.
How like a crocodile, or winged snake,

Yon sailing cloud bears on its dusky length !
And now transformed by the passing wind,
Methinks it seems a flying Pegasus.
Ay, but a shapeless band of blacker hue
Come swiftly after.—
A hollow murm'ring wind comes thro' the trees;
I hear it from afar; this bodes a storm.
I must not linger here—
            (*A bell heard at some distance.*)
           What bell is this?
It sends a solemn sound upon the breeze.
Now, to a fearful superstitious mind,
In such a scene, 'twould like a death-knell come:
For me it tells but of a shelter near,
And so I bid it welcome.   [Exit.

SCENE II.

*The inside of a Convent Chapel, of old Gothick archi-
tecture, almost dark; two torches only are seen at
a distance, burning over a new-made grave. The
noise of loud wind, beating upon the windows and
roof, is heard. Enter two* Monks.

    1*st Monk.* The storm increases: hark how dis-
      mally
It howls along the cloisters. How goes time?
    2*d Monk.* It is the hour: I hear them near at
      hand;
And when the solemn requiem has been sung
For the departed sister, we'll retire.
Yet, should this tempest still more violent grow,

We'll beg a friendly shelter till the morn.

1st Monk. See, the procession enters: let us
join.

*(The organ strikes up a solemn prelude Enter
a procession of Nuns, with the Abbess,
bearing torches. After compassing the grave
twice, and remaining there some time, whilst
the organ plays a grand dirge, they advance
to the front of the stage.)*

SONG, BY THE NUNS.

Departed soul, whose poor remains
This hallow'd lowly grave contains;
Whose passing storm of life is o'er,
Whose pains and sorrows are no more!
Bless'd be thou with the bless'd above!
Where all is joy, and purity, and love.

Let him, in might and mercy dread,
Lord of the living and the dead;
In whom the stars of heav'n rejoice,
To whom the ocean lifts his voice,
Thy spirit purified to glory raise,
To sing with holy saints his everlasting praise.

Departed soul, who in this earthly scene
Hast our lowly sister been.
Swift be thy way to where the blessed dwell?
Until we meet thee there, farewell! farewell!

Enter a LAY SISTER, *with a wild terrified look,
her hair and dress all scattered, and rushes forward amongst them.*

Abb. Why com'st thou here, with such disorder'd looks,

To break upon our sad solemnity?

Sist. Oh! I did hear, thro' the receding blast,
Such horrid cries! it made my blood run chill.

Abb. 'Tis but the varied voices of the storm,
Which many times will sound like distant screams:
It has deceiv'd thee.

    1st Sist. O no, for twice it call'd, so loudly
        call'd,
With horrid strength, beyond the pitch of nature.
And murder! murder! was the dreadful cry.
A third time it return'd with feeble strength,
But o'the sudden ceas'd, as tho' the words
Were rudely smother'd in the grasped throat;
And all was still again, save the wild blast
Which at a distance growl'd—
Oh! it will never from my mind depart!
That dreadful cry all i'the instant still'd,
For then, so near, some horrid deed was done,
And none to rescue.

    Abb. Where didst thou hear it?

    Sist.   In the higher cells,
As now a window, open'd by the storm,
I did attempt to close.

    1st Monk. I wish our brother Bernard were
        arriv'd;
He is upon his way.

    Abb. Be not alarm'd; it still may be deception.
'Tis meet we finish our solemnity,
Nor shew neglect unto the honour'd dead.

        (*Gives a sign, and the organ plays again: just
          as it ceases a loud knocking is heard without.*)
        3

Abb. Ha! who may this be? hush!

(*Knocking heard again.*)

2d Monk. It is the knock of one in furious haste.
Hush, hush! What footsteps come? Ha! brother
    Bernard.

Enter BERNARD *bearing a lantern.*

1st Monk. See, what a look he wears of stiffen'd
    fear!
Where hast thou been, good brother?

Bern. I've seen a horrid sight!

(*All gathering round him and speaking at once.*)
                    What hast thou seen?

Bern. As on I hasten'd, bearing thus my light,
Across the path, not fifty paces off,
I saw a murther'd corse stretch'd on its back,
Smear'd with new blood, as tho' but freshly slain.

Abb. A man or woman?

Bern.   A man, a man!

Abb. Did'st thou examine if within its breast
There yet is lodg'd some small remains of life?
Was it quite dead?

Bern.   Nought in the grave is deader.
I look'd but once, yet life did never lodge
In any form so laid.—
A chilly horrour seiz'd me, and I fled.

1st Monk. And does the face seem all unknown
    to thee?

Bern. The face! I would not on the face have
    look'd
For e'en a kingdom's wealth, for all the world.

O no! the bloody neck, the bloody neck!
(*Shaking his head, and shuddering with horrour.*
Loud knocking heard without.)
Sist. Good mercy! who comes next?
Bern. Not far behind
I left our brother Thomas on the road;
But then he did repent him as he went,
And threaten'd to return.
2d Monk. See, here he comes.

Enter brother THOMAS, *with a wild terrified look.*

1st Monk. How wild he looks!
Bern. (Going up to him eagerly.) What, hast thou
seen it too?
Thom. Yes, yes! it glar'd upon me as it pass'd.
Bern. What glar'd upon thee?
(*All gathering round* Thomas *and speaking at once.*)
O! what hast thou seen?
Thom. As, striving with the blast, I onward
came,
Turning my feeble lantern from the wind,
Its light upon a dreadful visage gleam'd,
Which paus'd, and look'd upon me as it pass'd.
But such a look, such wildness of despair,
Such horrour-strain'd features never yet
Did earthly visage show. I shrunk and shudder'd.
If damned spirits may to earth return
I've seen it.
Bern. Was there blood upon it?
Thom. Nay, as it pass'd, I did not see its form;

Nought but the horrid face.

Bern. It is the murderer.

1st Monk.   What way went it ?

Thom. I durst not look till I had pass'd it far,
Then turning round, upon the rising bank,
I saw, between me and the paly sky,
A dusky form, tossing and agitated.
I stopp'd to mark it, but, in truth, I found
'Twas but a sapling bending to the wind,
And so I onward hied, and look'd no more.

1st Monk. But we must look to't ; we must fol-
    low it :

Our duty so commands. (*To* 2*d* Monk.) Will you
    go, brother ?

(To Bernard.) And you, good Bernard ?

Bern.   If I needs must go.

1st Monk. Come, we must all go.

Abb.   Heaven be with you, then !
                       [EXEUNT Monks.

Sist. Amen, amen ! Good heaven be with us
    all !

O what a dreadful night !

Abb. Daughters retire ; peace to the peaceful
    dead !

Our solemn ceremony now is finish'd.

SCENE III.

A large room in the Convent, very dark. Enter the ABBESS, Lay Sister *bearing a light, and several* Nuns. Sister *sets down the light on a table at the bottom of the stage, so that the room is still very gloomy.*

Abb. They have been longer absent than I
    thought ;
I fear he has escap'd them.
 1*st Nun.*   Heaven forbid !
 Sist. No no, found out foul murder ever is,
And the foul murd'rer too.
 2*d Nun.* The good Saint Francis will direct
    their search ;
The blood so near his holy convent shed
For threefold vengeance calls.
 Abb. I hear a noise within the inner court,
They are return'd ; *(listening ;)* and Bernard's voice
    I hear :
They are return'd.
 Sist.   Why do I tremble so ?
It is not I who ought to tremble thus.
 2*d Nun.* I hear them at the door.
 Bern. (Without.) Open the door, I pray thee,
    brother Thomas;
I cannot now unhand the prisoner.
(All speak together, shrinking back from the door,
    and staring upon one another.) He is with
    them.
c c

(A folding door at the bottom of the stage is opened, and enter Bernard, Thomas, *and the other two* Monks, *carrying lanterns in their hands, and bringing in* De Monfort. *They are likewise followed by other* Monks. *As they lead forward* De Monfort *the light is turned away, so that he is seen obscurely; but when they come to the front of the stage they all turn the light side of their lanterns on him at once, and his face is seen in all the strengthened horrour of despair, with his hands and cloaths bloody.)*

*(*Abbess *and* Nuns *speak at once, and starting back.)*
Holy saints be with us!

Bern to Abb. Behold the man of blood!

Abb. Of misery too; I cannot look upon him.

Bern to Nuns. Nay, holy sisters, turn not thus away.

Speak to him, if, perchance, he will regard you:
For from his mouth we have no utt'rance heard,
Save one deep and smother'd exclamation,
When first we seiz'd him.

Abb. to De Mon. Most miserable man, how art
thou thus? *(Pauses.)*

Thy tongue is silent, but those bloody hands
Do witness horrid things. What is thy name?

De Mon. (Roused; looks steadfastly at the Abbess *for some time, then speaking in a short hurried voice.)* I have no name.

Abb. to Bern. Do it thyself: I'll speak to him
no more.

Sist. O holy saints ! that this should be the man,
Who did against his fellow lift the stroke,
Whilst he so loudly call'd.——
Still in mine ear it sounds : O murder ! murder !

De Mon. (*Starting.*) He calls again !

Sist. No, he did call, but now his voice is still'd.
'Tis past.

De Mon. (*In great anguish.*) 'Tis past !

Sist. Yes it is past, art thou not he who did it ?

(De Monfort *utters a deep groan, and is supported from falling by the Monks. A noise
is heard without.*)

Abb. What noise is this of heavy lumb'ring steps,
Like men who with a weighty burden come ?

Bern. It is the body : I have orders given
That here it should be laid.

(*Enter men bearing the body of* Rezenvelt, *covered with a white cloth, and set it down in
the middle of the room : they then uncover it.*
De Monfort *stands fixed and motionless with
horrour, only that a a sudden shivering seems
to pass over him when they uncover the corps.
The* Abbess *and* Nuns *shrink back and retire to some distance ; all the rest fixing their
eyes steadfastly upon* De Monfort. *A long
pause.*)

Bern. to *De Mon.* See'st thou that lifeless corps,
  those bloody wounds,
See how he lies, who but so shortly since
A living creature was, with all the powers
Of sense, and motion, and humanity ?

Oh! what a heart had he who did this deed !

   1st Monk. (*Looking at the body.*) How hard
     those teeth against the lips are press'd,

As tho' he struggled still !

   2d Monk. The hands, too, clench'd : the last
     efforts of nature.

     (De Monfort *still stands motionless. Brother*
     Thomas *then goes to the body, and raising*
     up the head a little, turns it towards De
     Monfort.)

   Thom. Know'st thou this gastly face ?

   De Mon. (*Putting his hands before his face in*
     violent perturbation.) Oh do not ! do not !
     veil it from my sight !

Put me to any agony but this !

   Thom. Ha ! dost thou then confess the dreadful
     deed ?

Hast thou against the laws of awful heav'n

Such horrid murder done ? What fiend could
     tempt thee ?

   (Pauses and looks steadfastly at De Monfort.)

   De Mon. I hear thy words but do not hear their
     sense—

Hast thou not cover'd it ?

   Bern. to Thom. Forbear, my brother, for thou
     see'st right well

He is not in a state to answer thee.

Let us retire and leave him for a while.

These windows are with iron grated o'er ;

He cannot 'scape, and other duty calls.

   Thom. Then let it be.

Bern. to Monks, &c. Come, let us all depart.
> (EXEUNT Abbess *and* Nuns, *followed by the*
> Monks.   *One* Monk *lingering a little*
> *behind.*)

De Mon. All gone! (*Perceiving the Monk.*)   O
stay thou here!

Monk.   It must not be.

De Mon. I'll give thee gold; I'll make thee rich
in gold,

If thou wilt stay e'en but a little while.

Monk. I must not, must not stay.

De Mon.   I do conjure thee!

Monk. I dare not stay with thee.   (*Going.*)

De Mon.   And wilt thou go?
> (*Catching hold of him eagerly.*)

O! throw thy cloak upon this grizly form!
The unclos'd eyes do stare upon me still.
O do not leave me thus!
> [Monk *covers the body, and* EXIT.

De Mon. (*Alone, looking at the covered body, but*
at a distance.) Alone with thee! but thou art
nothing now.

'Tis done, 'tis number'd with the things o'erpast,
Would! would it were to come!
What fated end, what darkly gath'ring cloud
Will close on all this horrour?
O that dire madness would unloose my thoughts,
And fill my mind with wildest fantasies,
Dark, restless, terrible! ought, ought but this!
> (*Pauses and shudders.*)

How with convulsive life he heav'd beneath me,

E'en with the death's wound gor'd.   O horrid,
    horrid!
Methinks I feel him still.—What sound is that?
I heard a smother'd groan.—It is impossible!
          (Looking steadfastly at the body.)
It moves! it moves! the cloth doth heave and
    swell.
It moves again.—I cannot suffer this—
Whate'er it be I will uncover it.
    (Runs to the corps and tears of the cloth in
    despair.)
All still beneath.
Nought is there here but fix'd and grizly death.
How sternly fixed! Oh! those glazed eyes!
They look me still.
          (Shrinks back with horrour.)
Come, madness! come unto me senseless death!
I cannot suffer this! Here, rocky wall,
Scatter these brains, or dull them.
    (Runs furiously, and, dashing his head against
    the wall, falls upon the floor.)

      Enter two MONKS, *hastily.*

1*st Monk.* See; wretched man, he hath destroy'd
    himself.
2*d Monk.* He does but faint.   Let us remove
    him hence.
1*st Monk.* We did not well to leave him here
    alone.
2*d Monk.* Come, let us bear him to the open air.
         [EXEUNT, *bearing out* De Monfort.

ACT V.—SCENE I.

Before the gates of the Convent. Enter JANE DE
MONFORT, FREBERG *and* MANUEL. *As they
are proceeding towards the gate,* JANE *stops short
and shrinks back.*

Freb. Ha! wherefore? has a sudden illness
    seiz'd see?
Jane No, no, my friend.—And yet I am very
    faint—
I dread to enter here!
Man.   Ay! so I thought:
For, when between the trees, that abbey tower
First shew'd its top, I saw your count'nance
    change.
But breathe a little here; I'll go before,
And make enquiry at the nearest gate.
    Freb. Do so, good Manuel.
          (Manuel *goes and knocks at the gate.*)
Courage, dear madam: all may yet be well.
Rezenvelt's servant, frighten'd with the storm,
And seeing that his master join'd him not,
As by appointment, at the forest's edge,
Might be alarm'd, and give too ready ear
To an unfounded rumour.
He saw it not; he came not here himself.
    Jane (*Looking eagerly to the gate, where Ma-
    nuel talks with the Porter.*) Ha! see, he
    talks with some one earnestly.

And sees't thou not that motion of his hands ?
He stands like one who hears a horrid tale.
Almighty God !

> (*Manuel goes into the convent.*)
> He comes not back; he enters.

Freb. Bear up, my noble friend.

Jane I will, I will ! But this suspence is
    dreadful.

> (*A long pause. Manuel re-enters from the
> convent, and comes forward slowly, with a
> sad countenance.*)

Is this the pace of one who bears good tidings ?
O God ! his face doth tell the horrid fact ;
There is nought doubtful here.

Freb.   How is it, Manuel ?

Man. I've seen him through a crevice in his
    door :
It is indeed my master.

> (*Bursting into tears.*)

> (Jane *faints, and is supported by* Freberg.—
> *Enter* ABBESS *and several* NUNS *from the
> convent, who gather about her, and apply
> remedies. She recovers.*)

1st Nun. The life returns again.

2d Nun.   Yes, she revives.

Abb. to Freb. Let me entreat this noble lady's
    leave
To lead her in. She seems in great distress :
We would with holy kindness soothe her woe,
And do by her the deeds of christian love.

Freb. Madam, your goodness has my grateful
    thanks.

    [Exeunt, *supporting* Jane *into the convent.*

SCENE II.

De Monfort *is discovered sitting in a thoughtful
posture. He remains so for some time. His face
afterwards begins to appear agitated, like one
whose mind is harrowed with the severest thoughts;
then, starting from his seat, he clasps his hands
together, and holds them up to heaven.*

De Mon. O that I had ne'er known the light of
    day !
That filmy darkness on mine eyes had hung,
And clos'd me out from the fair face of nature !
O that my mind, in mental darkness pent,
Had no perception, no distinction known,
Of fair or foul, perfection nor defect ;
Nor thought conceiv'd of proud pre-eminence !
O that it had ! O that I had been form'd
An idiot from the birth ! a senseless changeling,
Who eats his glutton's meal with greedy haste,
Nor knows the hand who feeds him.—
        (*Pauses ; then, in a calmer sorrowful voice.*)
What am I now ? how ends the day of life ?
For end it must ; and terrible this gloom,
The storm of horrours that surround its close.
This little term of nature's agony
Will soon be o'er, and what is past is past :
But shall I then, on the dark lap of earth

Lay me to rest, in still unconsciousness,
Like senseless clod that doth no pressure feel
From wearing foot of daily passenger;
Like steeped rock o'er which the breaking waves
Bellow and foam unheard? O would I could!

Enter MANUEL, *who springs forward to his master,
but is checked upon perceiving* De Monfort
draw back and look sternly at him.

   Man. My lord, my master! O my dearest
     master!
        (De Monfort *still looks at him without
        speaking.*)
Nay, do not thus regard me; good my lord!
Speak to me: am I not your faithful Manuel?
   De Mon. (*In a hasty broken voice.*) Art thou
     alone?
   Man. No, sir, the lady Jane is on her way;
She is not far behind.
   De Mon. (*Tossing his arm over his head in an
     agony.*) This is too much! All I can bear
     but this!
It must not be.—Run and prevent her coming.
Say, he who is detain'd a pris'ner here
Is one to her unknown. I now am nothing.
I am a man, of holy claims bereft;
Out from the pale of social kindred cast;
Nameless and horrible.—
Tell her De Monfort far from hence is gone
Into a desolate, and distant land,

Ne'er to return again.   Fly, tell her this ;
For we must meet no more.

Enter JANE DE MONFORT, *bursting into the chamber, and followed by* FREBERG, ABBESS, *and several* NUNS.

> *Jane* We must ! we must ! My brother, O my
> brother !
>> (De Monfort *turns away his head and hides
>> his face with his arm.* Jane *stops short,
>> and, making a great effort, turns to* Freberg,
>> *and the others who followed her ; and with
>> an air of dignity stretches out her hand, beck-
>> oning them to retire.   All retire but* Freberg,
>> *who seems to hesitate.*)

And thou too, Freberg : call it not unkind.

> [EXIT Freberg, Jane *and* De Monfort *only
> remain.*

> *Jane* My hapless Monfort !
>> (De Monfort *turns round and looks sorrowfully
>> upon her ; she opens her arms to him, and he,
>> rushing into them, hides his face upon her
>> breast and weeps.*)

> *Jane* Ay, give thy sorrow vent : here may'st
> thou weep.
> *De Mon.* (*In broken accents.*) Oh ! this, my
> sister, makes me feel again

The kindness of affection.
My mind has in a dreadful storm been tost ;
Horrid and dark.—I thought to weep no more.—

6

I've done a deed—But I am human still.

　　Jane I know thy suff'rings: leave thy sorrow free:
Thou art with one who never did upbraid ;
Who mourns, who loves thee still.

　　De Mon. Ah ! say'st thou so ? no, no ; it
　　should not be.

(Shrinking from her.) I am a foul and bloody
　　murderer,

For such embrace unmeet.　O leave me ! leave me !
Disgrace and publick shame abide me now ;
And all, alas ! who do my kindred own
The direful portion share.—Away, away !
Shall a disgrac'd and publick criminal
Degrade thy name, and claim affinity
To noble worth like thine ?—I have no name—
I am nothing, now, not e'en to thee ; depart.

　　　　(She takes his hand, and grasping it firmly,
　　　　speaks with a determined voice.)

　　Jane. De Monfort, hand in hand we have
　　enjoy'd

The playful term of infancy together ;
And in the rougher path of ripen'd years
We've been each other's stay.　Dark lowers our fate,
And terrible the storm that gathers over us ;
But nothing, till that latest agony
Which severs thee from nature, shall unloose
This fix'd and sacred hold.　In thy dark prison-
　　house ;

In the terrifick face of armed law ;
Yea, on the scaffold, if it needs must be,
I never will forsake thee.

De Mon. (Looking at her with admiration.)
Heav'n bless thy gen'rous soul, my noble Jane!
I thought to sink beneath this load of ill,
Depress'd with infamy and open shame ;
I thought to sink in abject wretchedness :
But for thy sake I'll rouse my manhood up,
And meet it bravely ; no unseemly weakness,
I feel my rising strength, shall blot my end,
To clothe thy cheek with shame.

    Jane Yes, thou art noble still.

    De Mon. With thee I am ; who were not so with
        thee ?
But, ah, my sister ! short will be the term :
Death's stroke will come, and in that state beyond,
Where things unutterable wait the soul,
New from its earthly tenement discharg'd,
We shall be sever'd far.
Far as the spotless purity of virtue
Is from the murd'rer's guilt, far shall we be.
This is the gulf of dread uncertainty
From which the soul recoils.

    Jane. The God who made thee is a God of
        mercy ;
Think upon this.

    De Mon. (Shaking his head.) No, no ! this
        blood ! this blood !

    Jane Yea, e'en the sin of blood may be forgiv'n,
When humble penitence hath once aton'd.

    De Mon. (Eagerly.) What, after terms of
        lengthen'd misery,
Imprison'd anguish of tormented spirits,

Shall I again, a renovated soul,
Into the blessed family of the good
Admittance have? Think'st thou that this may be?
Speak if thou canst: O speak me comfort here!
For dreadful fancies, like an armed host,
Have push'd me to despair. It is most horrible—
O speak of hope! if any hope there be.

> (Jane *is silent and looks sorrowfully upon him;*
> *then clasping her hands, and turning her eyes*
> *to heaven, seems to mutter a prayer.*)

De Mon. Ha! dost thou pray for me? heav'n
hear thy prayer!
I fain would kneel—Alas! I dare not do it.

Jane. Not so; all by th' Almighty Father
form'd
May in their deepest mis'ry call on him.
Come kneel with me, my brother.

> (*She kneels and prays to herself; he kneels by*
> *her, and clasps his hands fervently, but*
> *speaks not. A noise of chains clanking is*
> *heard without, and they both rise.*)

De Mon. Hear'st thou that noise? They come
to interrupt us.

Jane (*Moving towards a side door.*) Then let us
enter here.

De Mon. (*Catching hold of her with a look of*
horror.) Not there—not there—the corps
—the bloody corps.

Jane What, lies he there?—Unhappy Rezenvelt!

De Mon. A sudden thought has come across
  my mind ;
How came it not before ? Unhappy Rezenvelt !
Say'st thou but this ?
  Jane. What should I say ? he was an honest
  man ;
I still have thought him such, as such lament him.
          (De Monfort *utters a deep groan.*)
What means this heavy groan ?
  De Mon.   It hath a meaning.

Enter ABBESS *and* MONKS, *with two* OFFICERS
  *of justice carrying fetters in their hands to put
  upon* DE MONFORT.

  Jane (*Starting.*) What men are these ?
  1st Off. Lady, we are the servants of the law,
And bear with us a power, which doth constrain
To bind with fetters this our prisoner.
              (*Pointing to* De Monfort.)
  Jane. A stranger uncondemn'd ? this cannot be.
  1st Off. As yet, indeed, he is by law unjudg'd,
But is so far condemn'd by circumstance,
That law, or custom sacred held as law,
Doth fully warrant us, and it must be.
  Jane. Nay, say not so ; he has no power to
  escape :
Distress hath bound him with a heavy chain ;
There is no need of yours.
  1st Off. We must perform our office.
  Jane. O ! do not after this indignity!

1st Off. Is it indignity in sacred law
To bind a murderer ? (*To* 2*d* Officer.) Come, do
　thy work.

Jane. Harsh are thy words, and stern thy har-
　den'd brow ;
Dark is thine eye ; but all some pity have
Unto the last extreme of misery.
I do beseech thee ! if thou art a man—

(Kneeling to him.)

(De Monfort *roused at this, runs up to* Jane,
　and raises her hastily from the ground ; then
　stretches himself up proudly.)

De Mon. to Jane. Stand thou erect in native
　dignity ;
And bend to none on earth the suppliant knee.
Though cloath'd in power imperial. To my
　heart
It gives a feller gripe than many irons.
(*Holding out his hands.*) Here, officers of law, bind
　on those shackles,
And if they are too light bring heavier chains.
Add iron to iron, load, crush me to the ground ;
Nay, heap ten thousand weight upon my breast,
For that were best of all.

　　(*A long pause, whilst they put irons upon him.*
　　After they are on, Jane *looks at him sor-*
　　rowfully, and lets her head sink on her breast.
　　De Monfort *stretches out his hands, looks at*
　　them, and then at Jane ; *crosses them over*
　　his breast, and endeavours to suppress his
　　feelings.)

1st Off. I have it, too, in charge to move you
    hence,   *(To* De Monfort.)
Into another chamber, more secure.
De Mon. Well, I am ready, sir.
    (Approaching Jane, *whom the* Abbess *is en-*
    deavouring to comfort, but to no purpose.)
Ah! wherefore thus! most honour'd and most
    dear?
Shrink not at the accoutrements of ill,
Daring the thing itself.
                (Endeavouring to look cheerful.)
Wilt thou permit me with a gyved hand?
    (She gives him her hand, which he raises to his
    lips.)
This was my proudest office.
        [EXEUNT, De Monfort *leading out* Jane.

SCENE III.

*A long narrow gallery in the convent, with the
doors of the cells on each side. The stage dark-
ened. A* Nun *is discovered at a distance listening. Enter another* Nun *at the front of the
stage, and starts back.*

1st Nun. Ha! who is this not yet retir'd to rest?
My sister, is it you?
           (To the other who advances.)
2d Nun. Returning from the sister Nina's cell,
Passing yon door where the poor pris'ner lies,
The sound of one who struggl'd with despair
Struck on me as I went: I stopp'd and listen'd;

O God ! such piteous groans !

    1st Nun. Yes, since the ev'ning sun it hath
        been so.

The voice of mis'ry oft hath reach'd mine ear,
E'en in the cell above.

    2d Nun.   How is it thus ?

Methought he brav'd it with a manly spirit,
And led, with shackl'd hands, his sister forth,
Like one resolv'd to bear misfortune boldly.

    1st Nun. Yes, with heroick courage, for a while
He seem'd inspir'd ; but, soon depress'd again,
Remorse and dark despair o'erwhelm'd his soul,
And so he hath remain'd.

Enter Father BERNARD, *advancing from the further
    end of the gallery, bearing a crucifix.*

    1st Nun. How goes it, father, with your pe-
        nitent ?

We've heard his heavy groans.

    Bern. Retire, my daughters ; many a bed of
        death,

With all its pangs and horrour I have seen,
But never ought like this.

    2d Nun. He's dying, then ?

    Bern.   Yes, death is dealing
    with him.

From violent agitation of the mind,
Some stream of life within his breast has burst ;
For many times, within a little space,
The ruddy-tide has rush'd into his mouth.
God, grant his pains be short !

1st Nun.   Amen, amen!

2d Nun. How does the lady?

Bern. She sits and bears his head upon her lap;
And like a heaven-inspir'd angel, speaks
The word of comfort to his troubled soul:
Then does she wipe the cold drops from his brow,
With such a look of tender wretchedness,
It wrings the heart to see her.

    1st Nun. Ha! hear ye nothing?

    2d Nun. (Alarmed.)   Yes, I heard a noise.

    1st Nun. And see'st thou nothing?

               (Creeping close to her sister.)

Bern.   'Tis a nun in white.

Enter LAY SISTER *in her night cloaths, advancing
from the dark end of the gallery.*

(To Sister.) Wherefore, my daughter, hast thou
    left thy cell?
It is not meet at this untimely hour.

    Sist. I cannot rest. I hear such dismal
    sounds,
Such wailings in the air, such shrilly shrieks,
As though the cry of murder rose again
From the deep gloom of night. I cannot rest:
I pray you let me stay with you, good sisters!
                        (Bell tolls.)

    Nuns. (Starting.) What bell is that?

    Bern.   It is the bell of death.
A holy sister was upon the watch

To give this notice. (*Bell tolls again.*) Hark!
    another knell !
The wretched struggler hath his warfare clos'd ;
May heaven have mercy on him.
                          (*Bell tolls again.*)
Retire, my daughters ; let us all retire,
For scenes like this to meditation call.
                [EXEUNT, *bell tolling again.*

SCENE IV.

A hall or large room in the convent. The bodies of
DE MONFORT *and* REZENVELT *are discovered
laid out upon a low table or platform, covered with
black.* FREBERG, BERNARD, ABBESS, MONKS,
and NUNS *attending.*

  Abb. to Freb. Here must they lie, my lord,
    until we know
Respecting this the order of the law.
  Freb. And you have wisely done, my rev'rend
    mother.
    (*Goes to the table, and looks at the bodies, but
    without uncovering them.*)
Unhappy men ! ye, both in nature rich,
With talents and with virtues were endu'd.
Ye should have lov'd, yet deadly rancour came,
And in the prime and manhood of your days
Ye sleep in horrid death. O direful hate !
What shame and wretchedness his portion is
Who, for a secret inmate, harbours thee !
And who shall call him blameless who excites,

Ungen'rously excites, with careless scorn,
Such baleful passion in a brother's breast,
Whom heav'n commands to love. Low are ye
    laid :
Still all contention now.—Low are ye laid.
I lov'd you both, and mourn your hapless fall.
   Abb. They were your friends, my lord ?
   Freb. I lov'd them both. How does the Lady
    Jane ?
   Abb. She bears misfortune with intrepid soul.
I never saw in woman bow'd with grief
Such moving dignity.
   Freb.   Ay, still the same.
I've known her long ; of worth most excellent ;
But, in the day of woe, she ever rose
Upon the mind with added majesty,
As the dark mountain more sublimely tow'rs
Mantled in clouds and storm.

Enter MANUEL and JEROME.

   Man. (*Pointing.*) Here, my good Jerome, there's
    a piteous sight.
   Jer. A piteous sight ! yet I will look upon him :
I'll see his face in death. Alas, alas !
I've seen him move a noble gentleman ;
And when with vexing passion undisturb'd,
He look'd most graciously.
     (*Lifts up in mistake the cloth from the body of*
        Rezenvelt, *and starts back with horrour.*)
Oh ! this was bloody work ! Oh, oh ! oh, oh !

3

That human hands could do it!

> *(Drops the cloth again.)*

Man. That is the murder'd corps; here lies
De Monfort.

> *(Going to uncover the other body.)*

Jer. *(Turning away his head.)* No, no! I
cannot look upon him now.

Man. Didst thou not come to see him?

Jer. Fy! cover him—inter him in the dark—
Let no one look upon him.

Bern to Jer. Well dost thou show the abhor-
rence nature feels
For deeds of blood, and I commend thee well.
In the most ruthless heart compassion wakes
For one who, from the hand of fellow man,
Hath felt such cruelty.

> *(Uncovering the body of* Rezenvelt.*)*

This is the murder'd corse,

> *(Uncovering the body of* De Monfort.*)*

>   But see, I pray!

Here lies the murderer. What think'st thou here?
Look on those features, thou hast seen them oft,
With the last dreadful conflict of despair,
So fix'd in horrid strength.
See those knit brows, those hollow sunken eyes;
The sharpen'd nose, with nostrils all distent;
That writhed mouth, where yet the teeth appear,
In agony, to gnash the nether lip.
Think'st thou, less painful than the murd'rer's
knife
Was such a death as this?

Ay, and how changed too those matted locks!

Jer. Merciful heaven! his hair is grisly grown,
Chang'd to white age, what was, but two days
            since,
Black as the raven's plume.   How may this be?

Bern. Such change, from violent conflict of
        the mind,
Will sometimes come.

Jer.   Alas, alas! most wretched!
Thou wert too good to do a cruel deed,
And so it kill'd thee.   Thou hast suffer'd for it.
God rest thy soul! I needs must touch thy hand,
And bid thee long farewell.
                (Laying his hand on De Monfort.)

Bern. Draw back, draw back! see where the
        lady comes.

Enter JANE DE MONFORT.   FREBERG, *who has
been for sometime retired by himself to the bottom of
the stage, now steps forward to lead her in, but
checks himself on seeing the fixed sorrow of her
countenance, and draws back respectfully.* JANE
*advances to the table, and looks attentively at the
covered bodies.* MANUEL *points out the body of*
DE MONFORT, *and she gives a gentle inclination
of the head, to signify that she understands him.
She then bends tenderly over it, without speaking.*

Man. (To Jane, *as she raises her head.)* Oh,
    madam! my good lord.

Jane. Well says thy love, my good and faithful
    Manuel ;
But we must mourn in silence.
    Man. Alas! the times that I have follow'd him!
    Jane. Forbear, my faithful Manuel.   For this
    love
Thou hast my grateful thanks ; and here's my
    hand :
Thou hast lov'd him, and I'll remember thee :
Where'er I am ; in whate'er spot of earth
I linger out the remnant of my days,
I'll remember thee.
    Man. Nay, by the living God! where'er you are,
There will I be.   I'll prove a trusty servant:
I'll follow you, e'en to the world's end.
My master's gone, and I, indeed, am mean,
Yet will I show the strength of nobler men,
Should any dare upon your honour'd worth
To put the slightest wrong.   Leave you, dear
    lady !
Kill me, but say not this !
                (*Throwing himself at her feet.*)
    Jane. (*Raising him.*) Well, then ! be thou my
    servant, and my friend.
Art thou, good Jerome, too, in kindness come ?
I see thou art.   How goes it with thine age ?
    Jer. Ah, madam ! woe and weakness dwell
    with age :
Would I could serve you with a young man's
    strength !
I'd spend my life for you.

Jane.　　　　　　　　　Thanks, worthy Jerome.
O! who hath said, the wretched have no friends!
　Freb. In every sensible and gen'rous breast
Affliction finds a friend; but unto thee,
Thou most exalted and most honourable,
The heart in warmest adoration bows,
And even a worship pays.
　　Jane. Nay, Freberg, Freberg! grieve me not,
　　　my friend.
He to whose ear my praise most welcome was,
Hears it no more; and, oh our piteous lot!
What tongue will talk of him? Alas, alas!
This more than all will bow me to the earth;
I feel my misery here.
The voice of praise was wont to name us both:
I had no greater pride.

　　　(Covers her face with her hands, and bursts
　　　　into tears. Here they all hang about her:
　　　　Freberg *supporting her tenderly;* Manuel
　　　　embracing her knees, and old Jerome *catch-*
　　　　ing hold of her robe affectionately. Bernard,
　　　　Abbess, Monks, *and* Nuns, *likewise, gather*
　　　　round her, with looks of sympathy.)

　　　Enter Two OFFICERS *of law.*

　1st *Off.*　　　　　　　Where is the prisoner?
Into our hands he straight must be consign'd.
　Bern. He is not subject now to human laws;
The prison that awaits him is the grave.
　　1st *Off.* Ha! sayst thou so? there is foul play
　　　in this.

E E

Man. to Off. Hold thy unrighteous tongue, or
    hie thee hence,
Nor, in the presence of this honour'd dame,
Utter the slightest meatilng of reproach.

    1*st Off.* I am an officer on duty call'd,
And have authority to say, how died ?

    (*Here* Jane *shakes off the weakness of grief, and*
      repressing Manuel, *who is about to reply to*
      the Officer, *steps forward with dignity.*)

Jane. Tell them by whose authority you come,
He died that death which best becomes a man
Who is with keenest sense of conscious ill
And deep remorse assail'd, a wounded spirit.
A death that kills the noble and the brave,
And only them.   He had no other wound.

    1*st Off.* And shall I trust to this.

    Jane.   Do as thou wilt :
To one who can suspect my simple word
I have no more reply.   Fulfill thine office.

    1*st Off.* No, lady, I believe your honour'd word,
And will no farther search.

    Jane. I thank your courtesy : thanks, thanks to
    all !
My rev'rend mother, and ye honour'd maids ;
Ye holy men ; and you, my faithful friends,
The blessing of the afflicted rest with you :
And he, who to the wretched is most piteous,
Will recompense you.—Freberg, thou art good,
Remove the body of the friend you lov'd,
'Tis Rezenvelt I mean.   Take thou this charge :
'Tis meet that, with his noble ancestors,

!

He lie entomb'd in honourable state.
And now, I have a sad request to make,
Nor will these holy sisters scorn my boon ;
That I, within these sacred cloister walls
May raise a humble, nameless tomb to him,
Who, but for one dark passion, one dire deed,
Had claim'd a record of as noble worth,
As e'er enrich'd the sculptur'd pedestal.

[EXEUNT.

FINIS.

www.ingramcontent.com/pod-product-compliance
Lightning Source LLC
Chambersburg PA
CBHW030815110726
47900CB00006B/1632